MOSES

MOSES

MOSES AND EGYPT

The Documentation to the Motion Picture

The Ten Commandments

by

Henry S. Noerdlinger

with an introduction by

Cecil B. deMille

UNIVERSITY OF SOUTHERN CALIFORNIA PRESS

LOS ANGELES

Library of Congress Catalog Card Number: 56-12886

Published by
University of Southern California Press
University Park, Los Angeles 7, California

Printed in the United States of America
By Parker & Son, Inc., Los Angeles

ACKNOWLEDGEMENTS

The endeavors and contributions of research toward the making of *The Ten Commandments* find their culmination in the publication of this book. It has been made possible through the generous interest of Mr. Cecil B. deMille, Mr. Y. Frank Freeman and Paramount Pictures Corporation, to whom sincere appreciation is expressed.

To accomplish the vast research work for the film, 950 books, 984 periodicals, 1,286 clippings and 2,964 photographs were studied. In documenting the text of this work the source material has been selectively limited. Unusual care has been taken in noting the many references in order to provide the reader with an immediate awareness of the sources used. A compact list of these has been appended at the end of this book to serve not only as a bibliography but to make acknowledgement to their authors, editors and translators.

For reading the unedited manuscript in part, for giving encouragement and valued criticism, the author wishes to thank Professor James H. Butler, University of Southern California; Dr. Arthur P. Coleman, President, Alliance College; the Reverend James W. Fifield, Jr., First Congregational Church, Los Angeles; the Very Reverend Joseph Fulton, Dominican Provincial, Oakland; R. Dean Goodwin, Council of Missionary Cooperation, American Baptist Convention; Dr. Adolph Keller, Zurich, Switzerland; William J. Kerrigan, Iowa State College; Rabbi Rudolph Lupo, Los Angeles Jewish Community Library; Dr. James Z. Nettinga, American Bible Society; Dr. Lawrence Clark Powell, University of California at Los Angeles; the Reverend H. K. Rasbach, Hope Lutheran Church,

Hollywood; Dr. A. S. Raubenheimer, Educational Vice President, University of Southern California; Professor Keith C. Seele, Oriental Institute, University of Chicago; the Reverend J. Richard Sneed, First Methodist Church, Los Angeles; the Most Reverend Vincent S. Waters, Bishop of Raleigh; Professor Kyle M. Yates, Baylor University.

The criticisms and suggestions of Messrs. Art Arthur, Jack Gariss, Donald Hayne, and Henry Wilcoxon of the "deMille staff" are gratefully appreciated.

A debt of gratitude is owed to Miss Gladys Percey of the Paramount Research Department and her able staff for supplying the author with source material; and particularly to Miss Elizabeth Higgason, who, among her many other contributions, has compiled the index and the bibliography.

Mr. Bryant French, editor of the University of Southern California Press, deserves special acknowledgement for his untiring efforts in bringing this book to press. Thanks go to Mr. Earl C. Bolton for making the publication arrangements, and to Mrs. Audrey Hyland for typing the manuscript.

Last but not least I wish to praise my wife Eleanor and my children, Gale, Marie and Sue, for having been so patient with me as husband and father during the months spent on writing *Moses and Egypt*.

H.S.N.

CONTENTS

PAGE

ACKNOWLEDGEMENTS iii

ILLUSTRATIONS ix

INTRODUCTION 1

THE HISTORICAL PERIOD 5

MOSES 11
THE BIBLICAL ACCOUNT 11
WHAT IS HISTORY? 12
THE ANCIENT SOURCES 15
MOSES' AGE 16
THE NAME MOSES 18
MOSES, PRINCE OF EGYPT 19
MOSES, HEBREW SLAVE 20
MOSES, THE SHEPHERD 22
    a) Moses in Midian 22
    b) The Burning Bush and the names of God 23
MOSES, THE PROPHET 25
    a) The signs 25
    b) Goshen 26
    c) The plagues 26
    d) The Passover 28
MOSES, THE LEADER 31
    a) The length of the bondage and the Promised Land 31
    b) The Exodus 33
    c) The Red Sea 35
MOSES, THE LAWGIVER 37
    a) Mount Sinai 37
    b) The Ten Commandments 39
    c) The Golden Calf 43
    d) The Ark of the Covenant 45
    e) Mount Nebo 45

THE PHARAOHS 49
PHARAOH, GOD AND RULER 49
RAMESES I 55
SETHI I 55
RAMESES II 58
NEFRETIRI 60
EPILOGUE 61

THE MEN AND WOMEN OF THE BIBLE 63
HEBREWS, ISRAELITES, AND JEWS 63

AARON... 64
BITHIAH... 65
DATHAN... 66
HUR BEN CALEB.................................... 67
ISHMAEL... 67
JETHRO.. 68
JOSHUA.. 69
MERED.. 70
MIRIAM... 70
SEPHORA.. 70
YOCHABEL.. 71

THE HOLY SCRIPTURES............................. 73
  THE OLD TESTAMENT................................ 73
    a) Early transmission and composition............... 73
    b) The canon..................................... 75
    c) Ancient translations........................... 78
    d) English translations............................ 82
  THE KORAN... 86

THE ARMY.. 89

OF CAMELS, HORSES AND TRANSPORTATION......... 95
  THE CAMEL... 95
  THE HORSE... 97
  THE CHARIOT....................................... 98
  BOATS.. 99

BUILDING AND OTHER ARTS AND CRAFTS............ 101
  BUILDING... 101
    a) General observations........................... 101
    b) Materials...................................... 103
    c) Stone quarrying and working.................... 104
    d) Building methods............................... 105
    e) Buildings...................................... 107
    f) Tents.. 110
  SCULPTURE AND PAINTING.......................... 111
    a) General observations........................... 111
    b) Materials and tools............................. 112
    c) Working methods............................... 113
    d) Sculptures and paintings........................ 116
  FURNITURE... 121

COSTUMES AND ADORNMENTS...................... 125
  EGYPTIAN MATERIALS AND COSTUMES............... 125
    a) Materials...................................... 125
    b) Colored materials.............................. 127

c) Dyes... 130
d) Costumes.. 131
e) Royal costumes.................................. 133
f) Royal insignia.................................. 135
g) Costume accessories............................. 138
HEBREW MATERIALS AND COSTUMES..................... 139
a) Materials....................................... 139
b) General observations............................ 140
c) Men's costumes................................. 141
d) Head coverings................................. 142
e) Women's costumes.............................. 143
f) Footwear....................................... 144
HAIR STYLES... 144
a) Hair styles in Egypt............................ 144
b) Hair styles among Hebrews...................... 147
PERFUME, INCENSE AND COSMETICS.................... 148
EGYPTIAN JEWELRY.................................. 150
a) General observations............................ 150
b) Materials....................................... 151
c) Jewelry 152
HEBREW JEWELRY.................................... 155
a) General remarks................................ 155
b) The breastplate of the high priest.............. 155

FOOD AND ENTERTAINMENT....................... 159
FOOD... 159
SPORTS AND GAMES................................. 162
MUSIC AND DANCING................................ 163

POSTSCRIPT 167

BIBLIOGRAPHY..................................... 169

LIBRARIES AND MUSEUMS CONSULTED.............. 177

INDEX... 179
GENERAL INDEX.................................... 181
REFERENCES TO THE BIBLE.......................... 199
REFERENCES TO THE HOLY QUR'AN.................. 202

ILLUSTRATIONS

MOSES . . . . *Frontispiece*

GROUP I . . . . *following page 52*

The tables of the Law reproduced in early Canaanite lettering

Gebel Musa, the peak of Sinai where "the glory of the Lord abode"

Ras Safsafeh, the "Horeb" of the Bible

Mural painting in the tomb of Rekhmere showing captives making bricks (Thebes)

Brick pit scene photographed in Egypt for *The Ten Commandments*

Pylons and gate, obelisks and colossi at Luxor, as engraved for Napoleon I

Pylons, gate and colossi of the biblical treasure city Raamses, erected and photographed in Egypt

Sethi I in his war chariot riding against the Canaanites (Karnak temple)

Detail showing adaptation of the Karnak temple sculpture to the set erected in Egypt

Pharaoh offering sacrifice to Sokar (Abydos)

The shrine of Sokar adjoining the "Hall of Audience" set

Model showing the erection of an obelisk

The erection of an obelisk for Sethi I's jubilee

GROUP II . . . . *following page 116*

Pectoral representing the vulture, symbol of Nekhbet, goddess of Upper Egypt (Cairo Museum)

Replica of the vulture pectoral worn by Rameses II on the screen

Rameses II in his war chariot (Abu Simbel)

Rameses II, in his chariot, wearing the blue war crown and the armor of divine protection

Isis conducting Nefretiri to her tomb (Thebes)

Costume worn by Nefretiri in the film, inspired by murals in that queen's rock tomb

Mural in the tomb of the Vizier Mehou at Saqqarah presenting the performance of a dance

The ballet performed at Sethi I's court

Ancient Egyptian necklace on exhibit at the Metropolitan Museum in New York

The delicate necklace copied for the picture

ix

INTRODUCTION

by

CECIL B. DEMILLE

THERE is more to making a motion picture than putting action and sound on a strip of film.

Especially when the subject is historical or biblical, accurate research must precede and accompany every stage of production.

The research consultant on a producer's staff must become familiar with all the principal sources of information on the historical characters and the historical period of the picture; he must assemble an adequate working library for constant use as well as a voluminous collection of reference notes, photographs, photostats, excerpts, and other data from the great libraries and museums of the world; and he must approach his task with the steady objectivity of the scholar—even if this means that he must sometimes be, quite firmly, a "no-man" to the producer, the writers, the art department, and the others engaged in actual production!

The producer will sometimes overrule the research consultant, deliberately and without apology, for reasons of legitimate dramatic license; for, as Professor Keith C. Seele of the University of Chicago wrote to us, "The challenge which you meet . . . is even greater than that faced by the historian. What he does not know he may leave unexpressed; you, however, must solve every problem, no matter how small or detailed, for pictures can contain no gaps or lacunae and no uncertainties. Your decisions may be right or wrong, but decisions you must make; you cannot say, along with the historian, 'I do not know.'" But, to make these decisions intelligently, the producer must be aware of all that is known, with

1

certainty or probability, about his subject. Thorough research tells him.

I have sometimes likened the producer to the restorer of a broken mosaic. Some parts of the mosaic can be supplied by the historians. The missing parts, the gaps and lacunae, as Professor Seele calls them, the producer must supply; but the integrity of the whole work demands that what the producer supplies must fit in with what history knows. Thorough research is the producer's guide to both parts of this "restoration."

In our research for *The Ten Commandments*, we have consulted some 1,900 books and periodicals, collected nearly 3,000 photographs, and used the facilities of 30 libraries and museums in North America, Europe, and Africa.

This book summarizes that documentation.

In connection with some of my previous motion pictures, we have compiled similar books on a much smaller scale for our own reference and for limited distribution to certain universities, libraries, and individual scholars.

This book is the first to attempt a complete documentation of this kind of research and the first of its kind to be offered to the general public as well as to scholars.

I have been urged by numerous scholars and clergymen to compile and present this book since, as they have told me, there is no other single volume which brings together all these data from biblical, archaeological, and historical sources, bearing upon those great events which Sir Winston Churchill calls "the most decisive leap-forward ever discernible in the human story."

Here, I hope, Jewish, Christian, and Moslem believers and the clergy of all faiths will find the light of archaeological and historical science illuminating the Word of God.

Students will find here a distillation of materials for which otherwise they would have to search in many places, but which are here arranged and collated for ready reference.

Here film critics and the general motion picture audience will find answers to questions concerning our picture of the world in Moses' time—and perhaps they will find too a new insight into the amount of serious labor which goes into motion picture research to assure authenticity.

Hard, exacting, and costly labor it is. Motion picture producers have sometimes been criticized for spending so much money on research—in the case of *The Ten Commandments* more than ever before. I do not agree with the criticism. I consider it money well spent to bring to the screen the results of the work of so many patient and selfless scholars whose labors, with spade and with pen, have helped us make the days of Moses live again. Research does not sell tickets at the box office, I may be told. But research does help bring out the majesty of the Lawgiver and the eternal verity of the Law.

THE HISTORICAL PERIOD

IN the beginning were the Scriptures. From this beginning to the completion of the motion picture *The Ten Commandments* these sacred books served as our main guides.

In due time we had to set a date for the Exodus. The Scriptures did not give us one. Nor did they give us the name of the pharaoh of the oppression. The new ruler of Egypt "which knew not Joseph"[1] and the one who led his mighty host of chariots in pursuit of the Israelites[2] have remained nameless in these texts.

1. Ex. 1:8.

2. Ex. 14:6–.

In making a motion picture such as *The Ten Commandments,* we do not find ourselves in the relatively comfortable position of the Egyptologist or Bible scholar who can satisfy himself with a vague answer to the problem at hand or, awaiting concrete evidence, no answer at all. A decision has to be reached. A precise historical period has to be established—an actual pharaoh has to sit on the throne of Egypt. This is a motion picture. The characters who bring it to life must have actual names. They must live and perform in reality. An historical void cannot be portrayed on the screen.

The general and specific problem with which we deal here has received considerable attention by many learned men throughout many generations.

Among those who read the Bible in the literal

5

sense attempts have been made, time and again, to
construe an historical chronology from the various
ages given in the Old Testament. The classic work of
this school of thought is that of Archbishop James
Ussher (1561-1656), whose calculations fixed the creation of the world in 4004 B.C. Some editions of the
Bible have the Ussher chronology printed on the
margin of the corresponding text. Thus, the birth of
Moses was placed in the year 1571 B.C. and the
Exodus dated 1491 B.C.[3]

This chronology is based on the Hebrew text. An
interesting comparison arises if similar chronologies
are taken from the Greek Septuagint and the Samaritan Pentateuch. In these three Old Testament texts
of Genesis the period from the Creation to the Flood
is in the Hebrew text 1,656 years, in the Samaritan
Pentateuch 1,307 years and in the Greek Septuagint
2,242 years.[4]

With the evolution of knowledge in the natural
sciences and the rise of scholarly Bible investigation
which, among other forms of evidence, takes that
external to the Bible into account, the belief in a
chronology based on the Scriptures alone had to give
way to other concepts. It would prove difficult to
maintain that this earth and man came into being
precisely in 4004 B.C. A tiny speck within an ageless
universe, this earth is much older than man, and man's
memory of himself much too young.

The long lives given to men in the early books of
the Bible are beyond any natural comparison. The
desire to give the ancient ones of a nation or the
traditional progenitors of a people the extra quality
of extreme longevity can be read in the ancient
Sumerian King List.[5] Thus, also, it can be read in
the Bible. There, it is interesting to observe that the
later the person appears in the sequence of the Old
Testament books the more reasonable and normal his
life span becomes.

Adam, Methuselah and Noah, who lived before the
Deluge, each reached an age of over 900 years.[6] Abra-

3. J. Ussher,
*Annals of
the World*
(London,
1658), pp.
1-13; see,
for example,
*New Stand-
ard Alpha-
betical
Indexed
Bible*
(Chicago,
1936), *pas-
sim.*

4. W. G. Jor-
dan, in *Ab-
ingdon Bible
Commentary*
(New York,
1929),
p. 125.

5. A. L. Oppen-
heim, in
*Ancient Near
Eastern Texts*
(Princeton,
1950), p.
265.

6. Gen. 5:5,
27; 9:29.

ham died when 175 years of age[7] and, according to the Scriptures, Moses lived to be 120 years old.[8] But Rehoboam, king of Judah, reached the age of 58.[9]

The choice of this king as an example serves to illustrate another point as well. His life is involved with that of an Egyptian pharaoh who is named in the Bible and of whom contemporaneous Egyptian records exist, records which also describe his campaign in Palestine in about 926 B.C.[10] This "Shishak king of Egypt [who] came up against Jerusalem"[11]— the Sheshonk of Egyptian records—is mentioned once before when Jeroboam fled to his court during the reign of Solomon.[12] Here we have an example of external evidence to the Bible.

To return to the particular point of our discussion a general statement can be made: the biblical personalities achieve a more normal life span from about the Book of Judges onward. In Psalms 90:10 it says: "The days of our years are threescore years and ten; and if by reason of strength they be fourscore years, yet is their strength labour and sorrow; for it is soon cut off, and we fly away." This means an average life expectancy of seventy and, in rare cases, eighty years.

Many Bible scholars point out the uncertainty of a biblical chronology and consider the ages of the patriarchs as legendary.[13] In studying the Old Testament together with the contemporary documents of ancient nations and the findings of modern scholars it becomes evident that these Scriptures are not history in the concept of our day, documented with exact dates of events and the people of whom they speak— though history of the experiences of individuals and a nation they nevertheless are.

To relate the biblical events of Moses' birth and the significant Exodus with Egyptian history has proved to be a most difficult puzzle. No conscientious scholar has been able to set an exact date with absolute certainty for these events. No one can point his finger at this or that pharaoh and state accurately, "He is the one who reigned when Moses was born, and upon

7. Gen. 25:7.

8. Deut. 34:7.

9. I Kings 14:21.

10. J. H. Breasted, *History of Egypt* (New York, 1921), p. 529.

11. I Kings 14:25.

12. I Kings 11:40.

13. *a) Universal Jewish Encyclopedia* (New York, 1948), III, 193; VII, 186-187.
b) Catholic Encyclopedia, III (New York, 1908), 738; XI (1911), 548.
c) G. A. Barrois, in *Interpreter's Bible,* I (New York, 1952), 142, 152.

that king the Plagues were inflicted." The question
remains debatable with regard to the dynasty and the
particular pharaohs under whom the history of the
Book of Exodus took place.

The problem with which we deal here has received
considerable attention. We can state that neither the
period nor the pharaohs chosen for the picture *The
Ten Commandments* have been picked by whim.
Among scholars there are those who favor the thirteenth century B.C. as the general era of the Exodus.
Of course, this or any other proposed solution will remain controversial until conclusive evidence can be
established.

Related to this controversy is the answer to the
question, Who were the reigning pharaohs during
Moses' lifetime?

Some scholars have rendered an opinion which
establishes Rameses II—who reigned 1301-1234 B.C.—
as the pharaoh of the Exodus.[14] Since Rameses II was
preceded by his father Sethi I (1318-1301 B.C.), who
coreigned with Rameses I (1319-1318 B.C.) during
the last year of this pharaoh's short rule,[15] these kings
sat on the throne of Egypt during Moses' earlier years.

Influenced by the scholarly opinions established in
the foregoing paragraph, Cecil B. deMille set the historical period for the picture *The Ten Commandments* within the reigns of the pharaohs mentioned.
This period, therefore, also becomes the age of Moses.

Egypt, in this age of Moses, was a land of greatness. It was the power of the then known world—
an empire. In this land of the Nile lived a people of
great learning and refined living, a people whose creative ingenuity still amazes and delights the modern
eye, though most of their achievements are ruins now.

As elsewhere in that ancient world the heavy labor
was performed by men in "hard bondage, in mortar,
and in brick, and in all manner of service."[16] In Egypt
"they built for Pharaoh treasure cities, Pithom and
Raamses."[17]

14. *a) Westmin-
    ster Histori-
    cal Atlas to
    the Bible*,
    ed. Wright
    and Filson
    (Philadel-
    phia, 1945),
    p. 37.
    b) P. Hein-
    isch, *History
    of the Old
    Testament*
    (College-
    ville, Minn.,
    1952), p.
    83.
    c) Barrois,
    145.

15. Breasted,
    p. 408.

16. Ex. 1:14.

17. Ex. 1:11.

This city named Raamses in the Bible interests us. It is the Per-Ramses of ancient Egyptian records. Archaeologists have established its location at modern Qantir in the Nile Delta.[18] Labib Habachi is about to publish his findings to the effect that Raamses became the political capital built during the reigns of Sethi I and Rameses II, who imposed his name on it.[19]

The twelve tribes traditionally lived in the land of Goshen,[20] which is the present Wadi Tumilat.[21] It is located within close proximity of Raamses, i.e. the modern Qantir.

Sethi I and Rameses II were active builders who levied vast numbers of laborers. Though it is not possible to provide external evidence to the specific use of Hebrew or Israelite labor for these enterprises, it is a fact that Asiatic prisoners, i.e. Semites, were employed for such and other purposes in ancient Egypt.[22]

For the picture *The Ten Commandments* these archaeological facts are as a bridge connecting them with the biblical account of the "hard bondage"[23] and the building of Raamses. On a larger scale they establish the age of Moses.

18. G. Steindorff and K. C. Seele, *When Egypt Ruled the East* (Chicago, 1947), p. 256.

19. Conference with the author, Luxor, November, 1954.

20. Gen. 45:10.

21. W. M. F. Petrie, *Egypt and Israel* (London, 1931), p. 30.

22. J. A. Wilson, *Burden of Egypt* (Chicago, 1951), pp. 189, 191, 201, 255-256.

23. Ex. 1:14.

MOSES

The Biblical Account

The story of Moses as it is written in the Bible is well known. There, the description of his early life is presented in a most abbreviated manner. A few short verses tell of his birth under the terror of Pharaoh's persecution,[1] his exposure to the river by his worried mother,[2] and his adoption into the royal family of Egypt.[3] When Moses reaches manhood he kills an Egyptian and must leave Egypt abruptly.[4]

Starting with the scenes at the well in Midian, where Moses rescues Jethro's daughters,[5] the Bible becomes more explicit. One arrives at the conclusion that the scriptural account of Moses is concerned, in the main, with the liberation of the Israelites in bondage,[6] the giving of the Law and ordinances,[7] the wandering in the wilderness, and the eventual approach to the Promised Land.[8]

Of foremost importance in these Bible chapters and unmistakably originating these events is God, Who as "the God of Abraham, the God of Isaac, and the God of Jacob"[9] familiarizes Moses with the tradition of his forefathers and, with His name YHWH—I AM THAT I AM,[10] or, as translated in the Douay Version, I AM WHO AM — brings new meaning, new hope and a renewed religious faith to those distressed in bondage in Egypt. It becomes clear that the prime purpose of this biblical account is the establishment

1. Ex. 1:22; 2:2.
2. Ex. 2:3.
3. Ex. 2:10.
4. Ex. 2:12, 15.

5. Ex. 2:16—.

6. Ex. 3:7—.
7. Ex. 20—.

8. Numbers, Deuteronomy.

9. Ex. 3:6.

10. Ex. 3:14.

11

of the one God in the heart and mind of man—the
establishment of a people governed not by the whims
of man, but by law.

Thus we can understand that the events not closely
connected with the purposes indicated in the preceding paragraphs were not always set down in the good
Book. Still, these events must have taken place in
time and space—in history.

What Is History?

There does not seem to be any serious person
nowadays who would deny the historicity of Moses.
Whether he be a skeptic scholar or a devout theo-
logian, whether he be a psychiatrist like the late
Sigmund Freud[11] or the philosopher Martin Buber,[12]
to all of them Moses was a living man.

Moses was a human being. He was born. He did
grow from infancy to childhood, from adolescence to
manhood. He grew old and he died.

His formative years are suggested in the Bible by
two sparse clues only. He was adopted as a son into
the royal family of Egypt while a child[13] and "Moses
was learned in all the wisdom of the Egyptians, and
was mighty in words and in deeds."[14]

In relating the giving of the Ten Commandments
one cannot avoid portraying the life of Moses. The
life of a man is made up of many facets. Many things
happen and much occurs to him. In writing about such
a man, in re-creating a picture of him, whether it be
for a book or the motion picture *The Ten Commandments,* it is not enough to present the essence of his
being and the outstanding achievements of his life
in a few well-worded sentences or some chosen frames
of film. The events that shaped his life, the joys and
sorrows, the passions lived and the knowledge gained,
the people he knew, the men and women with human
failings and strength of will and heart—these must be
told, these must be shown. Thus only does the man
take form and grow to become a living human being.

To portray the life of Moses, the man who is re-

11. *Moses and Monotheism,* trans. K. Jones (New York, 1939).

12. Buber, *Moses* (Oxford, 1946).

13. Ex. 2:10.

14. Acts 7:22.

vered by the followers of three great religions—Judaism, Christianity and Islam—is an undertaking of great responsibility. It tests the conscience and intelligence of all who participate in this re-creation of biblical history. To bring these events and the man who lived them to the screen was approached with responsibility, with conscientiousness and with intelligence.

Cecil B. deMille's genius as a storyteller, his inherent talent as a dramatist in the direct and universal language of the cinema, are known and proven. For the picture *The Ten Commandments*, the facets of Moses' life that are not recorded in the Bible could have been invented and written into scenes harmonious with the Old Testament story. But Mr. deMille, his associate producer and writers—Messrs. Wilcoxon, MacKenzie, Lasky, Gariss and Frank—did not have to invent them. They had been set down in writing some 1,600 to 2,400 years ago. The missing years of Moses' life have survived in this very ancient literature.

As it was with the Bible, where many of the stories were first transmitted by word of mouth from father to son, around the campfires in the desert or at the gates of a city,[15] before they were set down in writing,[16] compiled and edited, so it must have been with some of the stories concerning Moses not included in the Scriptures. Undoubtedly, some of these had their origin in just such a fashion during the very lifetime of the great lawgiver. They are usually referred to as traditions, legends or sagas.

It has been said that a legend or tradition, regardless of the fanciful rendering into which it may have crystallized, contains an element of original actuality, a kernel of history.

The late archaeologist Ernst Herzfeld went a step further in stating that "saga and history have a simultaneous beginning. They start from the actual event. Each event can be and is told in different ways and each contemporary description is basically legendary. Historical research establishes the facts through the

15. Cf. I Kings 22:10.
16. A. Jeffery, in *Interpreter's Bible*, I (New York, 1952), 46.

consequences they have created, retrogressing from effect to cause, and based upon these effects judges the event as historical or not. The sagas are true to the event and are unconcerned about their effects. They tell what is of importance at the moment of happening. The doer is more important than the deed. As the event becomes more distant in time its details pale or disappear, but everything that satisfies emotion remains. Thus a unity, an inner relationship enters into these stories—something human which has no relationship with history, since history, like nature, is inhuman. However, these stories do have a relationship with psychological truth. . . ."[17]

No one can claim that all of the traditions, legends or sagas about Moses contain an actual kernel of history, nor that they started with the event. Dealing with a personality of Moses' importance and influence on his own and later generations, ancient storytellers and subsequent compiling scribes may have felt the need to supplement the actuality of a story with imaginative additions to fill in a detail where there seemed to be a void. In writing about Moses the profoundly religious scholar Martin Buber states, "the literature of the ages saw fit to round off the saga material by supplementary data. . . ."[18] This does not invalidate the saga by any means. Indeed, it would be impossible for any scholar to state always with absolute certainty which saga element is that of an actual event or that of popular imagination from among this very ancient material.

One more thing needs to be said on this subject. Again, it is best put into the words of Martin Buber: "There can be no certainty of arriving . . . at 'what really happened.' "[19]

What is meant by this "what really happened" is in the sense of objective documentation of the event, as we understand history today—the event, as recorded and judged by a disinterested outside observer looking in, as it were. We have seen, however, that a tradition or a saga is, in its original form, the con-

17. In *Archaeologische Mitteilungen aus Iran,* VI (December 1933), 102-103; translation by the author.

18. Buber, p. 16.

19. *Ibid.*

temporary account of an event as it impressed the mind of the participant, the "doer." Though of a different kind, this is history too, human history which takes the human being and his emotional reactions to an event into account.

Thus does Moses become a living person, a man with a human history and of history in the picture *The Ten Commandments.*

The Ancient Sources

The ancient authors who have provided us with extrabiblical information on the life of Moses need to be discussed briefly.

On the Life of Moses was written by Philo Judaeus of Alexandria. He lived shortly before and during the lifetime of Jesus. His purpose for writing the book was "to make the story and the character of the great legislator known to the outer world."[20] His approach to the subject at hand was to "tell the story of Moses as I have learned it, both from the sacred books . . . and from some of the elders of the nation; for I always interwove what I was told with what I read, and thus believed myself to have a closer knowledge than others of his life's history."[21] Philo wrote many other books concerning the Old Testament. From among these *The Decalogue* is of particular interest to the subject under discussion.

The historian Flavius Josephus (37-100? A.D.) produced a work of considerable importance, the *Jewish Antiquities.* With it Josephus wished to inform the Roman world with the history and traditions of his people. He based his writings on "Hebrew records."[22]

Of a slightly more recent date are the writings of an early church father, Eusebius of Caesarea (260?-340? A.D.). In his *Preparation for the Gospel* he quotes ancient authors who wrote about Moses and whose works are no longer extant anywhere else.[23]

Very ancient texts belonging to this group of source material are rabbinical compilations—the Midrashim.

"Midrash" is interpretation and explanation of cer-

20. *Philo,* trans. F. H. Colson, VI (Cambridge, Mass., 1950). xiv.

21. *Ibid.,* p. 279.

22. *Josephus,* IV, trans. H. St. J. Thackeray (London and New York, 1930), 5.

23. Eusebius, *Preparation* (trans. E. H. Gifford. Oxford, 1903), ix. 27-29.

24. *Jewish Encyclopedia,* VIII (New York, 1905), 548-549.

25. I. Epstein, "Foreword," *Midrash Rabbah,* ed. H. Freedman and M. Simon, I (London, 1951), x.

26. *a*) L. Ginzberg, *Legends of the Jews* (Philadelphia, 1946-1947).
  b) Jewish Encyclopedia, IX (New York, 1907), 46-54.
  c) A. S. Rappaport, *Myth and Legend of Ancient Israel* (London, 1928), II.
  d) J. Z. Lauterbach, *Mekilta de-Rabbi Ishmael* (Philadelphia, 1949).

27. *Universal Jewish Encyclopedia* (New York, 1948), X, 160-165.

28. Mishnah (trans. H. Danby. London, 1950).

29. Ex. 2:2.

30. Ex. 7:7.

31. Ex. 2:11.

32. Heinisch, *History of the Old Testament* (Collegeville, Minn., 1952), p. 82.

33. Koran, trans. G. Sale (London, n.d.), p. 361, n. 1.

34. *Midrash Rabbah,* III, trans. S. M. Lehrman (London, 1951), 82.

35. Ginzberg, V, 104.

tain Old Testament books. There are two general forms: Midrash Haggadah, whose aim is to stress instruction in moral and religious knowledge, and Midrash Halakah, which comments on legal matters.[24]

The Midrash particularly studied by us in our research was the Midrash Rabbah on Exodus, which is haggadic in character. It contains many valuable traditions told with religious devotion. The beginning of this Midrash seems to have taken place during the time of Ezra (fifth century B.C.) and reached its present form in the eleventh century of our era.[25]

There are other Moses traditions of this order whose edited texts we were able to consult.[26]

In addition to the laws contained in written form in the Old Testament, oral legal traditions came about. These were transmitted in a work known as the Talmud, which consists of two parts. The first, called Mishnah, was compiled and edited about 200 A.D. The commentaries to the Mishnah form the second part of the Talmud. They are the Gemaras, of which there are two, the Babylonian and the Palestinian (also called Jerusalem) Gemara. The Babylonian work is the commentary of rabbis and Jewish scholars who lived in Babylonia. It was compiled about 500 A.D. The Palestinian (Jerusalem) Gemara is a similar record executed in Palestine around 400 A.D.[27] In our studies we consulted the Mishnah.[28]

Moses' Age

From the time that Moses is three months old[29] to his reaching "fourscore years"[30] the Bible is silent on his age. It is for this reason that the interpretations to "when Moses was grown"[31] vary accordingly.

Paul Heinisch has Moses "about 20 years old,"[32] and the commentator to the Koran, Al Beidawi, interpreted that he lived thirty years at Pharaoh's court.[33] In the Midrash Rabbah his age is given as twelve[34] while in other similar sources Moses is twenty, twenty-two or forty years old when he leaves Egypt for Midian.[35]

We do not indicate the respective ages of Moses;

however, his physical appearance on the screen denies the biblical age of eighty at the time he and Aaron "spake unto Pharaoh."[36]

36. Ex. 7:7.

Many authorities are agreed that the ages given in the early books of the Bible are not to be taken literally. In our investigations concerning the problem of Moses' age the awareness arose that the Israelites at one time had two distinct beginnings of the year within a twelve months cycle. "The first day of Nisan [in the spring] marks the beginning of the year with regard to the computation of passover. For other purposes the year began in autumn, on the first of Tishri, which was solemnized as New Year's day."[37] "The new year of Nisan did not survive as a formal religious occasion, but was used only for legal and calendarical purposes."[38] Speculation is close at hand that such a double New Year might have caused a two count for a regular calendar year, thus increasing some of the biblical ages and periods twofold. This particular aspect and its possible influence upon related calculations has not been explored by any of the authorities we consulted.

37. G. A. Barrois, in Interpreter's Bible, I (New York, 1952), 152.

38. T. H. Gaster, Festivals of the Jewish Year (New York, 1953), p. 108.

The length of Moses' life runs in cycles of forty, and forty is a round figure frequently used in the Old Testament. It has been interpreted to indicate a generation.[39] The precise number of years composing a generation varies greatly. In Abraham's time it was one hundred years;[40] at another instance a generation stands for as few as ten years, while Herodotus wrote "three generations of men make one hundred years,"[41] which is the modern computation also. The meaning of the word *forty* used as an idiom is "any lengthy time,"[42] just as we say "many years," for example.

39. Univ. Jewish Encycl., III, 193.

40. Gen. 15:13, 16.

41. Cyclopaedia of Biblical Literature, ed. J. Kitto (New York, 1857), I, 748.

42. Midrash Rabbah, III, 258, n. 5.

Martin Buber writes that the actual age of Moses was far less than that given in the Bible.[43] Elsewhere it is stated that alterations of the figures in the Hebrew text of the Old Testament had taken place as late as the fourth century A.D.[44]

43. Buber, p. 201.

44. Catholic Encyclopedia, XI (New York, 1911). 548.

Unfortunately, archaeology has not unearthed any contemporary documentation on Moses.

The Name Moses

When Pharaoh's daughter names her adopted son Moses she explains, "Because I drew him out of the water."[45]

45. Ex. 2:10.

Both ancient and modern scholars have attempted to find the derivation of the name "Moses" through various means, and each explanation, whether propounded by Josephus, the rabbis or modern philologists, has found its opposition.

Philo and Josephus establish the name as Egyptian, claiming that the syllable *mou* means "water." This etymology, actually based on Coptic, is no longer adhered to.[46]

46. *Philo*, VI, 285. See also *Josephus*, IV, 263, note a.

The rabbis derive the name of the lawgiver from the Hebrew verb *mashah*, "to draw out."[47]

47. *Midrash Rabbah*, III, 34, n. 1.

Philological investigations of the last few decades have taken the ancient Egyptian language as the source of Moses' name. Among Egyptologists the opinion has been held that Moses is an incomplete name, actually meaning "child." According to this view, it occurs in the complete name of Thut-mose, for example,[48] meaning "child of Thut."

48. J. G. Griffiths, *Journal of Near Eastern Studies*, XII (1953), 227.

A recent analysis on this subject establishes good evidence for the name Moses to be of Egyptian origin,[49] just as the names Putiel,[50] Hophni and Phinehas[51] are Egyptian.[52] According to Mr. Griffiths the name "mose" does occur independently in ancient Egyptian records identifying several individuals. However, it is not a complete name like Ptahmose ("Ptah is born"), for example, but an abbreviated one.[53] We wonder, in our speculative thinking, whether this abbreviated name could be the reason why no archaeological evidence of the biblical Moses has ever been found in the records of ancient Egypt.

49. *Ibid.*, pp. 225-231.
50. Ex. 6:25.
51. I Sam. 1:3.
52. J. A. Wilson, *Burden of Egypt* (Chicago, 1951), p. 256.
53. Griffiths, pp. 225-231.

Moses was adopted into the royal family of Egypt, according to the Scriptures,[54] and traditions establish him as heir to the throne. With this in mind it is of interest to consider James Breasted's deductions derived from an altered relief on a temple wall at Kar-

54. Ex. 2:10.

nak. This relief shows Pharaoh Sethi I and Rameses II
as crown prince, with Rameses' carved figure superimposed above an erasure. Breasted deduces from this
that Sethi I did have a son older than Rameses II who
was to follow him on the throne. But Rameses elimi-
nated this older brother through intrigue and caused
the latter's figure and name to be erased from the temple wall.[55] Not denying that Rameses II may have had
an older brother, some archaeologists do not agree
with Breasted's thoughts on this point.[56] Possibly that
erased figure could have been the one of Moses, prince
of Egypt, and the name, forever lost, the complete one
of the leader of the Exodus.

Moses, Prince of Egypt

Moses a prince of Egypt? The Bible[57] and the
Koran[58] imply it; they refer to his adoption into the
royal family. From this precise moment to his killing
an Egyptian as a grown man[59] the Bible and the Scriptures of Islam become taciturn on Moses' life. This is
the moment when we draw fully from the ancient
sources to paint as complete a portrait of Moses as
possible for the film *The Ten Commandments*. It is a
fascinating task to bring a little-known Moses to life.

What do these sources say about Moses' becoming a
grown man?

Moses receives the attention "due to a prince." He
is considered as successor to the throne "and indeed
regularly called the young king." So says Philo;[60] and
Josephus also establishes Moses as heir to the throne of
Egypt.[61]

His education as a member of the royal family comprises all the fields of learning,[62] a statement which, in
essence, is substantiated by Stephen's testimony to the
Sanhedrin, "And Moses was learned in all the wisdom
of the Egyptians, and was mighty in words and in
deeds."[63]

The Midrash Rabbah tells of the great affection
shown Moses by his adoptive mother and Pharaoh.[64]
In the picture the mutual relationship of Moses with

55. J. H. Breast-
    ed, *History
    of Egypt*
    (New York,
    1921), pp.
    418-420.

56. K. C. Seele,
    *Coregency of
    Rameses II
    with Sethi I
    and the Date
    of the Great
    Hypostyle
    Hall at Kar-
    nak* (Chi-
    cago, 1940),
    pp. 23-26.

57. Ex. 2:10.

58. Holy Qur'an
    (trans. M.M.
    'Ali. Lahore,
    1951), 28:9.

59. Ex. 2:12.

60. *Philo*, VI,
    285-293.

61. *Josephus*, IV,
    265.

62. *Philo*, VI,
    287-289.

63. Acts 7:22.

64. *Midrash
    Rabbah*, III,
    33.

Bithiah and Sethi I is one of fond devotion.

Josephus and Eusebius deal at length with Moses in command of an Egyptian army. As a general he defeats the invading Ethiopians and succeeds in conquering their country. These accounts are made additionally interesting by court intrigues against the life of Moses.[65]

65. *Josephus*, IV, 269-275. See also Eusebius, ix, 27.

The picture presents Moses' victorious return from this campaign and his acclaimed welcome to the court of Sethi I amid the exotic tribute exacted from the conquered enemy. The element of intrigue, though not against Moses' life, but rather against his gaining the throne, has its inception here.

In ancient Egypt women were the nominal inheritors. The throne of Egypt was assured through the royal heiress. By marrying the heiress or heiresses a man could become pharaoh.[66] This custom accounts for the frequent brother and sister marriages, though in actuality such marriages more often took place between half brothers and half sisters.[67]

66. M. A. Murray, *Splendour that was Egypt* (New York, 1949), pp. 100-102.

67. Wilson, pp. 96-97.

The relationship between Moses and Nefretiri—as shown on the screen—whom he would marry if not for a radical change in the pattern of his life, is derived from such customs.

Moses' activity as chief architect of the new treasure city in the picture *The Ten Commandments* can be deduced not only from Acts 7:22, but also from a tradition contained in the Midrash Rabbah.[68] His concern for the welfare of the Hebrew slaves is expressed in the last-mentioned source and, expanding on it, we have Moses empty the temple granary to feed the hungry. The weekly day of rest that Moses obtains for the burdened Hebrews is documented in a tradition.[69]

68. *Midrash Rabbah*, III, 35.

69. *Ibid.*

Moses, Hebrew Slave

Traditions generally assume that Moses knew of his Hebrew parentage from earliest childhood and throughout the years he spent as a member of the royal family of Egypt. Actually, the Bible makes no such statement.

All the classic sources are expressive of Moses' honesty, sincerity and responsibility. Convinced of these qualities and desirous of creating this impression clearly in an audience, we could not portray Moses as a man of duplicity. A man of such high ethical and moral standards could not have been loyal both to Pharaoh and to the enslaved Israelites.

In the picture *The Ten Commandments* Moses is a grown man when he is confronted with the fact that he is not a master, but a slave. He has to find out by and for himself what it means to be a Hebrew. It is with this condition in mind that we render the meaning of "he went out unto his brethren and looked on their burdens."[70] It is in this fashion that we apply the tradition, "he used to shoulder [his brethren's] burdens and help each one"[71]—in the sweat and oppression of the brick pits. This interpretation is supported in the New Testament: "By faith Moses, when he was come to years, refused to be called the son of Pharaoh's daughter; Choosing rather to suffer affliction with the people of God, than to enjoy the pleasures of sin for a season."[72]

The biblical account of Moses killing an Egyptian[73] is also revealed in the Koran.[74] Philo deals with the incident briefly,[75] but Josephus omits it altogether.[76] In Eusebius this event is the outcome of a court intrigue in which Moses was to be assassinated. Moses successfully wards off the attacker and slays him.[77] An elaborate background to this deed is given in the Midrash Rabbah, where the Egyptian taskmaster, whom Moses kills, first seduces a Hebrew woman. Most important to the picture is the fact that this tradition names the observer and informer of the killing—Dathan![78]

In the Koran, Moses uses his fist to slay his foe,[79] and a like statement is made in the Midrash Rabbah, among other solutions.[80]

The Egyptian whom Moses kills is named Baka, the masterbuilder, in the film. It is indeed Dathan who observes the deed and informs prince Rameses. Moses

70. Ex. 2:11.

71. *Midrash Rabbah*, III, 34.

72. Heb. 11:24-25.

73. Ex. 2:12.

74. Holy Qur'an ('Ali tr.), 28:15.

75. *Philo*, VI, 299.

76. *Josephus*, IV, 277.

77. Eusebius, ix. 27.

78. *Midrash Rabbah*, III, 39.

79. Holy Qur'an ('Ali tr.), 28:15.

80. *Midrash Rabbah*, III, 39.

81. *Ibid.*

is imprisoned, an account not specified in the Book of
Exodus, but implied in one of the midrashic stories.[81]

82. Ex. 2:15.

In keeping with Moses' noble character we interpret
his flight from the face of Pharaoh[82] as a sentence of
banishment. He is exposed to a merciless desert and
left to die. The Midrash Rabbah contains the tradition
of a sentence of death, though Moses escapes miracu-

83. *Midrash
Rabbah*, III,
39.

lously.[83]

Moses, the Shepherd

a) Moses in Midian. Of Moses' stay in Midian the
Old Testament relates three major events that play an
important part in his life: he becomes a shepherd, a

84. Ex. 2:21,
Douay Ver-
sion.

nomad; he marries Sephora,[84] the daughter of Jethro,
and has a son by her named Gershom; God reveals
Himself at the Burning Bush, a revelation in which He
establishes His new name and commands Moses to

85. Ex. 2:15-25;
3; 4:1-23.

deliver the children of Israel from bondage.[85] All of
these events are shown in the picture *The Ten Commandments.*

At the well in Midian Moses comes to the aid of
Jethro's seven daughters and drives the offending
shepherds away. We name them Amalekites, after
Exodus 17:8. The Koran indicates the presence of only

86. Holy Qur'an
('Ali tr.),
28:23-28,
and n. 1877.

two daughters at the well and in the tent of Jethro.[86]

Moses' ability as an efficient shepherd is pointed out
in various sources. Philo particularly emphasizes the
integrity with which Moses applies himself to his new
occupation, how he becomes expert in keeping and in-

87. *Philo*, VI,
309-311.

creasing flocks.[87] This description gives rise to the
scene of Moses' successful business transaction in behalf of Jethro and several sheiks.

When Moses first apprehends the Burning Bush in
the film he is not alone, since he speaks to someone—

88. Ex. 3:3.

"I will now turn aside, and see this great sight."[88]
In the Koran Moses is with his family when he ob-

89. Holy Qur'an
('Ali tr.),
27:7; 28:29.

serves what he believes at first to be a campfire[89] and
the Midrash Rabbah describes him in the company

90. *Midrash
Rabbah*, III,
53.

of others.[90] The nomad shepherd always travels with
his family from pasture to pasture.

In Exodus 4:20 ". . . Moses took his wife and his
sons . . . and he returned to the land of Egypt." In
the film we show only one son, Gershom, the only one
so far mentioned by name in the Bible.[91] The name of
the second son, Eliezer, is not given until after the
Exodus, at Moses' reunion with his family near Mt.
Sinai.[92]

Considering the complexity of the biblical text as
indicated above, we find support for our rendition in
the statement "it is not impossible that we should here
read sons in the singular."[93] Paul Heinisch explains
that the second son was born in Midian during Moses'
absence,[94] i.e. after Sephora returns from Egypt to her
father's tent.[95] In Moffatt's translation the reference
to "sons" does not occur at all in the passage.[96]

Neither the Bible nor the picture establishes the
length of time spent by Moses in Midian as keeper of
Jethro's flocks. However, many interpretations exist.
In the Koran, the years number eight or ten.[97] In the
Book of Jubilees the period is given as lasting "5 weeks
and 1 year,"[98] while Heinisch presents the length of
time as two years.[99]

b) The Burning Bush and the names of God. The
experience gained at the Burning Bush and the revelation of God's new name mark another turning point
in the life of Moses and in the development of the faith
of Israel. A few notes are warranted in this context.

The bush itself is not classified in the Scriptures,
but the Midrash Rabbah emphasizes it as a lowly thorn
bush to teach that God is present everywhere.[100]

The account of Artapanus quoted by Eusebius elimi-
nates the bush or any other fuel altogether. The flame
blazes out of the earth.[101]

The Midrash Rabbah explains that God spoke to
Moses with the voice of his father,[102] while Philo tells
us that the revelation took place "with a silence that
spoke more clearly than speech [employing] the miracle of sight to herald future events."[103]

Commentators to the Koran explain that Moses saw

91. Ex. 2:22.

92. Ex. 18:2-5.

93. J. C. Rylaars-
dam and J.
E. Park, in
*Interpreter's
Bible,* I
(New York,
1952), 881.

94. Heinisch,
p. 84.

95. Ex. 18:2.

96. J. Moffatt,
*The Bible: A
New Trans-
lation* (New
York, 1935),
p. 64.

97. Holy Qur'an
('Ali tr.),
28:27.

98. *Apocrypha
and Pseude-
pigrapha of
the Old
Testament,*
ed. R. H.
Charles (Ox-
ford, 1913),
II, 78.

99. Heinisch, p.
84.

100. *Midrash
Rabbah,* III,
53.

101. Eusebius,
ix. 27.

102. *Midrash
Rabbah,* III,
58.

103. *Philo,* VI,
311.

the revelation with his "spiritual eye," that it was not a physical fire.[104]

What cannot be seen with the eye cannot be projected onto the screen, what cannot be heard with the ear cannot be recorded in a film with sound. It is left to the viewer to grasp the meaning beyond the physical manner in which this revelation is materialized in *The Ten Commandments.*

A modern occurrence in nature may be of interest to some. Ewald Schild reports that the Corsican maqui bush and the dittany of Germany exude highly inflammable gases. When ignited the plants are enveloped by a quickly consumed flame without damage to the bushes.[105]

In the Old Testament text God is addressed by various names. The name most frequently used in the Hebrew text is YHWH (Yahweh). In the King James Version, at the revelation of the Burning Bush, this name is translated "I AM THAT I AM . . . I AM hath sent me unto you."[106] The same passage in the Douay Version reads "I AM WHO AM . . . HE WHO IS hath sent me to you."[107] Philo, as translated from the Greek, has "I am He Who IS."[108]

In the English texts "Jehovah" occurs as a name of God. This name came into being through an inexact transliteration from the Hebrew combined form of *YHWH* and *Adonai.* The fact that YHWH is the name for God most frequently used in the Hebrew Old Testament indicates that in the English versions it has been translated into another form as well. That form is the title "Lord."

There are indications that the name Yahweh was readily pronounced by the faithful in ancient Old Testament times. By about the third century B.C., however, the name was considered too sacred to be spoken. Josephus states: "I am forbidden to speak [His name]."[109] While the Hebrew consonants of *YHWH* were not changed, the vowels of *Adonai* were added and the written name pronounced "Adonai."

Marginal notes:

104. Holy Qur'an ('Ali tr.), nn. 1578, 1842.

105. "Burning Bushes That Grow Today," *Literary Digest,* April 6, 1929, p. 72.

106. Ex. 3:14.

107. Ex. 3:14, Douay Version.

108. *Philo,* VI, 315.

109. *Josephus,* IV, 285.

The word usually translated as God stems from the Hebrew word *Elohim*. This is a plural, of which the singular is *Eloah*. *Elohim* stands for God as well as for gods and images. When God is addressed the singular form of a verb is written in connection with it. The original meaning of the word is obscure but seems to approximate "He Who is the Subject of reverence (or fear)."

Another word for God is *El*. Usually this title is connected with adjectives such as "Most High God," El Elyon; "God Almighty," El Shaddai; "Everlasting God," El Olam; "Living God," El Hai; "the God of Israel," El Elohe Israel.

The title Adonai, i.e. Lord, which has already been demonstrated to be a substitute for YHWH, also appears independently.[110]

Moses, the Prophet

a) The signs. The paying of tribute and the bringing of gifts by foreign ambassadors to the court of Egypt is an occasion that can be found painted in the tombs of ancient Egypt.[111] A tradition illustrates such a scene as well when Moses and Aaron arrive at the royal palace to demand the release of the Hebrew bondsmen.[112] These sources suggested the setting for Moses' and Aaron's appearance before Pharaoh as told in Exodus 5:1- and 7:10-. In the film *The Ten Commandments* we combine into one scene Pharaoh's pronouncement that no more straw shall be given for the making of bricks and the sign of the staff turned serpent.

The Bible indicates that Aaron throws down his staff to perform the commanded sign,[113] but on the screen Aaron uses Moses' staff. This rendition is substantiated by God's instructions to Moses to "take this rod in thine hand, wherewith thou shalt do signs."[114] Additional agreement with this interpretation can be found in Josephus,[115] in the Septuagint text, where Moses hands his staff to Aaron,[116] and in the Koran, where Moses performs the sign himself.[117] It is a sound conclusion to symbolize the staff hallowed at the Burn-

110. Sources for names of God:
a) *Jewish Encycl.*, IX, 160-162.
b) *Dictionary of the Bible*, ed. J. Hastings (New York, 1954), p. 299.

111. G. Steindorff and K. C. Seele, *When Egypt Ruled the East* (Chicago, 1947), pp. 107-108.

112. *Midrash Rabbah*, III, 94.

113. Ex. 7:10.

114. Ex. 4:17.

115. *Josephus*, IV, 289-291.

116. Septuagint Bible (trans. C. Thomson. Indian Hills, Colo., 1954), Ex. 7:9-10.

117. Holy Qur'an ('Ali tr.), 7:107.

ing Bush whenever the will of God requires its use for His purpose.

It is recorded that the Egyptian cobra can be put into a state of rigidity.[118] During our stay in Egypt in 1954 some of us observed a native snake charmer perform this feat, which we photographed. In fact, the Bible does designate the performance of Pharaoh's sorcerers a magician's trick.[119] The rabbis and the classical authors point out the commonplace of a serpent swallowing others of its kind, but the miracle that occurs here is that Moses' serpent reverts to its original state—the staff—without any change in its size, while the Egyptian's rods were serpents from the start.[120]

The "anguish of spirit" of the people in Goshen, consequent to the withdrawal of straw for the making of bricks, turns them against Moses and Aaron.[121] It can be seen on the screen as the beginning of a rebellion.

b) Goshen. Adjoining the Nile Delta to the east, Goshen is the land where the Israelites lived while in Egypt.[122] Geographically known as Wadi Tumilat, it is one of Egypt's most fertile districts.[123]

As early as the eighteenth century B.C. a canal was dug through this land of Goshen, the first to connect the Mediterranean, through the Nile, with the Red Sea.[124] Thus, the modern Suez Canal has had its predecessor at least 3,600 years ago.

As we proceed into the consequent phases of Moses' life an awareness arises that the events themselves overshadow the actions of the man. In the picture *The Ten Commandments* Moses expresses this feeling when he says, "By myself I am nothing. It is the power of God which uses me to work His will!"

c) The plagues. The will of God is expressed through Moses and Aaron in bringing about the afflictions that beset Pharaoh and his nation.[125] The Koran records the plagues also but uses the term "sign" instead.[126] In the picture we portray three plagues, while others

118. *Encyclopaedia Britannica,* 11th ed., VI, 613.

119. Ex. 7:11.

120. *Midrash Rabbah,* III, 125. See also *Philo,* VI, 323; *Josephus,* IV, 289-291.

121. Ex. 5:21; 6:9.

122. Gen. 45:10; Ex. 8:22.

123. *a)* W. M. F. Petrie, *Egypt and Israel* (London, 1931), p. 30. *b)* K. Baedeker, *Egypt and the Sudan* (Leipzig, 1914), p. 180.

124. Breasted, pp. 188, 276.

125. Ex. 7–10.

126. Holy Qur'an ('Ali tr.), 7:130-135, and nn. 345, 346.

are spoken of.

The first plague of the Bible[127] is the first plague we show on the screen, when Egypt's waters are turned into blood at the shrine of the "lord of the inundation," Khnum.[128] The next plague presented in the film is the seventh one of the Scriptures: thunder and hail and fire.[129]

The last plague, the death of all that is first-born in Egypt,[130] is brought about by God alone. In the picture Rameses II unknowingly pronounces the manner of this terrifying plague with his own mouth. A justification for this rendition could be based upon a verse contained in the Koran, where Pharaoh says, as the plagues are brought about, "We will slay their sons."[131]

It will be remembered that Moses brought his family with him from Midian to Egypt.[132] The Bible omits to explain but certainly implies that Sephora and Gershom left Egypt to return to Midian[133] before the event of the Exodus. There are traditions concerning Moses' separation from Sephora in Egypt.[134] On the screen a dramatic solution to the problem is presented.

A difficulty arose in the writing of the script *The Ten Commandments*. How can a man, a creature of God, make choice between good and evil of his own free will, if God hardens his heart?[135] Our solution is given, when Nefretiri says to Moses, "Who else can soften Pharaoh's heart—or harden it?" To which Moses replies that it may well be she through whom "God will work this wonder."

General observations have been made by Sir Flinders Petrie, Martin Buber and others that the majority of the plagues mentioned in the Bible are still recurring natural phenomena in Egypt.[136] At the time of the inundation (about July) the Nile does carry minute animal life and/or silt from beyond the cataracts which can produce a reddish tint in the water.[137] Frogs still breed in great numbers at about the same time. While visiting the temple of Luxor in 1954, shortly after the flood had abated, we observed innumerable little frogs on the still damp temple grounds. Flies and other in-

127. Ex. 7:20.

128. G. Rawlinson, *History of Ancient Egypt* (Boston, 1882), I, 338.

129. Ex. 9:22-26.

130. Ex. 11:5; 12:29-30.

131. Holy Qur'an ('Ali tr.), 7:127, and n. 319.

132. Ex. 4:20.

133. Ex. 18:2-6.

134. Ginzberg, III, 64.

135. Ex. 7:13, *et passim*.

136. Petrie, pp. 35-36. See also Buber, p. 61.

137. *Jewish Encycl.*, X (1905), 70.

sects can be a plague in Egypt to this day. The spread
of all manner of disease is not a thing of the biblical
past alone. Thunderstorms and hail do occur in the
winter season in the Land of the Nile. Under a recent
Cairo date line *The New York Times* reported locusts
destroying plant life in that city.[138] "Even darkness
which may be felt"[139] is another still existing phenomenon. It is the Khamsin, the sandstorm which can obscure the sun, or the Zobaa, a whirlwind which whips
the desert sand to rise in pillarlike fashion.[140]

Rabbi Hertz concurs with such views but stresses
the miraculous intensification of these phenomena to
illustrate man's impotence against God and God's judgment on the idols of Egypt.[141] In relation to the subject of Pharaoh and the land of Egypt the Koran says:
"Surely their evil fortune is only from Allah [God],
but most of them know not."[142]

d) The Passover. A reference in the Mishnah informs
that the Passover in Egypt differed from that celebrated in subsequent generations,[143] when it came to
be observed in the sense of a memorial, a thanksgiving
for the deliverance from bondage.[144]

Quite a different reason underlies the first Passover.
In the biblical sense it is particularly an ordinance to
invoke protection from the avenging "Lord [Who]
smote all the first-born in the land of Egypt."[145] The
ritual ordained by God for the Israelites cannot be interpreted as a festive occasion at this first occurrence.
The ordinance given for the "feast of unleavened
bread"[146] is for the future and not for that fateful night
which, with the death of Egypt's first-born, terminates
four hundred years of life and bondage in the land of
the Nile for the people of the Book.[147]

How did this first Passover differ in its rite from all
subsequent ones? We quote from the Mishnah: "At the
Passover of Egypt the lamb was got on the 10th [day],
sprinkling of the blood with a bunch of hyssop was
required on the lintel and on the two sideposts, and
it was eaten in haste and during one night; the pro-

138. Nov. 8, 1955.
139. Ex. 10:21.
140. *Encyclopae-dia Britan-nica,* 14th ed., VIII, 35.
141. J. H. Hertz, in *Pentateuch and Hafto-rahs* (U.S.A., 1941?), I, 400.
142. Holy Qur'an ('Ali tr.), 7:131.
143. Mishnah (Danby tr.), p. 148.
144. *Haggadah of Passover,* trans. M. Samuel (New York, 1942).
145. Ex. 12:29.
146. Ex. 12:14-20.
147. Gen. 15:13.

hibition of leavened bread lasted in the Passover of
Egypt but one day whereas the Passover of the generations that followed after continued throughout
seven days."[148] We read further that unleavened wheat,
barley, spelt, goat-grass and oats were admissible as
Passover food and the following uncooked fresh or
dried herbs: lettuce, chicory, pepperwort, snakeroot
and dandelion.[149]

In the picture *The Ten Commandments* Moses pre-
sides over the rite. We show the sprinkling of blood
with hyssop, the eating of the roast lamb, unleavened
bread and bitter herbs. All the participants are prepared for immediate departure. Other elements of
Jewish ritual are contained in the scene, such as the
confession of faith, the traditional questions asked (in
this instance, by Aaron's son Eleazar), the admission
of the stranger to partake of the Passover meal.[150]

There is a rabbinical tradition which makes Moses
the author of Psalms 90-100.[151] This tradition caused us
to use Psalm 91 to suggest the visible cause of death
of Egypt's first-born. In verse 6 it speaks of the "pesti-
lence that walketh in darkness." A portion of this Psalm
is chanted by Hur ben Caleb during the Passover meal.

Many of the religious holidays we celebrate today
have absorbed in their coming about much older and
more primitive festivals; historic-biblical events were
superimposed to give them added and new meaning.[152]
The Passover (Pesach) and the modern Seder cere-
mony held in the privacy of Jewish homes are no exception to these.

Two distinct festivals underlie the biblical Passover.
One pertains to a pastoral people owning flocks and
sacrificing animals; the other is that of an agricultural
people, where unleavened bread made from the new
field crops would be offered the gods in thanksgiving.[153]
Both of these festivals were celebrated in the spring,
close to the spring equinox,[154] i.e. about March 21st.
The twofold nature of the feast can still be discerned
in Leviticus 23:5-6, where the Passover of the Lord is
to be celebrated on the fourteenth day of the first

148. Mishnah
     (Danby tr.),
     pp. 148-149.

149. *Ibid.*, p. 138.

150. Ex. 12:
     48-49.

151. *Jewish
     Encycl.*, X,
     244.

152. *Jewish
     Encycl.*, IX,
     554.

153. *Ibid.*,
     pp. 553-554.

154. W. O. E.
     Oesterley and
     T. H. Robin-
     son, *Hebrew
     Religion*
     (London,
     1949),
     pp. 129, 165,
     180.

month and the feast of unleavened bread is to begin
on the fifteenth and to last seven days. In Exodus 23:15
and 34:18 the feast of unleavened bread is especially
emphasized.

It may be of some interest in this connection to note
that the Easter holiday, which to all Christians everywhere commemorates the resurrection of Jesus, was
once a pagan feast, as its name still implies. In Anglo-
Saxon the festival was called *Eastre,* or in the plural
Eastron (note the English *Easter* and the German
Ostern). It was held to honor a pagan goddess, Eostre,
at the time of the spring equinox, i.e. about March
21st. In several of the European languages the word
Passover, i.e. Pesach, has survived to express the Christian Easter. In French the holiday is called *Pâques,*
in Italian *Pasqua,* and in Spanish *Pascuas,* while the
English language contains the expression "paschal
lamb."[155]

The Passover is mentioned in several other instances
in the Old Testament. In Exodus 13:5, for example, it
is commanded that this day shall be observed after
reaching the Promised Land. A celebration of the holiday is indicated in Numbers 9:1-4 where we also find
evidence that a year has gone by since the Exodus
from Egypt. Preceded by an act of mass circumcision,
the Israelites hold the Passover at Gilgal, after they
have crossed the Jordan.[156]

A decided change in the celebration of this memorial
comes about during the time of the Temple. Heretofore we have had a family or local community rite.
Now, however, the sacrifice has to take place in the
Temple at Jerusalem, any other site being strictly pro-
hibited.[157] Even the partaking of the paschal meal has
to take place within the Temple walls and only the
following morning are the participants allowed to
leave for their homes.[158]

A notable mention of the Passover occurs in II Kings
23:21-23, which is also told in II Chronicles 35:1-18.
The implication is that the feast had not been held
since the days of the Judges. When Josiah (late sev-

155. J. T. Shipley,
*Dictionary
of Word
Origins*
(Ames, Iowa,
1955),
p. 131.

156. Josh. 5:2-11.

157. Deut. 16:
5-6.

158. Deut. 16:7.

enth century B.C.) is given the Book of the Covenant,[159] which is Deuteronomy, he rededicates his adherence to the Mosaic laws and reinstates the Passover on a lavish scale within the Temple.

159. II Kings 22: 8-10.

In the Old Testament, the holiday is last mentioned
in Ezekiel 45:21. After the destruction of the second
Temple (70 A.D.) the Passover meal reverts back to
the home. At this time also the sacrificial system ceases
to exist and, therefore, the sacrifice of a lamb is no
longer performed.[160]

160. Univ. Jewish Encycl., IX, 453-454.

It has been mentioned earlier on these pages that
the Passover had made use of already extant feasts by
giving new meaning to them. Now, an additional and
entirely new idea was incorporated in the ritual: the
hope for future redemption, the hope for the re-estab-
lishment of Jerusalem as the spiritual center of Judaism.[161]

161. Haggadah of Passover.

This ritual, celebrated in the home as it was during
that awesome night of long ago in Egypt, is known
now as Seder. The book which contains the regulations
for this service as well as the text to be read during
its performance, is known as the *Haggadah shel Pesach,* the Narration of the Story of the Passover.

The order on which the present-day ritual is based
goes back to about the middle of the third century
A.D. Additions and variations of the rite have taken
place since. Today, the procedure varies among different Jews, such as Yemenite and Sephardic Jews, as
well as those whose customs have been influenced by
cultures in other parts of the world.[162]

162. Jewish Encycl., XI (1907), 146.

Thus was the first Passover, ordained by God and
taught to slaves about to be redeemed by Moses. Thus
is the Passover throughout the ages for the Jews, and
for Christians the Lord's Last Supper contains a memory of it.

Moses, the Leader

*a) The length of the bondage and the Promised
Land.* Blasts of shofars announce the dawn of freedom
for the Israelites in the picture *The Ten Command-*

ments. The sounds of these traditional horns also punctuate the end of four hundred years of life in a land that was not theirs,[163] or, as we read in Exodus 12:40, "the sojourning of the children of Israel, who dwelt in Egypt, was four hundred and thirty years."

163. Gen. 15:13.

Rabbinic traditions explain the discrepancy of thirty years to mean that the Genesis account dates the four hundred years from the birth of Isaac; i.e. thirty years had elapsed from the time of Abraham's vision to the birth of Isaac.[164]

164. Hertz, I, 259.

The Bible tells us that the bondage of the Israelites in Egypt did not begin till after Joseph's death under a pharaoh "which knew not Joseph."[165] The traditions present this period of time as 210 years.[166]

165. Ex. 1:8-11.
166. *Midrash Rabbah*, III, 227.

The oppression of the Israelites is also described in the Koran. There, Pharaoh is called a "high-handed mischief maker" and he and his people are "arrogant," "guilty" and "iniquitous."[167]

167. Holy Qur'an ('Ali tr.), 10:75; 26: 10; 28:4.

The goal of the people who participate in the Exodus under the leadership of Moses is the Promised Land. The Lord's promise upon which all subsequent biblical hopes and their realization are based occurs first in Genesis 13:14-15: "And the Lord said unto Abram . . . Lift up now thine eyes, and look from the place where thou art northward, and southward, and eastward, and westward: For all the land which thou seest, to thee will I give it, and to thy seed for ever." The Lord's promise is brought to mind again, for example, in Exodus 12:25.

In Allah's (God's) revelations to His prophet Mohammed, that promise is also voiced: "I will . . . cause you to enter Gardens wherein rivers flow"[168]; "It may be that your Lord will destroy your enemy and make you rulers in the Land, then He will see how you act,"[169] to which the commentator adds, "By 'the Land' is meant the Promised Land."[170] In a later chapter it is written: "And We desired to bestow a favour upon those who were deemed weak in the land, and to make them the leaders, and to make them the heirs, And

168. *Ibid.*, 5:12.
169. *Ibid.*, 7:129.
170. *Ibid.*, n. 932.

to grant them power in the land."[171] The explanation
of the translator to this passage is: "heirs to a kingdom
in the promised land of Canaan. And this refers also
to the establishment of the kingdom of Islam and the
vanquishment of its persecutors."[172]

b) The Exodus. The shofars sound! Gone is the night
of terror! The angel of death has passed over and
spared the first-born in the houses marked with the
blood of the lamb. The Hebrews' possessions are en-
riched by what they can "borrow" from their Egyptian
neighbors.[173] Philo considers this spoil just wages for
services rendered.[174] Referring to Exodus 12:35-36
Josephus writes of gifts to the Hebrews to speed their
departure from Egypt.[175]

The "mixed multitude"[176] is interpreted as representing Semites other than Israelites,[177] or else those of
mixed blood and others who became converts to the
God of Moses.[178] On the screen, Israelites, Egyptians
and Negroes are shown.

The men, the women, the children, the cattle and
the fowl—all of them pour into the avenue of sphinxes
fronting the gate of Raamses, the treasure city that
Moses once had helped to build in the picture *The
Ten Commandments.*

A mixed multitude, indeed, happy in their new-found
freedom, the meaning of which they cannot fully com-
prehend after the years of affliction. Cherishing the
hope of reaching the Promised Land, they face an unknown road to take them over arid wastes to a para-
dise on earth—flowing with milk and honey—shimmer-
ing in their minds like a fata morgana.

Moses, the leader, is fully aware of the immense
responsibility that rests on him to bring this people
through a desolate wilderness to the mountain of God,
there to receive His Commandments and hence to
their other inheritance, Canaan.

Joshua, Moses' faithful helper, organizes the multitude according to tribes. True to the promise made,[179]
the bones of Joseph are carried along to be buried in

171. *Ibid.*, 28:
5-6.

172. *Ibid.*,
n. 1869.

173. Ex. 3:21-22;
11:2-3;
12:35-36.

174. *Philo*, VI,
349.

175. *Josephus,*
IV, 303.

176. Ex. 12:38.

177. Rylaarsdam
and Park,
p. 926.

178. *Philo*, VI,
353.

179. Gen. 50:25.

180. Ex. 13:19.
the land of his fathers.[180]

The moment of departure has arrived and Moses proclaims, "Hear, O Israel! remember this day when the strong hand of the Lord leads you out of bond-
181. Cf. Ex. 13:3.
age."[181] In reply the people shout the confession of
182. a) Author-
ized Daily
Prayer Book,
trans. J. H.
Hertz (New
York, 1948),
p. 117.
b) Septua-
gint Bible
(Thompson
tr.), p. 304.
c) Cf. Deut.
6:4.
faith, "The Lord is our God—the Lord is One."[182]

There is archaeological evidence of Semite tribes temporarily grazing their flocks in the verdant Nile Delta and withdrawing again after a season.[183] We have already spoken of Semitic war prisoners who were put to work in ancient Egypt. There are also contemporary records of fugitive slaves traveling east-
183. Wilson,
Burden,
p. 258.
ward, away from Egypt proper.[184] These accounts faintly echo the biblical Exodus which traditionally
184. J. A. Wilson,
in Ancient
Near Eastern
Texts
(Princeton,
1950),
p. 259.
took place at one time with the participation of a very large body of people. The number given is "about six hundred thousand on foot that were men, beside children. And a mixed multitude went up also with
185. Ex. 12:37-
38.
them."[185]

Assuming that each of these men represented a fam-ily of five, including women and children, the mixed multitude multiplies into the staggering figure of three million people.

The Koran in describing the event, states, "those who went forth . . . were thousands," which, as ex-
186. Holy Qur'an
('Ali tr.),
2:243, and
n. 319.
plained by the commentator, means just that and not hundreds of thousands.[186]

John Wilson supposes the population of ancient Egypt to have been about 1,600,000. Assuming this to have been the case, it would have meant a population density in the then habitable land, twice that of the state of Virginia in the United States of America, or
187. Wilson,
Burden,
p. 14.
three times that of Mississippi today.[187] The settled inhabitants of Palestine-Syria numbered about 36,000 during the period represented in the picture The Ten
188. Ibid., p. 201.
Commandments.[188]

Paul Heinisch, the Catholic scholar, states, "The impossibility of this figure [600,000] is generally acknowledged." He also informs that Palestine and Transjordan together hold about 1,250,000 inhabitants in this mid-century.[189] The impracticality of this vast number is also pointed out elsewhere.[190]

Investigating this aspect of the biblical text Sir Flinders Petrie has come forth with an interesting solution. According to him the Hebrew word *elef* that occurs in the biblical passage under discussion has two meanings, namely, "thousand," and "group" or "family." As the increase of years dimmed the past, the Bible scribes employed the word to mean "thousand." If, however, the meaning "family" or "group" is applied, we arrive at "six hundred families (or groups)," to which must be added the mixed multitude. "Six hundred families" add up to a more realistic figure than "six hundred thousand."[191] Petrie further estimates that the total average per tent, or that composing a family, was slightly over nine people.[192]

c) The Red Sea. With the arrival at the western shore of the Red Sea the Israelites' joy of freedom suddenly changes to despair when Pharaoh's chariots loom on the horizon. In the film a mutiny against the leadership of Moses is instigated by Dathan.[193] It is Moses' unshakable faith in God that saves the people in spite of themselves.

The Egyptians' pursuit is barred by the pillar of fire and cloud[194]—in Philo's words, "the light of which in the daytime was as the sun and in night as flame."[195] On the screen the visible manifestation of God is symbolized by the pillar of fire on this as well as on other occasions.

Masses of heavy clouds start to form and darkness oppresses the air. Upon God's command, Moses stretches out his hand over the sea. The east wind effects a phenomenon: the sea parts and permits the Israelites to cross to the eastern shore on dry ground.[196] Reaching the opposite shore the Israelites behold the "great work which the Lord did upon the Egyptians": the wind changes and a tumultous sea engulfs the pursuers.[197]

There is a thoughtful legend: when the Egyptians

189. Heinisch, pp. 88-89.
190. Rylaarsdam and Park, p. 925.

191. Ex. 12:37.

192. Petrie, pp. 42-46.

193. Cf. Ex. 14: 10-12.

194. Ex. 14:19-20, 24.
195. *Philo*, VI, 361.

196. Ex. 14:21-22.

197. Ex. 14:27-31.

were drowning the angels burst into song. God silenced them; the dying were His children too, the work of His hands.[198]

198. Ginzberg, VI, 12.

"And when We parted the sea for you, so We saved you and drowned the people of Pharaoh while you saw." Thus it is written in the Koran among other verses pertaining to the crossing of the Red Sea.[199] In these Scriptures the sea is not given a name.

199. Holy Qur'an ('Ali tr.), 2: 50; see also 10: 90-92; 20:77-80, and n. 82.

The naming of this body of water in Bible translations as "Red Sea" has a history of its own. The earliest texts in which this sea is named "Red Sea" are the Books of Judith, Wisdom and I Maccabees in the Septuagint. In the Hebrew Old Testament passages the sea is named *yam suph,* which does not mean "Red Sea" but rather "sea of reeds," "sea of seaweeds," "sea of seagrass" or "marsh sea." The name *yam suph* is also given to the Ælantic Gulf, i.e. the Gulf of 'Aqaba, in the Old Testament; for example, in Exodus 23:31, or in I Kings 9:26, where it is written "Solomon made a navy of ships in Ezion-geber . . . on the shore of the Red sea [*yam suph*], in the land of Edom." Scholars agree that the translation of *yam suph* into "Red Sea" is a mistaken one.[200] Nevertheless, this name is solidly established in Bible translations. The geographical Red Sea is called *ha-yam ha-adom* in modern Hebrew.[201]

200. a) Jewish Encycl., X, 345.
b) Heinisch, p. 80.
c) Westminster Historical Atlas to the Bible, ed. Wright and Filson (Philadelphia, 1945), p. 38.
201. University of Judaism, Los Angeles.

There are learned men who place the point of this particular crossing north of the modern city of Suez, either near Lake Timsah or at the Bitter Lakes. Early Greek and Latin authorities have placed it as far north as the city of Hero, i.e. Pithom, in the Wadi Tumilat, the land of Goshen.[202] It has been thought by others that the crossing of the *yam suph* took place at the Gulf of 'Aqaba. One of the reasons given is the Hebrew identity of the name with reference to I Kings 9:26 (see above), for example. Another justification for this theory is based on the implied volcanic activity of Mount Sinai in the Bible; the mountains near the western shore of this gulf were volcanic at one time, in contrast to the Sinai region.[203] Sir Winston Churchill, in his article "Moses," follows this view.[204]

202. Jewish Encycl., X, 345. See also Heinisch, p. 80; Westminster Atlas, p. 38.
203. Oesterley and Robinson, pp. 141-146.
204. W. S. Churchill, Amid These Storms (New York, 1932), p. 291.

Neither the correct translation of *yam suph* nor the geographical placements indicated above change the biblical account in the least: a body of water is crossed from Egypt to an eastern shore and the picture *The Ten Commandments* presents a literal interpretation of the Old Testament passage.[205]

Josephus, in his account of this crossing, refers to a related event which happened during the campaigns of Alexander the Great. He tells of the Pamphylian Sea drawing back for Alexander's army.[206] Arrian, Alexander's historian, describes that a north wind caused the waters to recede.[207]

On the very day of the Declaration of Independence of the Colonies, July 4, 1776, a committee consisting of John Adams, Benjamin Franklin and Thomas Jefferson was appointed to suggest a design for the Great Seal of the United States. On August 10, 1776, the following device for the reverse side of the seal was presented by them: "Pharaoh sitting in an open chariot, a crown on his head, and a sword in his right hand, passing through the divided waters of the Red Sea, in pursuit of the Israelites. Rays from a pillar of fire in the cloud, expressive of the Divine Presence and command, beaming on Moses, who stands on the shore and, extending his hand over the sea, causes it to overthrow pharaoh." The device was to contain the motto, coined by Cromwell: "Rebellion to Tyrants is Obedience to God." After many other suggestions, a different device, which is now the Great Seal of the United States, was adopted on June 20, 1782.[208]

Moses, the Lawgiver

a) Mount Sinai. God instructed Moses: "When thou hast brought forth the people out of Egypt, ye shall serve God upon this mountain."[209]

The mountain of God has two interchangeable names in the Bible, Mount Sinai and Mount Horeb.[210] Neither one of these names is given on survey maps of the Sinai Peninsula.[211] However, it appears that a particular mountain range located in the southern tip

---

205. Ex. 14: 15-31.

206. Josephus, IV, 317.

207. Arrian, Anabasis Alexandri, trans. E. I. Robson (Cambridge, Mass., 1946), I, 109.

208. G. H. Preble, Origin and History of the American Flag (Philadelphia, 1917), II, 683-691.

209. Ex. 3:12.

210. Ex. 19:20; 3:1. See also Jewish Encycl., XI, 381; Midrash Rabbah, III, 51.

211. a) Ordnance Survey of the Peninsula of Sinai (Southampton, 1868-69), Sheet 2. b) International Map of the World, 1:1,000,000, sheet NH-36, "Cairo," 2nd ed., Survey of Egypt (Giza, 1954).

of this peninsula is named Mount Sinai.

According to the monks at the monastery of St. Catherine, located at the base of the Sinai range, the biblical Sinai and Horeb are two separate peaks belonging to the Sinai mountain complex. The geographical names given them are Gebel Musa (Mountain of Moses) and Ras Safsafeh.[212] It is pointed out that Gebel Musa was the peak where "the glory of the Lord abode"[213] and where "he gave unto Moses . . . two tables of testimony, tables of stone, written with the finger of God." [214] Ras Safsafeh, which stands like a sentinel between Gebel Musa and the plain where the Israelites encamped, was the mountain upon which God descended to pronounce the Ten Commandments to the assembled people.[215]

Theories have been expressed that another mountain lying to the northwest of Gebel Musa might have been the biblical Mount Sinai. But the description left behind by the pilgrim Silvia of Aquitaine, who visited the peninsula in 385-388 A.D., agrees with the traditional location of Mount Sinai, the present Gebel Musa. Thus, this identification of the mountain of God is historically established as far back as the fourth century A.D. The history of the famous monastery of St. Catherine at the foot of Mount Sinai is equally as old.[216]

Some scholars hold the view that Mount Sinai should be placed east of the Gulf of 'Aqaba. This is the gulf bordering upon the east coast of the Sinai Peninsula. The theory is that the description contained, for example, in Exodus 19:18 represents an actual volcanic eruption. Sinai, according to geologists, was not volcanic, but some mountains immediately to the east of the Gulf of 'Aqaba were.[217] This view has already been touched upon in the discussion of the Red Sea crossing.

Other scholars are in agreement with locating Mount Sinai on the Sinai Peninsula. Several sites mentioned in the Bible in conjunction with the route taken by the Israelites have been established there.[218]

212. P. B. Meistermann, *Guide du Nil au Jourdain* (Paris, 1909), pp. 112-113.
213. Ex. 24:16.
214. Ex. 31:18.

215. Ex. 20:1-22. See also Meistermann, p. 153.

216. *Ibid.*, p. 100.

217. Oesterley and Robinson, pp. 141-148.

218. *Westminster Atlas.* See also Meistermann, pp. 49 ff.

In making the picture *The Ten Commandments* we
have not only adhered to, but photographed the biblical sites on the Sinai Peninsula. The atmosphere of
ancient and living traditions and the very nature of
that mountain fill one with exhilarating inspiration.

b) The Ten Commandments. In the Book of Exodus
the Commandments are given on three distinct occasions. The first time[219] God pronounces the Ten Commandments to all the assembled people and, conse-
quently, Moses writes down all the words the Lord
has spoken.[220] The second instance occurs when God
gives Moses "tables of stone, written with the finger
of God."[221] These are the ones Moses smashes when
he sees the idolatry of his people.[222] Later, God orders
Moses to make two tables of stone upon which He will
write the words again.[223]

In viewing the picture *The Ten Commandments* one
must assume that the giving of the Law, as described
in Exodus 20, has already taken place. We depict particularly the giving of the first tables of stone. The
event involving the second set of stone tables is not
shown on the screen.

The giving of the Law has stimulated much thought
among religious men. This becomes evident in reading the accounts contained in midrashic writings and
those of Philo and Josephus. Philo, whose mysticism
expressed in his metaphysical writings presents solutions beyond the plainly written word of Scripture,
suggested the idea of how to materialize these scenes
for the film. The use of the voice of God and the finger
of God in the form of fire is derived from his work.
It is best to quote excerpts from Philo's translated
writings, where he describes the event of Exodus 20:
"I should suppose that God wrought on this occasion
a miracle of a truly holy kind by bidding . . . sound
to be created in the air more marvelous than all instruments . . . [by] giving shape and tension to the air
and changing it to flaming fire. . . . Then from the
midst of the fire that streamed from heaven there

219. Ex. 20:2-17.

220. Ex. 24:4-8.

221. Ex. 31:18.
222. Ex. 32:19.

223. Ex. 34:1;
      Deut. 10:2.

sounded forth . . . a voice, for the flame became articulate speech. . . ."[224] Thus, on the screen, the flame becomes the divine voice and the finger of God which writes on the red granite stone of Sinai. It is this same divine flame which turns into the pillar of fire and cloud to protect the Israelites from the forces of Pharaoh at the Red Sea[225] and to serve as their guide on the road to the mountain of God.[226]

There are some interesting descriptions in midrashic writings concerning the giving of the Law; for example, the length of the tables of stone that God gave to Moses was six handbreadths, or about 20.64 inches.[227] The rabbis state that God addressed the people in Egyptian, since that was the language they knew. In another instance it is said that the voice of God could be heard by every person throughout the world, each in his own language, a total of seventy tongues.[228]

The lettering in which the Commandments are written on the red granite stone brought by us from the slopes of Mount Sinai to be used in the picture is of an early Canaanite type. It is a precursor of what was to become the square Hebrew alphabet with which the Hebrew Old Testament is written today. This text was set down by Ralph Marcus of the Oriental Institute at the University of Chicago. According to him, it was this type of writing which came about in the general area of Canaan during the late Bronze Age, which is the era of Moses.

There is no doubt in the minds of scholars that the Ten Commandments were set down originally as simple and brief statements, which later were expanded into the full text we now read in the Bible.[229] As a matter of fact, in teaching the Commandments today, a brief form is still used for good and practical reasons.

There are a few differences in the sequence of the Ten Commandments in some texts. In the Hebrew and in Josephus the respective Commandments concerning murder, adultery and theft are given in that sequence.[230] In the Septuagint, however, this sequence runs murder, theft, adultery;[231] while Philo enumerates

224. *Philo,* VII (1950), 23, 29.

225. Ex. 14:19-20.
226. Ex. 13:21-22.

227. *Midrash Rabbah,* III, 331.

228. Ginzberg, III, 94, 97.

229. *Jewish Encycl.,* IV (1907), 495. See also Rylaarsdam and Park, p. 979.

230. Ex. 20:13-15.

231. *Jewish Encycl.,* IV, 494.

them adultery, murder, theft.[232] The Vatican Codex, an early Bible manuscript written in Greek now located at the Vatican library in Rome, lists adultery, theft, murder.[233]

The Commandments are always ten in number in any religion which adheres to the Old Testament. Among these religions, however, different traditions have arisen and there are variances in the numbering of the Ten Words. (For ready survey, these differences are explained on the accompanying chart—see following page.[234]) These variances in the numbering have come about due to the fact that the Old Testament does not number the Law specifically.

The number of Commandments that each table of stone contained, therefore, also varies. Jewish tradition, which numbers Exodus 20:2 as a distinct Commandment, generally presents the division as an even one, i.e. five Commandments to each tablet. There are also ancient rabbinical views which claim that each tablet contained the complete wording of the Law.[235]

Catholics and Lutherans adhere to three Commandments for the first tablet and seven for the other, while practically all of the Reformed Churches divide them into four and six.

These respective divisions have one common meaning: the first tablet contains the Law dealing with the relationship of man to God, i.e. religious duties, while the second governs the relationship of man to man, i.e. moral obligations.

In copying the Commandments onto the red granite brought from Mount Sinai for practical use in the picture, we divided the Law into four and six. In the Monastery of St. Catherine there is an ancient portrait of Moses painted in an undated period. He is shown holding the tablets and the Commandments depicted thereon are divided into four and six.

The Koran does not list the Commandments in the manner of the Bible. But the giving of the Law is specifically mentioned in 7:142-147, where it says, for example: "And We ordained for him in the tablets

232. *Philo,* VII, 69-73.

233. *Jewish Encycl.,* IV, 494.

234. *a) Ibid.,* p. 495.
b) Rylaarsdam and Park, p. 979.
c) J. D. Davis and H. S. Gehman, *Westminster Dictionary of the Bible* (Philadelphia, 1944), p. 598.
d) E. Power, in *Catholic Commentary on Holy Scripture* (New York, 1953), p. 218.

235. *Jewish Encycl.,* IV, 495.

THE TEN COMMANDMENTS
Traditions of Their Order

			JEWISH	PROTESTANT	CATHOLIC AND LUTHERAN
vs.	2	I am the Lord thy God.	1st vs. 2		
vs.	3	Thou shalt have no other gods before me.	2nd vss. 3-6	1st vss. 2-3	1st vss. 2-6
vss.	4-6	Thou shalt not make unto thee any graven image.		2nd vss. 4-6	
vs.	7	Thou shalt not take the name of the Lord thy God in vain.	3rd	3rd	2nd
vss.	8-11	Remember the sabbath day to keep it holy.	4th	4th	3rd
vs.	12	Honour thy father and thy mother.	5th	5th	4th
vs.	13	Thou shalt not kill.	6th	6th	5th
vs.	14	Thou shalt not commit adultery.	7th	7th	6th
vs.	15	Thou shalt not steal.	8th	8th	7th
vs.	16	Thou shalt not bear false witness.	9th	9th	8th
vs.	17	Thou shalt not covet, etc.	10th	10th	divided into 9th and 10th

admonition of every kind and clear explanation of all
things."[236] Prohibitions are presented in Surah 6. These
are brought into connection with a "book" (the Pentateuch?) which Moses receives from the hands of
God.[237]

The assumption that the statement "We gave Moses
nine clear signs"[238] refers to nine Commandments
(not including the one concerning the Sabbath, which
would make it ten) is given by the commentator to
the Koran, Al Beidawi.[239] Another interpretation identifies these "nine signs" as the rod of Moses, his leprous
hand and seven of the biblical plagues.[240]

The Ten Commandments are the foundation upon
which a civilized world must build. Sir Winston
Churchill describes them as "those fundamental Laws
which were henceforward to be followed, with occa-
sional lapses, by the highest forms of human society."[241]

About the man Moses and the Law, Henry George
spoke these ringing words: "From between the paws
of the rock-hewn sphinx rises the genius of human
liberty, and the trumpets of the exodus throb with the
defiant proclamation of the rights of man . . . [the]
recognition of Divine law in human life. . . . From the
free spirit of the Mosaic law sprang that intensity of
family life that amid all dispersions and persecutions
has preserved the individuality of the Hebrew race:
that love of independence that under the most adverse
circumstances has characterized the Jew. . . . It kindled
that fire that has made the strains of Hebrew seers and
poets phrase for us the highest exaltations of thought;
that intellectual vigour that has over and over again
made the dry staff bud and blossom. And passing out-
ward from one narrow race it has exerted its power
wherever the influence of the Hebrew scriptures has
been felt."[242]

c) *The Golden Calf.* Considering Moses dead after
his absence of forty days, the Israelites express their
demand for visible gods to lead them.[243] Aaron com-

236. Holy Qur'an ('Ali tr.), 7:145.

237. *Ibid.*, 6:155.

238. *Ibid.*, 17:101.

239. Koran (Sale tr.), p. 282, n. 5.

240. Holy Qur'an ('Ali tr.), nn. 935, 1470.

241. Churchill, pp. 291-292.

242. George, *Moses*, an address delivered in Glasgow, Dec. 28, 1884, reprinted by Robert Schalkenbach Foundation (New York, n.d.), pp. 4, 7, 13.

243. Ex. 32:1-.

plies with their wishes; the Golden Calf is made and a riotous feast of idolatry ensues.

The screen being limited by code regulation in portraying what the biblical passage describes, a commentary is heard over these scenes, which attempts to make their enactment more complete. The wording used for this purpose is derived from the Bible either in direct quote or in adaptation.

Hot anger overcomes Moses when he sees the Israelites worshipping the Golden Calf and he breaks the tables of stone.[244] He asks the faithful to rally: "Who is on the Lord's side? let him come unto me."[245] Dathan, who personifies the opposition in the film, makes one last attempt to return the Hebrews to the flesh pots of Egypt.

The making of the Golden Calf, the faithlessness of the people and the breaking of the tables of the Law—all these events are part of Allah's (God's) revelation to Mohammed also.[246]

The manner of making such golden sculptures in ancient Egypt was, in some cases, in wood overlaid with thin gold.[247] This process can be observed on the screen.

The statement has been made frequently that the Golden Calf was derived from an Egyptian religious cult. It does seem so, but we cannot prove it one way or the other. It is true that certain animals were looked upon with religious reverence. Among them were three bulls, namely, the Mnevis Bull of Heliopolis, the Buchis Bull of Hermonthis and the Apis Bull of Memphis.[248] According to Étienne Drioton these bulls were not considered deities in themselves, but incarnations of important gods.[249]

At the ancient Egyptian turquoise mines in the Sinai Peninsula the goddess Hathor was worshipped. She is usually shown with cow horns on her human head, but sometimes even as a cow. Sir Flinders Petrie identifies her with the Semitic goddess Ashtaroth, whom we meet time and again in the Bible with varied spellings.[250]

244. Ex. 32:19.
245. Ex. 32:26.
246. Holy Qur'an ('Ali tr.), 7:148-151.
247. a) A. Lucas, Ancient Egyptian Materials and Industries (London, 1948), p. 264. b) Jewish Encycl., III (1907), 508.
248. Steindorff and Seele, p. 140.
249. In Introduction to Egyptian Archaeology (Cairo, 1946), p. 188.
250. W. M. F. Petrie, Researches in Sinai (London, 1906), pp. 137, 191.

The Golden Calf is revived in the Old Testament when Jeroboam sets up "two calves of gold . . . and he set the one in Beth-el and the other put he in Dan."[251] In this respect, is it not interesting that the "molten sea"[252] of Solomon's Temple should stand on "twelve oxen"?[253] We read that the ox or the bull was sacred to agricultural Semites and, perhaps because of this ancient meaning, or because it was a sacrificial animal, the ox formed part of the "molten sea" in the Temple.[254]

d) The Ark of the Covenant. The first mention of the Ark occurs in Exodus 25:10, when God orders Moses to make an "ark of shittim wood" (i.e. acacia wood) to hold the testimony.[255] The making of the Ark by Bezaleel is described in Exodus 37, but in the Book of Deuteronomy the order for its construction is not given by God till after the Golden Calf incident with the implication that Moses build it.[256] The second set of the tables of stone are to be placed in the Ark.

Once the Temple is built the Ark is placed therein and it ceases to be a movable sanctuary.[257]

The Ark is also mentioned in the text of the Koran. An explanation is appended to the effect that the word used for ark, *tabut,* represents a chest, or a box, and also the heart. Based on this last meaning, it is expounded that the heart is the real repository of the Lord.[258] According to Jallalo'ddin the Ark contained the shoes and staff of Moses, the miter of Aaron, manna and the broken pieces of the tables of the Law.[259]

To archaeologists the design of the Ark suggests an Egyptian pattern. In that ancient land such movable sanctuaries, housing gods, were carried in processions.[260]

As the picture *The Ten Commandments* comes to an end and Moses ascends Mount Nebo, he sees the Israelites approach the river Jordan in the far distance, carrying the Ark of the Covenant.

e) Mount Nebo. Nebo or Pisgah, from which Moses

251. I Kings 12:28-29.

252. I Kings 7:23.

253. I Kings 7:25.

254. Jewish Encycl., XI, 452.

255. Ex. 25:16.

256. Deut. 10:1-5.

257. I Kings 8:6-8.

258. Holy Qur'an ('Ali tr.), 2:248, n. 328.

259. Koran (Sale tr.), p. 36, n. 2.

260. Petrie, Egypt and Israel, p. 61.

surveys the Promised Land that he cannot enter, is
the mountain which he ascends to meet his final earthly destiny.[261]

261. Deut.
    32:49-52;
    34:1-6.

Nebo and Pisgah seem to be one and the same
mountain, though they may be two distinct peaks. As
a matter of fact, the view from the geographical Mount
Nebo does not correspond with that described in the
Bible. However, located on the same ridge a little
more than a mile to the northwest, there is a peak
named Gebel Sijagha. From this location a magnificent view is obtained and most of the land of which
we read in the Bible can be seen. In Deuteronomy
32:49 this point is called Abarim.[262] According to modern maps, Mount Nebo lies approximately eleven miles
in a straight line to the east from the entrance of Jordan into the Dead Sea. It is located in present Transjordan.[263]

262. *Jewish En-
    cycl.*, IX,
    200; X, 62.

263. *International
    Map of the
    World.*

On the screen, Moses is seen as he bids farewell to
those nearest him before his ascent to Mount Nebo
to die. Wisdom, majesty and sadness dwell upon the
face of Moses, but "his eye was not dim, nor his natural force abated."[264] He puts his mantle over the
kneeling Joshua and lays his hands upon the new
leader's head in ordination. This is the scriptural
source upon which this rite is founded.[265]

264. Deut. 34:7.

265. Deut. 34:9.
    See also
    *Jewish En-
    cycl.*, VI
    (1907), 211.

Pursuing the fact that the art of writing was known
in the age of Moses and the possibility that some written word by the hand of Moses, "who was learned in
all the wisdom of the Egyptians,"[266] may have existed
at one time, the film shows Moses giving Joshua five
papyrus scrolls.[267]

266. Acts. 7:22.

267. Jeffery, p. 47.
    See also
    Rylaarsdam
    and Park, p.
    842.

Of his death Philo writes, "the time came when he
had to make his pilgrimage from earth to heaven, and
leave this mortal life for immortality, summoned
thither by the Father Who resolved his twofold nature
of soul and body into a single unity, transforming his
whole being into mind, pure as the sunlight."[268]

268. *Philo*, VI,
    593.

269. Deut. 34:6.

"No man knoweth of his sepulchre unto this day."[269]
To this, Henry George—whom Moses inspired, as the

Lawgiver did and does inspire so many men, both
great and small—adds, "but the name of the Hebrew
who, revolting, strove for the elevation of his fellow-
men, is yet a beacon light to the world. It is in the
Mosaic institutions that we may read the greatness of
the mind whose impress they bear—of one of those
star souls that dwindle not with distance, but, glowing
with the radiance of essential truth, hold their light
while institutions and languages and creeds change
and pass."[270]

The Liberty Bell in Philadelphia, upon its metal
cast carries the same message with which the picture
The Ten Commandments closes. Here Moses ad-
dresses not only the Israelites, but all the world and
all the generations to come when he pronounces the
words of God: "GO, PROCLAIM LIBERTY THROUGHOUT
ALL THE LANDS UNTO ALL THE INHABITANTS THERE-
OF!"[271]

270. George, pp.
12, 15;
edited by the
author.

271. Cf. Lev.
25:10.

THE PHARAOHS

Pharaoh, God and Ruler

Why was the pharaoh accepted by his people as a god who ruled on earth? In order to gain some knowledge about this god-king we must transpose ourselves into the psychology of the ancient Nile dwellers and attempt to visualize what the pharaoh meant to his contemporaries who lived under his rule and looked up to this god with practical satisfaction.

Contrary to other Near-Eastern countries of that period, where the king ruled as a deputy for the gods, the pharaoh was one of the gods in Egypt.[1] The origin of this religious concept with its political and economic implications lies unrecognizably buried in Egypt's prehistory. It appears as an already established fact during the early dynasties of the Old Kingdom (circa 2700 B.C.). This concept of government continued successfully for about 2,000 years till the Empire started to decay and the dogma of the god-king became nothing but a mummified idea carried forward by the sheer weight of centuries of ossified tradition.

John Wilson has developed some revealing theories on this doctrine and its reasons for existence. He writes that the dogma grew out of the natural geographic isolation and self-sufficiency of the rich Nile valley, and the dualism of its innate political components,

1. J. A. Wilson, *Burden of Egypt* (Chicago, 1951), p. 45.

Upper and Lower Egypt. Only a god who was not a
citizen of either one of the two lands could successfully rule over both and hold them and their people
together.[2]

2. *Ibid.,*
pp. 45-46.

But why a god—why not a king who through his
ability, knowledge and diplomacy was able to keep
Upper and Lower Egypt unified as one land? In actuality that is what also took place, but it is a modern
afterthought.

In this period of human development man's mind
did not look for logical causes. According to William
Albright, James Baldwin termed this age the "prelogi-
cal" stage,[3] when man's observations were purely sub-
jective. The relationship between the impressionable
human being and nature, events and his gods, was one
in which man's mind animated everything in the universe. John Wilson says: "[The Egyptian] saw no essential difference in substance in the several components of the universe. To him the various visible and
tangible phenomena of his existence were only superficially or temporarily different, but essentially of one
substance, blended into a great spectrum of overlap-
ping colors without sharp margins."[4] In analyzing
man's mental attitude toward the world Henri Frankfort arrived at an excellent conclusion: "The fundamental difference between the attitudes of modern and
ancient man . . . is this: for modern, scientific man
the phenomenal world is primarily an IT; for ancient—
and also for primitive—man it is a THOU . . . THOU
is not contemplated with intellectual detachment; it is
experienced as life confronting life."[5] This IT is man's
objective observation of phenomena and their com-
prehension in logical thought. To the ancient Egyptian, as well as to ancient people elsewhere, "natural
phenomena were regularly conceived in terms of human experience and that human experience was conceived in terms of cosmic events."[6]

The ancient Egyptians were of an easy-going dis-
position. The world surrounding them undoubtedly
encouraged such an attitude: bright blue skies and a

3. W. F.
Albright,
*Archaeology
and the Re-
ligion of
Israel*
(Baltimore,
1946), p. 26.

4. Wilson,
pp. 46-47.

5. H. and H. A.
Frankfort,
in *Before
Philosophy*
(Harmonds-
worth, Eng-
land, 1951),
pp. 12-14.

6. *Ibid.,* p. 12.

brilliant sun; the permanence of the life-giving Nile; a land to itself, isolated and protected by the mountains bordering upon both sides of the valley as well as by arid deserts. If there was more than one solution to any problem they did not bother to systematize, scrutinize and make an intelligent choice. "Those people were neither mystics nor modern scientific rationalists. . . . Their reasoning never sought to penetrate to the essence of phenomena, and their easy-going pragmatism did not attempt to find the one single way; rather, different and disparate ways were acceptable if they gave some indication of practical effectiveness."[7] And why not! After all, the Nile kept on flowing, the fields grew with wheat after the inundation, the sun rose in the east each morning to bring warmth and joy after the dreary darkness and the cold of night. All this happened and continued to happen with regularity, season after season, year after year, century after century. And the pharaoh was a good god. Indeed, why not? Egypt and its people were secure while the pharaoh was their god.

To modern man the ancient Egyptian is a paradox. Traditional to the extreme, he kept the customs handed down to him by his ancestors with insistence and without change, yet he was also open-minded in his own fashion and accepted new ideas, new gods with ease and without contradiction to previously held concepts. In this, to him, practical attitude, he superimposed one concept over the other and formed combinations that are bewildering to us. The many gods were no problem to him. He identified some with others and accepted foreign gods as well. He united the sun-god Ra with the creator-god Amon into Amon-Ra, while considering them individually as well. The Semitic Ashtaroth and Baal had their own cult within Egypt.[8] When the invading Hyksos brought their god Baal to the Delta, the Egyptians had no difficulty in identifying him with Seth, their god of foreign countries.[9] (This god's name is commemorated in that of Sethi.) An Egyptian could worship different godly trinities[10]

7. Wilson, p. 46.

8. a) *Ibid.*, p. 192.
b) G. Steindorff and K. C. Seele, *When Egypt Ruled the East* (Chicago, 1947), p. 115.

9. Steindorff and Seele, p. 25.

10. É. Drioton, in *Introduction to Egyptian Archaeology* (Cairo, 1946), pp. 185-186.

without reproach to himself. It was all good, the old and the new; "they were only superficially different" and "blended into" each other "without sharp margins."[11] There were no precise delineations. "It was easy to move comfortably from the human to the divine and to accept the dogma that this pharaoh . . . was actually a god, graciously residing upon earth in order to rule the land of Egypt."[12] This was an ancient dogma, a tradition that solved the problem of government for the Egyptian. It worked and he was content.

This, of course, presents only a partial insight into the mentality of the ancient Egyptian. It may have created the erroneous picture of a thoughtless, careless people, lacking in intellect. A people able to build the pyramids with geometric precision, a nation that produced sculptures and paintings which cause us to marvel today must have contained within their midst individuals capable of creative and contemplative thought. So it must have been within the vastness of their religion. A text of about 2000 B.C. speaks of the equality of men and has the god Amon state, "I made every man like his fellow. I did not command that they do evil, but it was their hearts which violated what I said."[13] It has been established that Psalm 104 was derived from a much older Egyptian hymn.[14]

Still more intriguing is the Memphite theology, which considered the creation of the world intellectually, as an act of thought. It is a logos doctrine, set down originally about 2700 B.C., in which the god Ptah of Memphis conceived the world in his mind and brought its various composing elements into physical existence through the power of the spoken word.[15] The search in man's mind for one cause, one reason underlying all and permeating everything started early. It is interesting in this regard that the philosophy of the logos should come back to Egypt from Greece—through Plato to Philo Judaeus of Alexandria—some 2,700 years later.

Another concept also holds fascination. This one

11. Wilson, pp. 46-47.

12. *Ibid.*, p. 47.

13. J. A. Wilson, in *Ancient Near Eastern Texts* (Princeton, 1950), p. 8.

14. Wilson, *Burden*, p. 227.

15. Wilson, *Ancient Texts*, p. 4.

The tables of the Law reproduced in early Canaanite lettering
(Page 40)

Gebel Musa, the peak of Sinai where "the glory of the Lord abode." *(Page 38)*

Ras Safsafeh, the "Horeb" of the Bible. *(Page 38)*

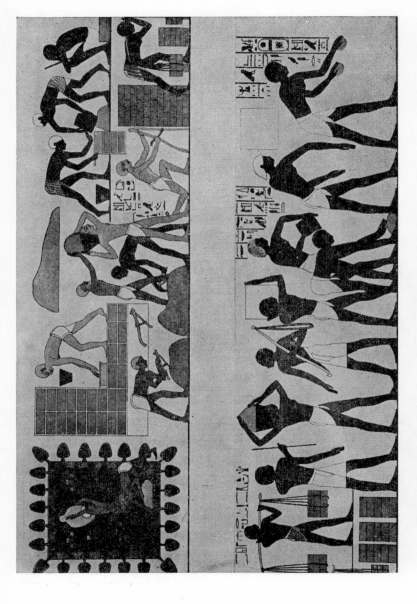

Mural painting in the tomb of Rekhmere showing captives making bricks (Thebes). (From Lepsius, *Denk-maeler aus Aegypten . . .* Berlin, 1849-1856. Part 3, Pl. 40.)

Brick pit scene photographed in Egypt for *The Ten Commandments*. (*Pages 21, 103*)

Pylons and gate, obelisks and colossi at Luxor, as engraved for Napoleon I. (From *Description de l'Égypte* . . . Paris, 1809-. Vol. III, Pl. 6.)

Pylons, gate and colossi of the biblical treasure city Raamses, erected and photographed in Egypt
(*Pages 33, 107, 116, 117*)

Sethi I in his war chariot riding against the Canaanites (Karnak temple). (From Schaefe
and Andrae, *Kunst des Alten Orients*. Berlin, 1925.)

Detail showing adaptation of the Karnak temple sculpture to the set
erected in Egypt. *(Pages 117, 120)*

Pharaoh offering sacrifice to Sokar (Abydos). (From Lange, *Aegypten, Landschaft und Kunst.* Berlin, 1943. Pl. 53.)

The shrine of Sokar adjoining the "Hall of Audience" set
(Pages 108, 117)

(Upper) Model showing the erection of an obelisk. (From Engelbach, *Problem of the Obelisks*. Courtesy of Bruce Humphries, Inc.)

(Lower) The erection of an obelisk for Sethi I's jubilee
(Pages 56, 106)

applies to pharaoh and government. It was called *ma'at*. The word defies precise translation because it is expressive of a number of ideas related to one another. It has the quality of truth, justice, order, righteousness; it is something that is morally good. The god-king was endowed with it and in expressing it he was executing the divine function of his rule.[16]

Pharaoh was thought of as being divinely conceived—the sun-god incorporating himself in the body of the reigning pharaoh at the time of conception. Thus, when the old pharaoh died, the divine descent of the new king was assured and he could rule as a god upon earth.[17] This dogma was applicable even when a new dynasty, a new family of pharaohs, came into power. The Egyptian god-king doctrine shows a religious father-son relationship, though the practical use to which it was put is another matter.

The legitimacy of divine kingship was insured in still another manner. In marrying his sister, the daughter of the queen, the god-king would firmly establish his throne against many possible claimants from among the offspring of his father's lesser wives. In this fashion the divine genealogy was kept theoretically intact.[18]

The god-king had five distinct titles, which served to illustrate his divine descent and the legitimacy of his rule, his power and the unity of Upper and Lower Egypt. His fourth title, "he of the Sut-Plant and of the Bee," which symbolized him as king of Upper and Lower Egypt, preceded the pharaoh's prenomen, which, when written, was enclosed in a frame called a cartouche.[19] These are the names of Sethi I and of Rameses II that we have copied[20] and properly applied to all manner of objects shown in the picture *The Ten Commandments*. The fifth title, the sun-god name, established the pharaoh's connection with that deity. It preceded the personal name of the king, which again was enclosed in a cartouche.[21] It is by these personal names that we

16. Wilson, *Burden*, p. 48.

17. *Ibid.*, p. 97.

18. *Ibid.*, pp. 96-97.

19. *Ibid.*, pp. 102-103. See also Steindorff and Seele, pp. 84-85.

20. E. A. W. Budge, *Kings of Egypt* (London, 1908), I, 162, 174.

21. Wilson, *Burden*, pp. 102-103. See also Steindorff and Seele, pp. 84-85.

know the Egyptian pharaohs as Sethi and Rameses.

Pharaohs were not addressed by their proper names, but instead they were spoken of as "the good god," "the ruler" or "his majesty." It was not until the New Kingdom (about sixteenth century B.C.) that the title "pharaoh" came into usage. Pharaoh, as he is called in the Bible,[22] derived from the Egyptian word *per-o*. It means "big house" and was used originally in a manner similar to "the White House announces," meaning of course the President of the United States; or "Buckingham Palace," standing for Elizabeth II; or "the Kremlin," representing whoever is in power in the U.S.S.R.[23]

The god-king was the supreme power of the land. As such he was high priest, commander in chief of the armed forces, chief justice, administrator, and so forth. But, after all, he was only a man of flesh and blood; he could not possibly execute all these responsibilities in person. Therefore, he delegated power; he appointed officers and surrounded himself with a bureaucracy of councilors for the many departments of government. He had to be shrewd and consider one political faction against the priesthood, or another against the army, and beware of intrigues hatched against him even within his own palace.[24]

The pharaoh was a man of flesh and blood indeed. As such he incorporated within himself little that was godly and all that was human: strength, nobility, weakness, ambition, love and hate. All these good gods had the divine gift of *ma'at*. But it was according to a pharaoh's character that he administered it —for good or for evil. In this manner are the pharaohs portrayed in the picture *The Ten Commandments:* an inhuman Rameses I, who orders the destruction of Israel's new-born sons; Sethi I, a kind but stern father, a humane ruler; and Rameses II, whose ambition was power.

Now, that we have discussed the pharaoh as god and ruler of Egypt, we must realize that out of this con-

22. Ex. 1:11, *et passim.*

23. A. Erman and H. Ranke, *Aegypten* (Tübingen, 1923), p. 62.

24. *Ibid.,* p. 55. See also Steindorff and Seele, pp. 85-86.

flict with a human god arose a Moses to establish a new nation of men and women who owed their allegiance to no man and to no earthly idol, but to one God, YHWH; to the one and only God, Who created all, Who is worshipped as the Father of all his sons and daughters by the brotherhood of Jews, Christians and Moslems and, in a wider sense, by the followers of other religions as well.

Rameses I

Rameses, who had been vizier of Upper Egypt, was chosen by Har-em-Hab to become his successor, when this childless pharaoh died.[25] With Rameses I a new dynasty, the nineteenth (1319-1222 B.C.), came into being, establishing new god-kings and bringing new names to the throne of Egypt.[26]

When he came to rule (1319-1318 B.C.), Rameses I was already an old man and he appointed his son Sethi I to coreign with him.[27] This information helped us solve a dilemma in writing the script for *The Ten Commandments.* In the dramatists' minds it would not do to have one and the same pharaoh pronounce the cruel edict over the Hebrews and be the king who, according to ancient tradition, "used to hug and kiss" Moses.[28] The duality of this kingship was applied to the picture by having Rameses I issue the inhuman verdict, while Sethi I becomes a just father to two princes of Egypt.

Sethi I

After a reign of only two years Rameses I died.[29] The new pharaoh, Sethi I (1318-1301 B.C.), vigorously engaged in military activities to strengthen the Empire, which still suffered from the decline brought about during the reign of the idealistic but impractical Akhnaton (1380-1362 B.C.). Sethi's campaign into Asia served to check the rising menace of the Hittites who were pressing southward from Asia Minor. He succeeded in re-establishing the borders of Egypt's possessions in northern Syria. Once his military pursuits had borne fruit, Sethi I became an

25. Steindorff and Seele, p. 247.

26. Wilson, *Burden,* p. 239.

27. J. H. Breasted, *History of Egypt* (New York, 1921), p. 408.

28. *Midrash Rabbah,* III, trans. S. M. Lehrman (London, 1951), p. 33.

29. Breasted, p. 409.

active builder to which his temples and other monuments still bear witness.[30]

To rule an empire is arduous business, even for
a god-king. The distances that had to be covered
to watch over it were time-consuming. Both Libya
to the west and Palestine-Syria to the east required
active vigilance and supervision from the pharaoh.
For this purpose Sethi I started to rebuild Tanis in
the Delta, which had been the Hyksos seat of government (1730-1580 B.C.). Such is the view held by
archaeologists up to now.[31] According to Labib Habachi, however, the new capital was Per-Ramses—
the biblical treasure city Raamses—at modern Qantir.[32]

It is at this moment of Egypt's history that we
pick up the thread of Sethi's life in the picture.
Moses has just returned victoriously from his Ethiopian campaign when Sethi I entrusts him with the
assignment to complete the construction of the new
capital in time for the jubilee.

The building of the new capital in the Delta and
the preparation for Sethi's jubilee are historical
facts.[33] Such jubilees were celebrated to honor the
pharaoh usually after thirty years had gone by since
his official presentation as heir to the throne. They
were punctuated by the erection of obelisks.[34] The
process of building the city; the memorial obelisks;
and the day of jubilee are shown on the screen. This
is also the day chosen by Sethi to announce who is
to succeed him on the throne.

The kindness of the historical Sethi I is pointed
out in the humane treatment and increased food
provisions he bestowed upon laborers.[35] As a man
of justice, he enacted severe legislation against cor-
ruption in government.[36] These laws, enacted to
maintain integrity in Egypt, gave rise to one of the
most critical scenes in the picture: Sethi has to judge
a man who threatens the honor of the state. That
man is Moses! Sethi I orders the name of Moses—
once Prince of Egypt—to be erased from every docu-

30. Wilson, *Burden*, pp. 240-241. See also Steindorff and Seele, p. 248; Breasted, pp. 409-413.

31. Wilson, *Burden*, p. 239. Also Steindorff and Seele, p. 256.

32. Conference with the author, Luxor, Nov. 1954.

33. Breasted, p. 418.

34. Wilson, *Burden*, pp. 213, 252. Also Steindorff and Seele, p. 63; Breasted, p. 418.

35. Breasted, p. 414.

36. Wilson, *Burden*, p. 241.

ment, from all pylons and obelisks, from all the monuments of Egypt. In conclusion he gives advice to him who now will be his heir, Rameses II. The wording used in the picture is derived from an ancient document of the twelfth dynasty (1990-1780 B.C.), translated by James Breasted, in which the aged pharaoh Amenemhet lectures his son as follows:

> Hearken to that which I say to thee,
>
> . . . .
>
> Harden thyself against all subordinates.
> The people give heed to him who terrorizes them;
> Approach them not alone.
> Fill not thy heart with a brother,
> Know not a friend,
> Nor make for thyself intimates,
> Wherein there is no end.
> When thou sleepest, guard for thyself thine own heart;
> For a man has no people,
> In the day of evil.
> I gave to the beggar,
> I nourished the orphan;
> I admitted the insignificant,
> As well as him who was of great account.
> But he who ate my food made insurrection;
> He to whom I gave my hand, aroused fear therein.[37]

37. Breasted, pp. 178-179

This quotation of Egyptian wisdom is reminiscent of a passage in the Old Testament of a much later date. It is to be found in Micah 7:5-6: "Trust ye not a friend, put ye not confidence in a guide: keep the door of thy mouth from her that lieth in thy bosom. For the son dishonoreth the father . . . a man's enemies are the men of his own house."

The effacing of a name, even of entire monuments, did occur from time to time in ancient Egypt. It was a most severe punishment. The belief was that the elimination of a name was equal to death.[38] A name that cannot be read and cannot be spoken is soon forgotten and lost to the memory of later generations.

38. Wilson, *Burden*, p. 225. Also Erman and Ranke, p. 190.

There is an incised relief on a Karnak temple wall representing Sethi I and Rameses II as crown prince.

In the opinion of James Breasted, Rameses II, upon
gaining the throne through intrigue, had the name
and figure of an elder brother effaced and his own
superimposed instead.[39]

39. Breasted,
    pp. 418-420.

In the picture *The Ten Commandments* Sethi I is
portrayed as a kind but stern ruler with a wry
humor. He is aware of strengths and weaknesses in
others. On his deathbed he breaks his own edict by
speaking the name of the man who ate his bread
and made rebellion against Egypt—the man whom
he still loves as a son: Moses.

Rameses II

Rameses II still carries the epithet "the great."
A pharaoh who reigned for sixty-seven years (1301-
1234 B.C.)[40] had much time to build temples and
to commemorate his factual or fanciful exploits on
sculptured monuments, to impose the cartouche bearing his name wherever he chose and sometimes take
credit for what was not his.[41] Even those who sat
on the throne of Egypt in the following—the twentieth—dynasty (1200-1090 B.C.) were so impressed
by Rameses II's reputation that they accepted all
the records left behind him as actual history and
adopted his name as their own for whatever greatness and glory it implied.[42] Some careless guide who
leads an awed tourist through the maze of Egyptian
antiquities today is apt to ascribe to Rameses more
than even this pharaoh claimed for himself.[43]

Rameses II was a warring pharaoh. Many campaigns were conducted by him to safeguard the
Empire,[44] the contemporary effect of which seemed
to help maintain Egypt and her possessions. Today
we can ascertain the causes through the effects they
have created and we are fortunate to be able to
establish what Rameses and his contemporaries could
not know about their own times. During those centuries the pattern of the history of the world was
about to change. New people were pressing into the
Mediterranean area from the northeast,[45] new na-

40. Steindorff
    and Seele,
    p. 252.

41. *Ibid.*, p.
    275. Also
    Breasted, p.
    445.

42. Steindorff
    and Seele, p.
    253. Also
    Breasted,
    pp. 462-463.

43. Steindorff
    and Seele,
    p. 66.

44. Breasted,
    pp. 423-441.

45. Wilson,
    Burden,
    p. 244.

tions were in the making that would appear with greater clarity and definition some centuries later. The age of copper and bronze, of which Egypt had so much, was on its way out, to be superseded by iron, of which Egypt had none. All these causes had started to stir faintly in the Near East and kept on stirring during the long reign of Rameses II. He could not know, just as we could not know that Hitler's coming to power in 1933 would sow the evil seed for World War II; or that the October Revolution of 1917 would bring about a world divided by an Iron Curtain and a new form of hostility, the Cold War. The real causes of events are buried in the past and their significance unearthed in the future.

It is for the impact created by his buildings and the sculptured accounts of his wars, actual and assumed, that Rameses II is still called "the great." Is he still called "the great" perhaps, because, in a sense, he was the last great god-king of Egypt? Soon after his reign this concept gradually lost vitality to an extent that permitted the assassination of a god-king like Rameses III (1195-1164 B.C.).[46] It remained a tradition, but without the power of moral conviction—a dogma kept alive against the current of new thoughts and events which were about to make themselves felt outside Egypt to influence the world as time became both future and past.

James Breasted describes Rameses II as "inordinately vain and . . . ostentatious [who] loved ease and pleasure and . . . voluptuous enjoyments."[47] John Wilson analyzes him as "a stupid and culpably inefficient general [who] was personally courageous [but] arrogant." With regard to the battle of Kadesh against the Hittites this same author states that the event does not invoke "much admiration for his intelligence or foresight."[48] Lack of foresight led him into a Hittite trap at Kadesh, but it was his personal courage that got him out of it.[49]

46. Steindorff and Seele, p. 256.

47. Breasted, pp. 460-461.

48. Wilson, Burden, pp. 247, 245.

49. Ibid., pp. 245-247. Also Steindorff and Seele, p. 251.

Rameses II was an avid builder who, among many other edifices, finished the imposing hypostyle hall of the Karnak temple which had been started by his grandfather, Rameses I, and continued by his father, Sethi I.[50] The obelisk which stands in the Place de la Concorde in Paris[51] and at least three others now located at Rome[52] are his. But in his lust for power and fame, his vanity for eternal recognition, he also usurped buildings and monuments which were a credit to earlier pharaohs.[53] The Delta city started by Sethi I bears his name, Per-Ramses. George Steindorff and Keith C. Seele call him "the greatest of Egyptian boasters."[54]

According to James Breasted it was through a palace intrigue that Rameses II gained the throne[55] and intrigues do play their part in the film.

This pharaoh had over one hundred sons and daughters, but it was his thirteenth son, Merneptah (1234-1222 B.C.), who ruled over Egypt in due time. The twelve older sons had died.[56] The first among these, as far as our interpretation on the screen shows, was Rameses' first-born son, who met the fate of "all the first-born in the land of Egypt"[57] that night of the first Passover.

A pharaoh with these characteristics does fit the biblical Pharaoh of the Exodus. His personal courage, his arrogance and stubborn conceit as well as his lack of foresight can be recognized when he defies Moses, the spokesman of God, which leads him to ruin and sorrow at the Red Sea. Thus Rameses II, as he is painted onto the canvas of the picture *The Ten Commandments*.

Nefretiri

Beyond the fact that Nefretiri was Rameses II's wife and queen of Egypt[58] there is not very much that we have been able to learn about her. Her name barely appears in authoritative texts dealing with the history of ancient Egypt consulted by us.

Wallis Budge lists her cartouches,[59] and we read

50. Steindorff and Seele, p. 257.
51. *Ibid.*
52. Breasted, p. 445.

53. *Ibid.* Also Wilson, *Burden*, pp. 247, 252; Steindorff and Seele, p. 275.
54. Steindorff and Seele, p. 275.
55. Breasted, p. 418.

56. Wilson, *Burden*, p. 253; Breasted, p. 461.
57. Ex. 11:5.

58. Steindorff and Seele, p. 266; Breasted, p. 446.

59. Budge, I, 177.

in another book of his that Rameses II built a temple
dedicated to the goddess Hathor and to his wife
Nefretiri at Abu Simbel.[60] We have seen one of the
famous colossi of Rameses at the temple of Luxor,
whereon this queen is also sculptured. Most impressive of all that remains of Nefretiri today is her
rock tomb located in the Valley of the Queens on
the west bank of the Nile, near ancient Thebes. The
murals portraying Nefretiri in that tomb impress the
viewer with her grace and beauty.[61]

We read in a little-known book that she was a
hereditary princess of Egypt, the daughter of a pharaoh.[62] Whether she was a sister, half-sister or cousin
to Rameses II we do not know. The same book informs us that she was already married to Rameses II
in the first year of his reign,[63] which is the interpretation contained in the film. Presumably Nefretiri
had two sons whose names are lost to history.[64] Merneptah, who became pharaoh after Rameses II, was
the latter's son by another wife.

The fact that a temple had been built in which
Nefretiri shared honors with the goddess Hathor
indicates that her influence upon Rameses II must
have been great. The weight of her influence upon
Rameses' decisions is dramatically portrayed in the
picture *The Ten Commandments*.

Epilogue

During the decades following the expulsion of the
Hyksos, Egypt started on its road to Empire. Egypt
became the master of the then known world—until
the Rameses of the twentieth dynasty reigned over
its decline when Palestine and Syria were lost and
with them Egypt's foothold in Asia. Gradually the
Empire disintegrated and with it the power of Egypt.

Beyond the borders of Egypt new concepts were
being thought which would create a theocracy in
Palestine to establish the belief in one God for all
time, and in Greece bring about that philosophy
which made logic and science possible. On all of

60. E. A. W.
Budge, *The
Nile* (Lon-
don, 1912),
p. 818.

61. N. M. Davies,
*Ancient
Egyptian
Paintings*
(Chicago,
1936), II,
Pls. 91, 92.

62. C. Campbell,
*Two Theban
Queens*
(London,
1909), p. 13.

63. *Ibid.*

64. Campbell,
pp. 13-14.

these western civilization is founded.

In the meantime Egypt became a Persian province in 525 B.C. and within two hundred years after that Alexander the Great made the land of the Nile a part of the Greek world. In due time Egypt was incorporated in the Roman Empire. When Cleopatra died (30 B.C.) all that was left of Egypt's three thousand years of glory were the magnificent ruins of a once great nation and civilization. The ability to read Egypt's written records was forgotten and with it the knowledge of its historic and cultural accomplishments. Only the pyramids and a few monuments continued to amaze the onlooker. But ancient Egypt lay buried under the sands of time and its deserts for many centuries.

As history goes, it was but a short time ago that modern man started to rediscover the magnitude of ancient Egypt, to relearn what had been forgotten and to recognize the debt civilization owes these remarkable Egyptians.

THE MEN AND WOMEN
OF THE BIBLE

Hebrews, Israelites, and Jews

Throughout the picture the people of the Egyptian bondage and those who journeyed to Sinai are generally referred to as Hebrews or "children of Israel."[1] It would have been an anachronism to call them Jews.

In biblical tradition the Semites were sired by Shem, and his descendant Eber is the progenitor of the Hebrews.[2]

The first time the word *Hebrew* appears in the English text of the Bible is when Abraham is called "Abram the Hebrew."[3]

In the Old Testament the designation Hebrew or Hebrews is used infrequently and, generally speaking, applied as a denominator in contrast to other people, such as Egyptians and Philistines, for example.

The Hebrew word *eber* and its variations have, among others, the meaning of "beyond" or "across" —usually a region across or beyond a river and more particularly east or west of the Jordan or the Euphrates. Its use as a proper name has been indicated previously. Collectively, *eber* also stands for a country or a nation.[4]

Historically, the word *Habiru (Apiru)* appears quite early in Egyptian records, particularly in the cor-

1. Ex. 1:1.

2. Gen. 10:21, 25.

3. Gen. 14:13.

4. a) *Jewish Encyclopedia*, VI (New York, 1907), p. 305. b) Num. 24:24.

respondence of the vassal kings of Canaan to Egypt from about the fifteenth or fourteenth centuries B.C. These Habiru are identified as nomads, as desert or Aramaean Semites. This composite people were not the biblical Hebrews, according to scholars. The people who made the covenant with YHWH derived from many different ancestries, probably including the many-strained Habiru.[5]

The common characteristic of these Habiru and the early biblical Hebrews is that they were nomads. The fact that Hebrews existed before there were Israelites can be read clearly in the Book of Genesis when Jacob's name is changed to Israel.[6] The Bible frequently refers to the twelve tribes (sons) of Israel.[7]

The earliest historical record of the people of Israel is contained on the famous Merneptah stele where this Egyptian king, the successor of Rameses II, claims a victory over Israel (about 1225 B.C.) in the following exaggerated terms:

> . . . Carried off is Ascalon; seized upon is Gezer; . . .
> Israel is laid waste, his seed is not;
> Palestine is become a widow for Egypt![8]

The Hebrew adjective of Judah is *Yehudi*. This word traveled through many languages, undergoing change till it was incorporated in Old French as *Juieu*. Later it was written *Giu* and in this form entered the Middle English vocabulary where, among many varied spellings, it reached the form *Jew* in use today. At first the designation *Yehudi* applied only to the people living in the southern part of the divided kingdom (tenth century B.C.). In passage of time, particularly during the Exile (see Book of Esther, among others), the word *Jew* had absorbed the older word *Israelite*, though the latter term was revived in more modern times.[9]

Aaron

Aaron, the older brother of Moses,[10] was married to Elisheba,[11] by whom he had four sons. Of these

5. *a*) J. A. Wilson, *Burden of Egypt* (Chicago, 1951), pp. 201, 255.
b) J. H. Breasted, in *Cambridge Ancient History*, II (Cambridge, England, 1931), 108, 124.

6. Gen. 32:28.

7. Gen. 49:28, *et passim.*

8. Wilson, p. 225.

9. *a*) *Jewish Encycl.*, VII (1906), 174.
b) *Dictionary of the Bible*, ed. J. Hastings (New York, 1954), p. 465.

10. Ex. 7:7.

11. Ex. 6:23.

sons only Eleazar is portrayed in the picture. He was destined to become high priest of Israel.[12]

Aaron holds an important position in the Old Testament as appointed spokesman and particularly as Israel's first high priest. Nevertheless, the Book of Exodus leaves no doubt about Aaron's lesser position in relation to Moses, nor of his deed at the mountain of God where he was instrumental in making the Golden Calf.[13]

When the Temple priesthood became firmly established, efforts were made to impress greater importance upon Israel's first high priest. Therefore, later accounts do show Aaron in a better light.[14]

In the Koran, as in the Bible, Aaron is presented as the more eloquent speaker and as the appointed spokesman for Moses. The making of the Golden Calf is also part of the scriptures of Islam, but Aaron is not implicated in this act, according to the commentator.[15]

We depict Aaron being persuaded against his will into making the idol in the film *The Ten Commandments*.

Bithiah

The Midrash Rabbah[16] led us straight to the Bible to give us the name of Moses' foster mother: "Bithiah the daughter of Pharaoh, which Mered took."[17]

Bithiah means "daughter of God." There is a tradition in which God says to her: "Moses was not your son, yet you called him your son; you, too, though you are not My daughter, yet will I call My daughter."[18]

Though the rabbis have given Moses many other names, the name by which he has been known throughout the ages is the one which Bithiah, the Egyptian princess, gave him.[19]

That strangers may partake of the Passover meal is stated in Exodus 12:48. The participation of foreigners is expounded in the Midrash Rabbah.[20] In agreement with these texts we have the Egyptian

12. Num. 20:26.

13. Ex. 32:1-6.

14. *Jewish Encycl.*, I (1906), 2-5.

15. Holy Qur'an (trans. M. M. 'Ali. Lahore, 1951), 7: 148; 20:87-94; 28:34-35; n. 1599.

16. *Midrash Rabbah*, III, trans. S. M. Lehrman (London, 1951), 34.

17. I Chron. 4:18.

18. *Midrash Rabbah*, IV, trans. J. Israelstam (London, 1939), 6.

19. *Midrash Rabbah*, III, 34.

20. *Ibid.*, p. 223.

Bithiah partake of the first Passover in Moses' hut in the picture. On this occasion also, she meets her husband to be, Mered.[21]

21. Cf. I Chron.
4:18.

The reference in the Book of Chronicles leads to the logical conclusion that Bithiah participated in the Exodus.

Dathan

The modern word *Quisling* aptly describes Dathan in his characterization on the screen.

In the Bible this man's activities are linked with his brother Abiram, and Korah. Chapter sixteen of the Book of Numbers contains the first and only extensive biblical account concerning Dathan. Here Dathan, Abiram and Korah rebel against the divinely appointed leadership of Moses. God's judgment upon these men is executed as the earth opens and swallows them.

The traditions contained in the Midrashim have Dathan appear on the scene at a much earlier time. He is established there as an antagonist and schemer against Moses in connection with events set down in the Book of Exodus.[22] We have followed the sense of these traditions in writing the script.

22. *Midrash
Rabbah*, III,
36-39. See
also *Jewish
Encycl.*, I,
66.

Dathan is one of the Hebrews set over the Israelites to make them perform their labors.[23] He observes Moses killing the Egyptian and informs[24] Prince Rameses.

23. Cf. Ex. 5:6,
et passim.
24. *Midrash
Rabbah*, III,
39.

In the development of the biblical drama on the screen Dathan appears as the instigator against Moses' authority during the Exodus, particularly at the Red Sea[25] and at the idolatry of the Golden Calf.[26]

25. Cf. Ex.
14:11-12.
26. Cf. Ex.
32. Also
*Midrash
Rabbah*, III,
37.

It is here that we take dramatic license in the picture. We telescope into one scene the deaths of Dathan, Abiram and Korah,[27] and the destruction of the Golden Calf.[28] They die as the idol is destroyed by fire—the earth opens and swallows them.

27. Num. 16.
28. Ex. 32:20.

It is interesting to note that the Psalmist used a similar device in combining these and related events into a few verses.[29]

Hur ben Caleb

Hur is described as the son of Caleb in I Chronicles 2:19. Josephus names him as the husband of Miriam,[30] a suggestion we have incorporated in the picture.

Ishmael

Ishmael does not appear in the picture *The Ten Commandments*. In one of the scenes, however, Jethro states that he is a descendant of Abraham through Ishmael. The biblical genealogy establishes Abraham as Jethro's ancestor through the patriarch's wife Keturah, who bore Midian.[31] Ishmael, who was Abraham's first-born, had Hagar as mother.[32]

The Arabs of the desert—the nomadic Bedouins— are considered the descendants of Ishmael.[33] Surprisingly enough there is no genealogical indication to that effect in the actual text of the Koran. However, the verse "And the begetter and he whom he begot!" is interpreted to mean that the begetter is Abraham, the father of the Arab people; and he begat Ishmael.[34] Clearer information about this genealogy can be gathered from the Bible, where Ishmael is established as the progenitor of the Arab people.[35]

Tradition holds that Abraham and Ishmael were the ancestors of Moslems. This, together with a Jewish legend which identifies Keturah with Hagar,[36] justifies the statement made in the picture about Jethro's ancestry.

In the Scriptures of Islam Ishmael is named a prophet.[37] We further read that Ishmael helped his father Abraham in the building of the Kabah, the sacred shrine within the great mosque at Mecca.[38] Hagar, Ishmael's mother, is not mentioned by name in the Koran, though she figures prominently in Arab traditions. One of these relates that the spring Zamzam, which God produced to save her and her

29. Ps. 106: 16-20.

30. *Josephus*, IV, trans. H. St. J. Thackeray (London and New York, 1930), 345.

31. Gen. 25: 1-2.

32. Gen. 16:11.

33. *a*) G. W. Murray, *Sons of Ishmael* (London, 1935), p. 8. *b*) T. P. Hughes, *Dictionary of Islam* (London, 1935), p. 217.

34. Holy Qur'an ('Ali tr.), 90:3, and n. 2735.

35. Gen. 25: 12-18.

36. *Midrash Rabbah*, II, trans. H. Freedman (London, 1951), 542.

37. Holy Qur'an ('Ali tr.), 19:54, and n. 1552.

38. *Ibid.*, 2:127, and n. 170-a.

infant son from dying of thirst, was at the site of
Mecca and is the one located near the Kabah. There
is a popular belief that Abraham, Hagar and Ishmael
are buried in the Holy House at Mecca.[39]

Jethro

When Moses' father-in-law first appears in the
Old Testament, he is named Reuel.[40] In the very
next chapter, however, his name is Jethro, a priest
of Midian[41] and as Jethro he is known thereafter
throughout the Book of Exodus.

In Numbers 10:29 he is referred to as Raguel,
which is the Greek form of Reuel. Here, he also
has a son named Hobab, while in Exodus 2:16 only
seven daughters are indicated. To confuse the issue
still more, Hobab is established as Moses' father-
in-law in Judges 4:11.

Shu'aib is the name for Jethro in the Koran.[42]
This text makes him the father of two daughters.[43]

Much speculative thought has been given to the
problem of the three biblical names indicated above.
Among rabbinical views, one simplifies the issue in
stating that Jethro had several names.[44] Other opinions make Reuel the father of either Jethro or Hobab.[45] Thus, Jethro would have been Moses' brother-
in-law. Upon Reuel's death Jethro would have become sheik of his tribe and as such assumed the
traditional function of father to his sisters.[46]

In the Hebrew text the word for "father-in-law"[47]
is *chosan*. It has several associated meanings, all
dealing with relationships arising out of marriage:
for example, father-in-law, mother-in-law, son-in-law,
or a relative by marriage through the bride.[48]

In the picture, Jethro's reference to God as "He Who
has no name" is in agreement with the Old Testament,
where His specific name YHWH—I AM THAT I
AM—is not revealed until He speaks to Moses out
of the Burning Bush.[49]

A whole theory called the Kenite theory has been
evolved indicating that YHWH was known to the

39. H. A. R. Gibb and J. H. Kramers, *Shorter Encyclopaedia of Islam* (Leiden, 1953), *passim.*

40. Ex. 2:18.

41. Ex. 3:1.

42. Holy Qur'an ('Ali tr.), 7:85-93, and n. 919.

43. *Ibid.,* 28:22-28.

44. *Midrash Rabbah,* III, 327.

45. *Jewish Encycl.,* VII, 173-174.

46. G. Rawlinson, *Moses* (New York, 1887), p. 66.

47. Ex. 3:1.

48. J. Strong, *Exhaustive Concordance of the Bible* (New York, 1953): "Hebrew Dictionary," p. 45.

49. Ex. 3:14.

Kenite Jethro[50] before His revelation to Moses.[51]

Joshua

Joshua does not appear in the Bible until Moses chooses him to be his general to fight Amalek.[52] This is another instance of biblical writing where that part of a man's life not directly concerned with the religious-historical development of Israel was not considered for the text. Nor—to differ from Moses —could we find any ancient extrascriptural traditions to enlighten us on Joshua's life before the battle of Rephidim. There is one exception, an obscure comment which does place Joshua in Egypt before the first Passover.[53]

It should not need explanation that Joshua was alive before he reached biblical importance. Moses would not select a man to lead his army of whom he knew nothing. It is for this reason, to show that the future conqueror of Canaan developed the ability to become a leader and organizer, that we portray him as a Hebrew slave imbued with the spirit of freedom.

On the screen Joshua is the Hebrew whom Moses sees smitten by an Egyptian.[54] Joshua is the one who realizes that Moses could be the man to deliver them out of bondage.[55]

Egypt worked copper and turquoise mines on the Sinai Peninsula from the earliest times of its history.[56] The labor for these mining operations during the New Kingdom was performed by Asiatic prisoners who "presumably . . . were captives held in the Delta and brought out seasonally, under armed escort, for the mining."[57] We assume Joshua to have been one of these captive miners. He escapes and during his flight finds Moses near Sinai.

In the translation of the Koran generally used as a reference in this book, Joshua is not mentioned in the actual text. In footnotes, however, it is set forth that he is spoken of in 5:23 and 18:60.[58] In the Sale translation of the Koran Joshua is men-

50. Cf. Judg. 1:16.

51. W. O. E. Oesterley and T. H. Robinson, *Hebrew Religion* (London, 1949), pp. 146-150.

52. Ex. 17:9.

53. *Midrash Rabbah*, III, 236.

54. Ex. 2:11.

55. Cf. Gen. 15: 13; Ex. 3:8; 12:40-41.

56. A. Lucas, *Ancient Egyptian Materials and Industries* (London, 1948), pp. 231-235.

57. Wilson, p. 191.

58. Holy Qur'an ('Ali tr.), nn. 683, 1510.

tioned by name in Surah 18. It is possible that in translating the Koran, Sale unwittingly included commentary in the text.

Mered

His name is derived from I Chronicles 4:18, where he is mentioned as the husband of Bithiah, the daughter of Pharaoh.

In the Midrash Rabbah Mered is identified with Caleb.[59] This is the same Caleb who was sent with the others to spy on the land of Canaan.[60]

Miriam

Miriam is the older sister of Aaron and Moses. She is mentioned as a midwife in a legend[61] and, in the picture *The Ten Commandments,* we have adapted this information when Miriam performs as nurse and midwife during the Exodus.

Josephus indicates that she was the wife of Hur.[62] She is named a prophetess in the Old Testament[63] and the rabbis consider her as a deliverer of the Israelites.[64]

Sephora

The name of Jethro's daughter whom Moses marries is given as Sephora in the Douay Version.[65] In the film this rendition has been given preference over Zipporah, as the name appears in the King James Version and the Hebrew text.[66]

In Numbers 12:1 Moses is said to have married an Ethiopian woman. In the Hebrew text and Revised Standard Version it is a Cushite woman.[67] From the biblical point of view Cush and Ethiopia are identical.

This verse has given rise to various interpretations. Traditions indicate, for example, that "Ethiopian (or Cushite) woman" refers to Sephora because she distinguished herself from others by her beauty and virtue, just as an Ethiopian distinguishes himself from others by his physical appearance.[68]

59. *Midrash Rabbah,* IV, 6.
60. Num. 13:6, 17.

61. *Midrash Rabbah,* III, 16.

62. *Josephus,* IV, 345.
63. Ex. 15:20.

64. *Midrash Rabbah,* III, 317.

65. Ex. 2:21, Douay Version.

66. *Pentateuch and Haftorahs,* ed. J. H. Hertz (U.S.A., 1941?), I, 212.
67. a) *Ibid.,* II, 618.
   b) *Interpreter's Bible,* II (New York, 1953), 200.

68. L. Ginzberg, *Legends of the Jews* (Philadelphia, 1946-1947), VI, 90.

An entirely different version is presented by Josephus, who takes the "Ethiopian woman" literally. In his work her name is Tharbis, the daughter of the Ethiopian king. When, during his campaign as commander of Egypt's army, Moses is unable to conquer the Ethiopian stronghold, Tharbis offers him the city under condition of marriage. This is the Ethiopian woman whom Moses marries, according to this historian.[69]

In the poem by Ezekiel quoted by Eusebius, Sephora is described as a dark-skinned Ethiopian.[70] Concerning her appearance on the screen, we show Sephora according to rabbinic tradition.

Yochabel

She is the mother of Miriam, Aaron and Moses. In the King James Version her name is written *Jochebed*.[71] In the Douay Version it is spelled *Jochabed*.[72] In the Greek text of Josephus the name is, in transliteration, *Iochabel(e)*.[73]

For reasons of euphony, Cecil B. deMille decided to use the name given by Josephus. As pronounced at the beginning of a word, the transliterated *J* or *I* of the Hebrew or Greek has the sound of *Y* in English. Hence our use of *Y* in Yochabel's name.

69. *Josephus,* IV, 275.

70. *Preparation for the Gospel* (trans. E. H. Gifford. Oxford, 1903), ix, 28.

71. Ex. 6:20.

72. Ex. 6:20, Douay Version.

73. *Josephus,* IV, 258.

THE HOLY SCRIPTURES

The Old Testament

a) Early transmission and composition.[1] Long before the art of writing became known to the ancient Hebrews, stories of the Creation, the Flood, the lives of the patriarchs and important events that befell them were told by word of mouth from generation to generation.

Quite early, too, some independent scribe wrote on stone, papyrus or leather the story of a tribal tradition or a leader set down some legislation. The earliest elements of the Old Testament were in the form of poetry. No original has ever been found, but their existence can be detected in the present text by experts.

The form in which we know the first six books of the Bible today is, according to many Bible scholars, the final composition of several separate narrative, legislative and priestly source materials, fused into one. Though all of the Old Testament books can also be considered Near-Eastern literature, they were not written or edited with that intention. The purpose was edification, the establishment of monotheism and religious unity.

The attempt to set down in continued written form the early traditions of the Hebrew people did not take place till the ninth century B.C. At that

1. Bibliography:
   a) *Universal Jewish Encyclopedia* (New York, 1948), II, 288-293.
   b) J. Moffatt, *The Bible: A New Translation* (New York, 1935), pp. ix-xvi.
   c) *Encyclopaedia Britannica* (Chicago, 1951), III, 502-503.

time two separate documents came into existence. One is referred to as J. It was written in the southern kingdom of Judah, and the text has a preference for YHWH as the name of God.

The E document, which predominantly uses the word *Elohim* for God, came about in the northern kingdom of Israel. Generally speaking, both scribes or schools of scribes dealt with the same early history of the Hebrews and the development of the Israelites as a people, but in their own detectable style and approach.

In the reign of Hezekiah (seventh century B.C.) J and E were combined into one text, JE. Moffatt suggests that this new edition may have filled the need to have one religious text for one united people. Apparently no particular preference was given to one source over the other, since the same event is often told twice.

During the late seventh century B.C. legal and religious reforms were needed to establish the Temple in Jerusalem firmly and to strengthen the common faith against prevailing idolatry. A new code came into being for this purpose. It is named D and contains both old and new legislation. This, in part at least, was the book found in the Temple under the reign of Josiah. Portions of the present Book of Deuteronomy formed its nucleus.

There are some scholars who believe that during and after the Exile the so-called Priestly Code (P) came into existence. The writers of P used already existing documents from which they copied certain parts without any change. Sometimes they reworded the texts and in other cases they abstracted them. To this they added their own original writings which dealt particularly with genealogy, the priesthood and ritual. This final fusion of the first six books of the Old Testament, frequently called Hexateuch, is the text as we know it today. This is the prevailing view about the composition of the Hexateuch, with which, however, not all scholars agree.

The content of the Old Testament with which we
are familiar today was established between the
eighth and second centuries B.C. The oldest completed books in this sense are Amos and Hosea,
while Daniel and possibly Psalms and Zechariah are
the latest. Nearly all of them were edited from older
texts.

It must be pointed out that the Old Testament
was formed by a selection of books, called the canon.

b) The canon.[2] The formation of the Old Testament canon is not mentioned in the Bible, though in
Nehemiah (9:38-10:29) the canonization of the Law
of Moses is described. In the prologue to Ecclesiasticus
in the Douay Version, the existence of a canon is indicated with "a diligent reading of the law, and the
prophets, and other books" (i.e. the Writings).

The division of the Old Testament into three cate-
gories set forth in the prologue to Ecclesiasticus—
the Law, the Prophets and the Writings (Hagiographa)—is an ancient Jewish tradition.

It is generally concluded that the Pentateuch,
popularly called the Five Books of Moses, was completed and accepted in the fifth century B.C. For
the Prophets the latter part of the third century
B.C. is indicated and for the Writings the era from
150 to 100 B.C.

The Catholic Versions of the Old Testament contain seven more books than the respective Jewish
and Protestant texts. They are called deuterocanonical by Catholics, while to Protestants and Jews they
are known as the Apocrypha. To Catholics the name
Apocrypha has an entirely different meaning. It
comprises what is elsewhere known as the Pseudepigrapha. Before continuing with the subject of the
canon it is best to describe these two sets of very
ancient books briefly.

The Apocrypha, or deuterocanonical books, formed
part of the Greek translation of the Hebrew Scriptures accomplished in Alexandria from the third to

2. Bibliography:
a) Holy
Bible, Douay
Version.
b) Moffatt,
p. ix.
*c) Apocry-
pha and
Pseude-
pigrapha
of the Old
Testament,*
ed. R. H.
Charles
(Oxford,
1913), I,
vii-x; II,
iii-xi.
*d) Jewish
Encyclope-
dia,* II (New
York, 1903),
1-6; III
(1907),
141-145,
147-148,
186.
*e) Univ.
Jewish En-
cycl.,* I, 422-
423.
f) R. J.
Foster, in
*Catholic
Commentary
on Holy
Scripture*
(New York,
1953), pp.
13-16.
g) W. O. E.
Oesterley
and T. H.
Robinson,
*Hebrew Re-
ligion* (Lon-
don, 1949),
pp. 396-
400.
*h) Encyclo-
paedia Bri-
tannica,* III,
501-503.

the first centuries B.C. This translation is known as the Septuagint, commonly abbreviated LXX. Later, these books were also included in the Latin Vulgate.

The additional books contained in the Catholic canon are Tobias, Judith, Wisdom, Ecclesiasticus, Baruch, I and II Machabees and certain parts of Esther and Daniel (Esther, 10:4–16:24; Daniel, 3:24-90; 13; 14).

The naming of these books outside the Jewish and Protestant canons as "Apocrypha" (from the Greek *apocryphos*, "hidden") and the meaning that the word *apocryphal* has achieved in this connection as something false, spurious or heretical are unfortunate.

The terminology came about due to a misinterpretation of the Hebrew *sifrim ganozim* as "hidden books" in the sense of books not considered sacred. The Hebrew verb *ganoz* means to "store away" for safekeeping of something precious. The books that did not fall within the concept of sacred books were designated *sifrim hisonim*, i.e. "outside books." According to R. H. Charles, "to this class the Apocrypha were never relegated," and the true meaning of the Hebrew *sifrim ganozim* indicates that the books had religious value. In its earliest application "Apocrypha" referred to these books in approbation.

There were numerous discussions about the canonicity of these books within the Catholic Church itself and the question was finally and officially settled at the Council of Trent (sixteenth century A.D.).

The Pseudepigrapha of Jews and Protestants is called the Apocrypha by Catholics. The authors of the books contained in this collection were either anonymous or else adopted the alias of a biblical personality of importance. They were written somewhere between 200 B.C. and 100 A.D. and do not form part of any Old Testament canon, though their prophetic content and ethical teachings are impressive.

The authors of these books attempted to establish

a more spiritual interpretation of the Law, giving new life and new hope for the future. In contrast to them, the powers that were insisted on a most orthodox and therefore rigid and dogmatic adherence to the already existing text.

Originally written in Hebrew or Greek, Charles lists them as follows:

The Book of Jubilees
The Letter of Aristeas
The Books of Adam and Eve
The Martyrdom of Isaiah
I Enoch
The Testaments of the Twelve Patriarchs
The Sibylline Oracles
The Assumption of Moses
II Enoch, or the Book of the Secrets of Enoch
II Baruch, or the Syriac Apocalypse of Baruch
III Baruch, or the Greek Apocalypse of Baruch
IV Ezra
The Psalms of Solomon
IV Maccabees

The order of the Old Testament books as established in the Septuagint remained in Christian usage till the Reformation. At that time the Protestants reverted to the Hebrew canon, eliminating the books called by them the Apocrypha. The Protestant canon, therefore, is based on the Hebrew, while the Catholic Church follows the canon as found in the Septuagint and the Vulgate.

Why is the Apocrypha, i.e. the deuterocanonical books, an integral part of the Catholic Old Testament, and why is it not in the Jewish and Protestant canon? As already mentioned, the Septuagint contains these additional books. It is probable that certain religious practices differed between the Jews of Egypt and those of Palestine. There are indications, however, that some of the apocryphal books were also read by the Jewry of Palestine. Whatever questions arose in consideration of the canonicity of these books among the rabbis in Palestine, they

seem to have settled them at Jamnia in 90 A.D.
However, discussions on this subject continued to
the end of the second century A.D.

In searching for the reasons which made a book
acceptable for inclusion in the Hebrew canon it is
sometimes stated that it had to be written originally
in the Hebrew language. This cannot be used as an
explanation for the exclusion of the Apocrypha, since
several of these books were written originally in
Hebrew.

The rabbinical view of old, that no book more
modern than Ecclesiastes (second century B.C.)
could be considered Scripture, is more certain. To
this must be added that each biblical book was
thought of as written through divine inspiration by
a prophet, such as Moses, Joshua, Samuel, David,
Solomon, etc. According to the rabbis, therefore,
books which originated after 200 B.C. were post-
prophetic, hence not to be considered Holy Writ.
Exceptions to this rule are the books of Daniel and,
possibly, Psalms and Zechariah.

The fact that the Greek Septuagint of Alexandria
was used by the early Christians evidently added its
weight to the decision reached at Jamnia. The *Jewish Encyclopedia* states (Vol. 3, p. 186): "[The Septuagint's] divergence from the accepted text was
too evident; and it therefore could not serve as a
basis for theological discussion or for homiletic interpretation. This distrust was accentuated by the
fact that it had been adopted as Sacred Scripture
by the new faith."

c) Ancient translations.[3] The oldest written frag-
ment of the Old Testament in Hebrew is the Nash
Papyrus, which was discovered in the Faiyum, in
Egypt. It contains on one single page the Ten Commandments and Deuteronomy 6:4. Scholarly estimates
establish the date of this papyrus from 200 to 100 B.C.
The Dead Sea scrolls have been much in the headlines
in recent times. They are purported to have been writ-

3. Bibliography: a) Holy Bible, Douay Version. b) *Jewish Encycl.*, VI (1907), 463; VIII (1906), 365-371. c) E. Power, in *Catholic Commentary*, pp. 25-33, 104. d) A. Jeffery, in *Interpreter's Bible*, I (New York, 1952), 56-61. e) H. G. G. Herklots, *How Our Bible Came to Us* (New York, 1954), pp. 70-71. f) J. Strong, *Exhaustive Concordance of the Bible* (New York, 1953): "Hebrew Dictionary," p. 105. g) *English-Hebrew Dictionary*, ed. J. I. S. Kaufman (Tel Aviv, 1947). h) *Sculptures of Michelangelo* (New York, 1940), pp. 11-13.

ten in the second century B.C., but, since there is no precise and conclusive knowledge available at this time, we cannot consider them here.

Generally speaking, the oldest known Hebrew manuscripts of the Old Testament are masoretic texts of the late ninth century A.D. Briefly, the Masorah is a fixed text established to provide uniformity among all copies of the Hebrew Scriptures, presumably derived from an original form kept in the Temple at Jerusalem. Many technical safeguards were established for the copyists and, among others, the vowel signs for the square Hebrew alphabet were invented and applied. Since the translations of the Septuagint and Vulgate were made from a Hebrew text older than any Hebrew manuscripts existing today, they are of the greatest importance for comparative studies.

Traditional usage reserves the word *targum* for translations of the Old Testament from Hebrew into Aramaic. In a wider sense, however, any translation of the Scriptures can be named in this fashion, even the translations, also called versions, which gave us the King James and Douay Bibles. The word is of Babylonian origin—*targamanu*—and stood for the interpreter who translated for foreigners at the court of Babylon. It is still alive today in the Arabic word *dragoman.*

The knowledge of Hebrew among ancient translators was not always precise. Sometimes a Hebrew word was given another meaning in translation. Since there is one such word that has affected Moses' physical appearance for centuries it is most suitable as a selected illustration in this context.

The famous statue of Moses by Michelangelo (tomb of Pope Julius, San Pietro in Vincoli, Rome) shows his head with horns. Many other painters and sculptors have pictured Moses similarly. Among unsuspecting viewers these horns can cause consternation.

The artists who modeled Moses in this fashion

followed the text of the Latin Vulgate, where the
corresponding verses have persisted in the Douay
Version to this day. There, these verses have been
translated as follows: "And when Moses came down
from the mount Sinai, he held the two tables of
the testimony, and he knew not that his face was
horned" (Ex. 34:29). "And they saw that the face of
Moses when he came out was horned" (Ex. 34:35).

The original Hebrew word translated in this
fashion is *keren*. It has two possible meanings:
"horn" and "beam (or ray) of light," i.e. shining
with light. Under the circumstances the latter is the
true meaning of the word.

The oldest translations of any of the Old Testament books were rendered into Aramaic. Of these,
the most important translation of the Pentateuch
took place in Babylonia and in honor of its pre-
sumed author it is known as the Targum of Onke-
los, though it is also referred to as the Babylonian
Targum. A still older targum of the Torah, the Jerusalem Targum, originated in Palestine, where Aramaic
had become the spoken language. In due time the
Prophets and the Writings were also translated into
Aramaic.

Many Jews had settled in Greek-speaking Alexandria who no longer knew Hebrew. For them, certain sections of the Scriptures were translated into
Greek. Between 300 and 100 B.C. a new translation into
Greek comprising the entire Old Testament was accomplished. As has already been noted on a previous page it was named the Septuagint. According
to a legend seventy scholars had been engaged in
translating the text. When the LXX became the
Scripture of the early Christians, the Jews undertook new Greek translations based on the accepted
Hebrew text.

The earliest Latin translations of the Old Testament were derived from the Greek LXX. They came
about in the second century A.D. and were only
partial. When St. Jerome first undertook his famous

translation he revised the older Latin texts on the basis of the LXX. Later, however, he learned both Hebrew and Aramaic from Jewish teachers in order that he could use the texts written in these languages as additional source material. The Catholic Church owes its Latin Bible principally to St. Jerome (*circa* 340-420 A.D.), whose work is popularly known as the Vulgate.

There are many other ancient translations. The oldest manuscript of the Samaritan Pentateuch dates from the thirteenth century A.D. but the text originated in the second century B.C. The Scriptures of this small sect consist of the Five Books of Moses to this day.

For Syriac-speaking Jews and Christians a translation was accomplished perhaps as early as the second century A.D. The oldest existing manuscripts date from the fifth and sixth centuries A.D. In the ninth century the Syriac version received the proper name of Peshitta, which means "simple"; a simple text for ordinary people in contrast to the Hebrew read by learned men.

In the early centuries of our era the popular languages of Egypt consisted of several Coptic dialects. To the Christians living there the Greek Bible could not be understood. Therefore, translations into Coptic were made in the third and fourth centuries A.D. These were derived from the Septuagint, and the Version in use by the Coptic Church today is the one taken from the Bohairic dialect.

Arabic translations were accomplished between the eighth and tenth centuries; Armenian and Georgian texts originated in the fifth century. Further to be noted among early Bible translations are the Ethiopic and Gothic (fourth century A.D.). St. Cyrillus, in order to accomplish the Slavonic wording of the Scriptures (ninth century A.D.), actually invented the alphabet which is still in use in Russia, Bulgaria and parts of Yugoslavia today.

4. Bibliography:
a) Encyclo-
paedia
Britan-
nica, 14th
ed., III,
529-534.
b) A. Wik-
gren, in In-
terpreter's
Bible, I, 84-
100.
c) H. Pope,
in Catholic
Commen-
tary, pp.
34-39.
d) Herklots,
passim.
e) The
Bible, trans-
lated accord-
ing to the
Ebrew and
Greeke . . .
(London,
1586).

d) English translations.[4] If Hebrew, Greek or Latin had remained the only languages in which the Bible could be read, most of us would never have had the opportunity to study the text. Stimulated by the possibilities the new invention of printing presented, as well as the upheaval that the Reformation produced in Western Christendom, the efforts to translate the Bible into living languages became that much more productive.

Education being what it was before and during the Middle Ages, very few people would have been able to read the Bible had it been freely available. Nevertheless, some stories of the Scriptures became popularly known to the people at large through sermons, dramas, paintings, sculptures and even picture books. A seventh century peasant named Caedmon made verses of Bible stories which he sang and which were set down in Anglo-Saxon. Other minstrels used biblical subjects in their song. It is very likely that the Gospels had been written in this language in the eighth century.

When King Alfred (849-899 A.D.) established his laws he preceded them with a translation of Chapters 20-23 of Exodus in Anglo-Saxon. These early translations, as well as later ones, were made from the Latin Vulgate. Relatively numerous among the partial translations of the Bible texts were the rsalms, usually called Psalters.

The oldest such manuscript still in existence today is the Vespasian Psalter of the ninth century A.D. It is written in Latin with an interlinear translation in Anglo-Saxon. A partial translation of the Old Testament is ascribed to Ælfric (late tenth century).

Due to the Norman conquest and the impression of a new language, little was accomplished in English Bible translation during the eleventh, twelfth and thirteenth centuries. During the early fourteenth century the entire Old Testament had been translated into the Anglo-Norman tongue.

In due time English established itself again, but it was a new language now incorporating many French words. The Midland Psalter is an early product of that period (fourteenth century). It is a Latin text taken from the Vulgate with English glosses. Frequently separate renderings of certain passages were made—for example, of the Ten Commandments.

Dating from this period are the efforts of John Wyclif and his co-workers, John Purvey and Nicholas of Hereford. The translation is based on the Vulgate. An early and a revised version are known. It became immensely popular and remained the only English Bible until the sixteenth century. The book was evidently so widely distributed that in spite of bans and book burnings, 150 manuscript copies still exist today.

Heretofore we have dealt with English Bible texts that were written by hand. We now come to the age of printing. In 1505 the *Penitential Psalms* was the first partial Bible text to be published in English by this method. It is strange that it was not until 1536 that the first biblical text was printed in England proper, in view of the fact that the Bible had already been printed repeatedly in other languages as early as the fifteenth century on the Continent.

The first English text of the Pentateuch was printed by Hans Luft in 1530 in the German city of Marburg, and the *Epistles of the Old Testament* appeared in Antwerp in 1534. In 1536 this Antwerp edition was reprinted in England, the first biblical text to be printed in that country.

The author of these respective translations was William Tyndale, who used as his sources Hebrew and Greek originals, the Vulgate, the Latin version by Erasmus and Luther's German Bible for prefaces and marginal notes. To a large extent Tyndale's English wording is still extant in the Authorized Version of the Bible. Tyndale's original printed editions had a worse fate than the often copied manuscripts of the Wyclif translation. Very few specimens have survived. To translate the Bible, Tyndale had to find refuge in Germany, where he lived in Hamburg, Wittenberg (where he met Luther), Cologne, Worms, etc.

The first complete Bible printed in English is that translated by Miles Coverdale in 1535. The translation is based on German and Latin versions and possibly the English translation made by Tyndale. It seems that the first edition was printed abroad, but the second edition was printed in England by Nicolson in 1537.

Matthew's Bible followed next. It was published in England in 1537. Thomas Matthew seems to have been an alias for John Rogers, a co-worker of Tyndale. His text was not a new translation but a compilation of both Tyndale and Coverdale.

In 1539 Richard Taverner published a Bible which appears to have been in the form of a revision of Matthew's Bible. The "Great Bible" came about in 1539 and was printed with royal and church approval. Supervising the work was Miles Coverdale, who followed Matthew's Bible. In addition, a Latin version with Hebrew text was consulted for the Old Testament, while the Vulgate and the Greek text of Erasmus served for the New Testament. It became the first Authorized Version; other previous versions were banned.

Coverdale and others had fled to Geneva, where they started to plan a new revision of the Bible. In 1560 the Geneva Bible appeared, known popularly to this day as the "Breeches Bible." This name is derived from the translation "they sewed figge tree leaves together and made themselves breeches" (Genesis 3:7). It was the first complete Bible to have the now familiar division of chapters into verses. Even though it was not authorized it became extremely popular, more so than the Great Bible or its follower in England, the Bishops' Bible, which was published in 1568 as another Authorized Version.

The Catholic Church did not oppose translations into the vernacular as such, but did reject versions it considered heretical. Therefore, the Catholic refugees from England found it necessary to make an official English translation from the Latin Vulgate. The Old Testament was translated at Douay between 1609 and 1610, chiefly by Gregory Martin and Cardinal Allen, both former Oxford men.

The famous English Bible, called the Authorized Version or the King James Version, is known wherever English is spoken. It was accomplished by order of James I and first published in 1611. Actually, the Authorized Version is not a new translation but a revision of the Bishops' Bible. We should like to present some of the contemporary rules that served as a guide for the worthy scholars:

> The ordinary Bible read in the Church, commonly called "the Bishops' Bible" to be followed and as little altered as the truth of the original will permit. . . . These translations to be used when they agree better with the text than the Bishops' Bible; viz. Tyndale's, Matthew's, Coverdale's . . . Geneva . . .

In the preface to this Version, Dr. Miles Smith, who became bishop of Gloucester in 1612, stated:

> . . . truly (good Christian Reader) we never thought from the beginning, that we should neede to make a new Translation, nor yet to make of a bad one a good one . . . but to make a good one better . . .

In 1749-50 Richard Challoner revised the Douay Version.

Charles Thomson, once secretary of the Continental Congress, was the first American to undertake the translation of the Old Testament. It appeared in Philadelphia in 1808 and was based on the Septuagint, omitting the Apocrypha.

In 1870, initiated by the Church of England, the Protestant Churches of England and America undertook a revision of the Authorized Version, which is known as the Revised Version. Knowledge of, and scholarship in, the Hebrew language had made considerable advances so that a more faithful translation of the Hebrew text was made possible.

English translations for Jewish readers were put into print by Isaac Delgado (1785), David Levi (1787), Benisch (1851-56) and Friedlander (1884), and by the Jewish Publication Society in 1917.

During the last few decades many translations undertaken by individual scholars have appeared.

Due to further advances in the field of Bible learning the present age again has brought revisions of the biblical text by Protestant and Catholic scholars. The Revised Standard Version of the former has appeared recently. Catholic scholarship is in the process of producing the Confraternity Version, undertaken by the "Episcopal Committee of the Confraternity of Christian Doctrine." All these revisions and retranslations add to clearer reading and better understanding of the Old Testament.

Not every translation has been enumerated in this article, since it would be beyond its scope.

5. Bibliography:
a) Holy Qur'an (trans. M. M. 'Ali. Lahore, 1951), pp. xi-xiii.
b) E. D. Ross, in introduction to The Koran, trans. G. Sale (London, n.d.), pp. v-x.
c) H. A. R. Gibb and J. H. Kramers, Shorter Encyclopaedia of Islam (Leiden, 1953), passim.

The Koran[5]

To 322,000,000 faithful followers throughout the world, the Koran holds the same sacred position as the Bible does for 800,000,000 Christians and 12,000,000 Jews.

To Moslems the Koran is the word of Allah (God) as He revealed it to the last and greatest of His prophets, Mohammed. The Koran teaches strictest monotheism. Its text also forms the basis of civil law in Moslem countries.

In the times in which we are living it may be well for Western people to realize fully that the fundamental message of the Koran is identical with that of the Bible: Love of and obedience to the one God. The doctrine of faith of Islam, "there is no God but He" (3:17), is the same as the statement of Jews and Christians, "the Lord our God is one Lord" (Deut. 6:4).

. The Holy Scripture of Islam respects the Torah and the Gospels in stating "He revealed the Torah and the Gospel aforetime, a guidance for the people" (3:3). Prophets and revelations of earlier times are recognized by "We sent messengers before thee . . . nor was it possible for a messenger to bring a sign except with Allah's permission" (40:78).

Many of the events described and many of the prominent leaders spoken of in the Old and New Testaments are contained in the Koran. Among these are the following, presented in alphabetical order with the English name preceding the transliterated Arabic spelling:

Abraham	*Ibrahim*
David	*Dawud*
Elias	*Ilyas*
Isaac	*Ishaq*
Ishmael	*Isma'il*
Jacob, Israel	***Ya'kub, Isra'il***
Jeremiah	*Irmiya*
Jesus	*'Isa*
Jethro	*Shu'aib*
Jonah	*Yunus*
Joseph	*Yusuf*
Moses	*Musa*
Noah	*Nuh*
Solomon	*Suleiman*

The word *Koran* has the meaning of "reading" or "reciting." This holy Book is divided into 114 *surahs* (chapters) and the longer surahs are subdivided into *rukus* (sections). The Revelation *(al-Tanzil)*, which is one of many names given the Koran, has 6,247 *ayats* (verses) not counting the opening verse to each chapter. For the daily ritual the Koran is divided into thirty parts so that the devout Moslem can recite the whole book in one month.

According to Moslem tradition, the Koran was not revealed to Mohammed all at once, but over a period of twenty-three years. Ninety-three of the chapters originated at Mecca and twenty-one at Medinah. The chapters were not necessarily revealed in the order now established in the Koran. It is believed that the first five verses of the ninety-sixth chapter were the first revelation.

The first chapter is called "The Opening" *(Al Fatihah)* and consists of the following prayer:

In the name of Allah, the Beneficent, the Merciful.
Praise be to Allah, the Lord of the worlds,
The Beneficent, the Merciful,
Master of the day of Requital.
Thee do we serve and Thee do we beseech for help.
Guide us on the right path,
The path of those upon whom Thou hast bestowed favours,
Not those upon whom wrath is brought down, nor those
who go astray.   (1:1-7)

THE ARMY

DURING the early dynasties—long before the era in which the picture *The Ten Commandments* unfolds itself—Egypt's military needs were met with the conscription of a militia in times of war. The New Kingdom (1465-1165 B.C.) witnessed the establishment of a standing army of professional soldiers, composed of Egyptians and foreign mercenaries. The latter frequently were hired from among the conquered enemies.[1] This composite army must have presented a sight as colorful and varied as do the many different corps and nationalities forming the forces of more modern empires.

The main components of the Egyptian army were the infantry and chariotry. A professional police force, whose members apparently were recruited from Nubia, existed[2] and there is evidence of a corps of marines.[3]

Cavalry in the modern sense was unknown[4] and the horsemen of the early books of the Bible represent chariotry. Nevertheless, some rare representations of armed men on horseback of this period have been discovered, according to the well-known Egyptologist Keith C. Seele.[5]

The infantry was made up of spearmen and archers. The former were equipped with long spears tipped with copper or bronze points and long shields covered with leather. The archers were armed with bows and arrows. In addition, these troops carried either small

1. *a)* G. Steindorff and K. C. Seele, *When Egypt Ruled the East* (Chicago, 1947), pp. 89-90.
   b) J. A. Wilson, *Burden of Egypt* (Chicago, 1951), p. 187.
   c) A. Erman and H. Ranke, *Aegypten,* (Tübingen, 1923), pp. 621, 649.

2. Steindorff and Seele, pp. 89-91.

3. R. O. Faulkner, *Journal of Egyptian Archaeology,* XXVII (1941), 15.

4. *a)* Steindorff and Seele, p. 91.
   b) J. H. Breasted, *History of Egypt* (New York, 1921), p. 234.

5. In letter to the author, Mar. 3, 1953. See also Steindorff and Seele, p. 91.

6. Stein-
   dorff and
   Seele, p. 90.
   See also
   Erman and
   Ranke, pp.
   624-627,
   633, 652.
7. Steindorff
   and Seele,
   p. 91.
8. Wilson,
   p. 187.

9. Steindorff
   and Seele,
   p. 90.

10. Erman and
    Ranke,
    p. 652.

11. Steindorff
    and Seele,
    p. 91. See
    also Wilson,
    pp. 240-241;
    Faulkner, p.
    17.

12. Erman and
    Ranke, pp.
    651-653;
    also 237,
    253.

13. Ibid., p. 652.

14. Wilson,
    p. 244.

15. W. C. Hayes,
    in Everday
    Life in
    Ancient
    Times
    (Washing-
    ton, D.C.,
    1951),
    p. 160.

clubs or battle axes—short swords, daggers or scimitars in the days of the New Kingdom.[6]

The Egyptian chariot was manned by two soldiers, the driver and the fighter, whose weapons were the spear and the bow.[7] Members of this corps had a higher social standing,[8] just as the cavalry of more recent armies felt itself superior to the common footsoldier.

We do not know what insignia indicated the various ranks of officers. It has been established that low-ranking officers bore lighter arms than their men, while those of higher commissions would carry a ceremonial fan,[9] consisting of a single feather set into a more or less ornate handle. The traditional swaggerstick used by English officers of today has had its precedent in ancient Egypt.[10]

Upper and Lower Egypt were each garrisoned by two distinct army corps. These were organized into divisions and regiments named after a god, a pharaoh or a city.[11]

Distinctions in uniform between the different armed bodies existed, though an exact knowledge has been lost to us. Generally speaking, the soldiers were lightly dressed to permit freedom of movement. In the early days the only element of protective clothing consisted of a piece of leather to cover the abdominal region. During the Empire armored tunics came into use. In the work of Messrs. Erman and Ranke greaves are shown[12] and, though their military use has not been indicated, we have applied them as an item of protective uniform in the film. Helmets seem to have been worn primarily by mercenary troops.[13] An exceptionally striking and distinctive uniform was worn by the corps of Sardinians (technically named Sherden).[14] William Hayes states that these mercenaries served also as royal bodyguards; as such they perform in the picture.[15]

Military and naval standards of varied shapes containing heraldic emblems distinguished the many divisions, regiments and ships. They were affixed to poles and long, unicolored streamers were attached to them.[16] In the pursuit of the Israelites to the Red Sea, Rameses II's chariotry carries such standards in the picture *The Ten Commandments.*

16. Faulkner, pp. 12-18.

While dealing with this subject we take the liberty of departing from the Egyptian army for a moment to illustrate the use of standards among the Israelites. In Numbers 2:2 we read, "Every man of the children of Israel shall pitch by his own standard, with the ensign of their father's house. . . ."

In the Midrash Rabbah a detailed account of the design of these standards is given. Their heraldry is derived from the Bible and we shall present the related reference after each one in the following list:

Reuben: Mandrake—Gen. 30:14

Simeon: Town of Shechem—Gen. 24:26

Levi: Urim and Thummim—Deut. 33:8

Judah: Lion—Gen. 49:9

Issachar: Sun and moon—I Chron. 12:33

Zebulun: Ship—Gen. 49:13

Dan: Serpent—Gen. 49:17

Gad: Camp—Gen. 49:19

Naphtali: Hind—Gen. 49:21

Asher: Woman and olive tree—Gen. 49:20

Joseph: Bullock and wild-ox, or unicorn—Gen. 49:20

Benjamin: Wolf—Gen. 49:27[17]

Some of the emblems presented above do not lend themselves readily for identification with the verse indicated. Nevertheless, they have been derived in the manner noted by the ancient authors of the Midrash Rabbah. We have applied this information realistically to the screen, even though some of the heraldic ideas seem to be of a later date than the one represented. The use of them is justified by the precedent of Egyptian standards and their mention in the Bible, where their existence is established in the wilderness of Sinai.

17. a) *Midrash Rabbah*, V, trans. J. J. Slotki (London, 1939), 29-30.

b) *Jewish Encyclopedia*, V (New York, 1907), 405.

In Egypt, all the armed forces were under the command of the pharaoh. Frequently he made the crown prince commander in chief, but outsiders were appointed to this position as well, as the history of Harem-Hab proves before he became pharaoh at the end of the eighteenth dynasty.[18] Some of the actual titles for officers were "standard bearer," "commander of archers," "chief army commander" or "overseer of soldiers."[19]

An officer who distinguished himself on the battlefield would earn a decoration, the "gold of valor." It consisted of golden flies or lions suspended from a neck chain.[20] This "gold of valor" is worn in the picture by prince Moses and by Pentaur, Pharaoh's Commander of the Host. Other rewards consisted of participation in the conquered booty, gifts of land and slaves, or positions within the bureaucratic government.[21] Soldiers also partook of the loot and sometimes were given a piece of land to settle on in times of peace, with slaves to work it. Others remained in conquered countries to man the many garrisons and outposts.[22]

During a campaign a large baggage train composed of donkeys and two- and four-wheeled ox carts carried the tents and vast amount of provisions for the army.[23] To facilitate the progress of such a traveling army roads were built. Sethi I, for example, built roads into the wilderness of Sinai and had water wells dug at intervals. While these roads also served to approach the turquoise and copper mines, they functioned as a military highway for strategic access to Asia. They were guarded by fortified posts.[24]

Elsewhere along strategic points and within conquered countries, the pharaohs had fortifications built consisting of walls and towers enclosing functional buildings. Curiously enough the Egyptian language adopted a Semitic word for them, *migdol*.[25] This word occurs in the Old Testament also, when the route to the Red Sea is described: ". . . and encamp before

18. Wilson, p. 188.

19. *Ibid.*, pp. 187-188. See also Steindorff and Seele, p. 92.

20. Steindorff and Seele, p. 91.

21. *Ibid.* See also Wilson, p. 188.

22. Steindorff and Seele, pp. 92-93.

23. *Ibid.*, p. 91. Also Erman and Ranke, p. 636.

24. Steindorff and Seele, p. 105.

25. Wilson, pp. 181, 231, 240.

Pihahiroth, between Migdol and the sea. . . ."[26] It has been established archaeologically that such a fortification, a *migdol,* had been built between the Bitter Lakes and the Wadi Tumilat, the biblical Goshen.[27]

26. Ex. 14:2.

27. *a*) J. A. Wilson, in *Ancient Near Eastern Texts* (Princeton, 1950), p. 259.

b) Erman and Ranke, p. 628.

OF CAMELS, HORSES AND TRANSPORTATION

The Camel

The camel has become the most controversial animal in Hollywood when the making of a motion picture involves ancient Egypt. Scholars usually claim that camels did not become domesticated animals in Egypt proper till the Greek period,[1] while the Bible places them there when the nomadic patriarch Abraham sojourned in that land.[2] At the time of Moses they are mentioned in connection with the plague of murrain in Exodus 9:3.

The historical period represented in the picture *The Ten Commandments* is the nineteenth dynasty and particularly the thirteenth century B.C. In agreement with the biblical text we do show camels in a caravan and in the momentous Exodus.

It can be argued that the scribes who set the Old Testament down in writing unwittingly committed an anachronism. But let us consider what archaeologists have to say on the subject of camels.

The word *camel* of our vocabulary derives from a Babylonian-Semitic word, *gammalu,* which R. C. Thompson translates "the ass from the sealands."[3] Keith Seele writes that the word for camel does not occur in the ancient Egyptian language as expressed

1. A. Erman and H. Ranke, *Aegypten* (Tübingen, 1923), p. 586.
2. Gen. 12:16.

3. R. C. Thompson, in *Cambridge Ancient History,* I (Cambridge, England, 1928), 501.

95

4. In letters to the author, Mar. 31, 1953; Mar. 8, 1956.

5. a) A. E. Robinson, in Sudan Notes and Records, XIX, 57-58. b) A. Fakhry, Necropolis of El-Bagawat in Kharga Oasis (Cairo, 1951), p. 47, n. 1.

6. A. Lucas, Ancient Egyptian Materials and Industries (London, 1948), p. 160.

7. Robinson, p. 64.

8. Ibid., p. 61.

9. M. S. and J. L. Miller, Harper's Bible Dictionary (New York, 1954), p. 87.

10. Judg. 6:2.

11. Westminster Historical Atlas to the Bible, ed. Wright and Filson (Philadelphia, 1945), p. 45.

12. Fakhry, p. 47, n. 1.

13. Robinson, p. 66.

14. W. M. F. Petrie, Social Life in Ancient Egypt (London, 1923), p. 139.

in hieroglyphs of that time.[4] In other sources we read that modeled forms of camels of early dynasty dates have been excavated,[5] and A. Lucas has established a "two-strand rope of camel hair" pertaining to the Old Kingdom period (2700-2200 B.C.).[6] A. E. Robinson in his article "The Camel in Antiquity" points out that the camel may have been in Egypt up to the sixth dynasty (2350-2200 B.C.), but believes that it disappeared from that land thereafter.[7] As already indicated scholars hold that the domesticated camel appeared historically in Egypt during the Greek period. However, A. E. Robinson writes that "the remarkable success of the Assyrian invasion of Egypt in 671 B.C. is attributed to the use of camels by the eastern army."[8] We can assume that the Egyptians certainly did become acquainted with the camel in a painful manner at that time, whether they wanted to or not.

It is the lack of concrete Egyptian evidence of the camel from about 2200 B.C. to the Greek period that causes archaeologists to negate its existence in that land during that time.

There is other evidence which, while not derived from ancient Egyptian records, must be considered here.

In one of the books consulted on this subject W. F. Albright is quoted as authority that "our earliest certain evidence of the widespread domestication of the camel does not antedate the end of the 12th century, B.C. . . . but the beast was previously known."[9] When "Midian prevailed against Israel,"[10] "Bedouins . . . for the first time were using domesticated camels on a large scale."[11] Ahmed Fakhry writes, "the camel was not used as a means of transportation in Middle Asia before 1100 B.C."[12] while A. E. Robinson deduces the date for the domestication of the camel to be about 1200 B.C.[13]

Sir Flinders Petrie ascertains that camels may have been in use close to the borders of Egypt during the nineteenth dynasty,[14] i.e. thirteenth century B.C. Important data is provided by R. C. Thompson, who states that at the time of Hammurabi (2000 or 1800 B.C.)—the era usually ascribed to Abraham—Semites of the desert were known to ply the camel caravan trade "rarely showing their beasts in the towns. . . . That the camels were not led into the cities is not unusual, as their drivers prefer to park them outside."[15]

Holding with Sir Flinders Petrie that camels appeared at the borders of Egypt during the nineteenth dynasty, and with R. C. Thompson, who speaks of Semites plying the desert caravan trade with these animals at an even earlier date, it can be considered as at least possible that camel caravans penetrated into Egypt proper without entering cities. It is also within the realm of possibility that desert Semites would bring their camels with them when they sought refuge from drought and pasturage for their animals in Egypt's open Delta.[16]

In conclusion, it must be pointed out that the dating of the "widespread domestication"[17] in either 1200 or 1100 B. C. and the "large scale" use[18] of this animal by necessity imply that camels were domesticated and put to work earlier, even if on a lesser scale. Their use may have been restricted to the caravan trade plied by desert Semites,[19] whom the Egyptians might well have scornfully ignored, since they felt rather superior about these "despised" Asiatics, whom they called "sand-dwellers."[20]

The Horse

The horse was domesticated in Asia as early as 2000 B.C.,[21] and the generally accepted idea is that the Hyksos introduced this animal and the chariot into Egypt when they conquered that country in the eighteenth century B.C.[22] In a recent revision of *When Egypt Ruled the East* undertaken by Keith C. Seele (now in process of being published) this Egyptologist informs us of new evidence to the effect that the horse and chariot had already been in Egypt in the late Hyksos period.[23] This would mean that the horse and chariot were acquired by the Hyksos in Egypt.

15. Thompson, p. 501.

16. Cf. J. A. Wilson, in *Ancient Near Eastern Texts* (Princeton, 1950), p. 259.

17. M. S. and J. L. Miller, p. 87.

18. *Westminster Atlas,* p. 45.

19. Thompson, p. 501.

20. *a*) Wilson, *Ancient Texts,* pp. 227-228.
    b) J. A. Wilson, *Burden of Egypt* (Chicago, 1951), p. 112.

21. Robinson, p. 53.

22. *Ibid.* See also Wilson, *Burden,* p. 155.

23. In letter to the author, Mar. 8, 1956.

There is but little evidence of horseback riding in ancient Egypt; for example, a small statue is exhibited in the Metropolitan Museum of Art in New York showing an Egyptian in simple dress riding a horse. It is conjectured that the rider represents a groom who is taking the horse to the stable.[24] In the chapter "The Army" we have made reference to some rare representations of armed men on horseback and the fact that the "horsemen" of the Bible do not represent cavalry. The first cavalry seems to become evident during the reign of Sargon II in the late eighth century B.C.[25] A statement is made elsewhere that the Hittites, who lived where modern Turkey lies today, were experts in horsemanship and, aside from chariotry, also had cavalry in the early second millennium B.C.[26]

Judged by the names they gave these animals, the ancient Egyptians must have thought highly of their chariot horses. Sethi I, for example, had two teams named "Amon gives Strength" and "Amon orders Victory."[27] Rameses II owned a team which he called "Nura" and "Victory of Thebes"[28] and these are the names of his horses in the picture *The Ten Commandments.*

During the Exodus scenes Joshua is shown riding a horse. We assume that he had observed this phenomenon in Egypt and copied the idea as a practical one.

The Chariot

The fast-moving and greatly maneuverable chariot had revolutionized warfare in the ancient world just as much as did the tank in the twentieth century A.D. The Egyptians waged war, using it with telling effect.[29]

The chariot was driven for peaceful pursuits as well, to provide transportation.[30] An account of Amenhotep II (fifteenth century B.C.) tells of its use as a sporting vehicle.[31]

The Egyptian chariot normally had wheels of six spokes, the rim of each wheel being covered with a leather tire.[32] The sides of the upper body were usually

24. W. C. Hayes, in *Everyday Life in Ancient Times* (Washington, D.C., 1951), pp. 122, 137.

25. Robinson, p. 53.

26. T. L. Shear, quoted in W. R. Brown, *Horse of the Desert* (New York, 1947), p. 38.

27. Erman and Ranke, p. 585.

28. O. B. Miller, *Picturesque Tale of Progress* (Chicago, 1953), Part 1, p. 231.

29. G. Steindorff and K. C. Seele, *When Egypt Ruled the East* (Chicago, 1947), p. 91. See also Wilson, *Burden*, p. 163.

30. Steindorff and Seele, p. 91.

31. Wilson, *Ancient Texts*, p. 244.

32. R. Engelbach, in *Introduction to Egyptian Archaeology* (Cairo, 1946), p. 125.

covered with a network of leather thongs[33] and the chariot altogether executed in a most practical manner. Pharaoh's chariots, however, were beautifully decorated with overlaid gold and inlays of jewelry. Carefully designed friezes embellished the body, representing heraldic emblems as well as scenes of conquest.[34]

The chariots used so extensively in the picture were adapted from originals on exhibit in the Egyptian Museum in Cairo. Since the Egyptian chariots were not pulled by means of traces, the men who were to drive them during action of the film had to be specially trained.

Boats[35]

The oldest boats used on the Nile and adjoining swamplands probably were those made of papyrus. Such craft are still in use today in Upper Egypt and other parts of Africa. It is this boat with upturned bows that served as a general design pattern in ancient Egyptian shipbuilding.

A great variety of boats were built—for example, to transport the deceased from the eastern land of the living to the western shores of the Nile, where the dead were buried. There were pleasure boats and those that simply provided transportation, ships and rafts that moved heavy commercial loads and warships.

Boats were propelled both by oar and sail; the latter were of a rectangular shape. The sails were not manipulated with the help of pulleys, but rather with ropes that led through holes drilled into, or rings attached to, the mast. The direction in which the boat was to travel could be governed by a huge single or double rudder located at the stern of the boat.

On the screen, the boats that can be seen are the royal barge at the river shrine, the grain vessels, Nefretiri's ship and the primitive papyrus boat carried on the shoulders of Negroes participating in the Exodus.

33. Erman and Ranke, p. 584.

34. a) Ibid., pp. 584-585.
b) P. Fox, Tutankhamun's Treasure (London, 1951), pp. 15-16; Pls. 5 and 6.

35. Bibliography:
a) R. Engelbach, in Legacy of Egypt (Oxford, 1947), pp. 138-142.
b) W. C. Hayes, Scepter of Egypt, Part I (New York, 1953), pp. 267-270.

BUILDING AND OTHER ARTS
AND CRAFTS

Building

a) General observations. What we know of ancient
Egyptian architecture is, in the greatest number of
cases, derived from temples and tombs and to a lesser
extent from palaces, villas and homes in which royalty,
nobility and the common people lived. The temples
were built of durable stone. The funerary establish-
ments, such as the pyramids, also were constructed of
this imperishable material, or else cut into the native
rock as witnessed by the magnificent tombs in the
Valley of the Kings near ancient Thebes.

In domestic architecture, on the other hand, mud
bricks were used almost exclusively. The buildings
erected with this material have long since decayed, or
rest below fertile soil now tilled for agriculture to nur-
ture those living today. In other instances—and this is
typical of Bible lands—such houses served as founda-
tions for later building sites, a process that repeated
itself over and over again.

In some places archaeologists have uncovered the
outlines of buildings on ground level, combined with
rare remnants of walls. In this fashion not only floor
plans reappear but complete "maps" of cities. One of
these is the Middle Kingdom (2050-1800 B.C.) city of

101

1. A. Erman
   and H. Ran-
   ke, *Aegyp-
   ten* (Tübin-
   gen, 1923),
   pp. 196-207.

Kahun and another is El Amarna, once the capital of
Akhnaton (fourteenth century B.C.).[1] These discoveries and ancient clay models of dwellings, as well as
wall paintings, have enabled modern scholars to reconstruct to some extent the buildings wherein the living dwelt.

For obvious reasons, the ancient Egyptian buildings
that impress modern man most are those which have
remained for him to see readily. The general and popular idea of what was the architecture of the Nile
valley is, therefore, influenced by these clearly discernible features, i.e. the temples and tombs.

In making a motion picture, such as *The Ten Commandments,* it is advisable in certain cases to project
onto the screen what is considered typical, to present
that which an audience can readily recognize. In our
case this has influenced the design of certain sets.
There may be an exacting scholar who might identify
elements of temple architecture within the royal palace
or in the execution of the pylons flanking the gate of
the biblical treasure-city. These sets do represent what
can quickly be recognized as Egyptian architecture.
There is substantiation to support in a general sense
the choice of set designs made by Cecil B. deMille and
the art directors Hal Pereira, Walter Tyler and Al
Nozaki. Egyptian "temples were arranged in imitation

2. G. Steindorff
   and K. C.
   Seele, *When
   Egypt Ruled
   the East*
   (Chicago,
   1947),
   p. 157.

of human dwellings."[2] In actuality palaces were connected with temples at El Amarna, at the Ramesseum
built by Rameses II and at Medinet Habu.[3]

3. Erman and
   Ranke,
   p. 201.

The process of constructing Pharaoh's treasure city,
Raamses,[4] plays an important part in the picture. Generally, archaeologists have assumed that Tanis (or

4. Ex. 1:11.

Avaris) was the Delta capital rebuilt by Sethi I and
finished under Rameses II. Near it a royal residence
was erected which bore the name Per-Ramses

5. Steindorff
   and Seele,
   p. 256.

(House of Rameses).[5] Today, there is evidence that
Raamses (Per-Ramses) was in actuality the capital
and not Tanis. James Breasted states that Per-Ramses

6. J. H. Breas-
   ted, *History
   of Egypt*
   (New York,
   1921), p.
   443.

became the seat of government, where all records of
state were kept.[6] The Egyptian archaeologist Labib

Habachi is about to publish his evidence that Per-Ramses was the Delta capital of Egypt during the nineteenth dynasty. The location of this ancient city is identified with modern Qantir.[7] Here we have one of many instances where archaeology establishes a biblical place name in history and geography.

b) Materials. In most ancient times primitive shelters were constructed out of reeds to give protection from the hot sun. A little later such structures were covered with mud to make a more permanent building.[8] On the screen the combined use of mud and reeds may be seen in two typical columns which support the roof of Moses' hut in Goshen.

In historic times wood was used but little in building. It was employed for doors, and upon occasion for roofs and columns.[9]

The basic and outstanding materials for building in ancient Egypt were stones and Nile mud. Limestone and sandstone were used predominantly and, to a lesser degree, granite, alabaster, basalt and quartzite.[10]

In spite of the remarkable temples and tombs built of stone, which stand as a monument to the greatness of ancient Egyptian architecture to this day, the building material most widely used from early to modern times was and is the Nile mud in the form of sun-dried bricks.[11] The clay, gained from this Nile alluvium, was formed into bricks as found, or binding materials such as sand, straw or animal dung were added.[12] This mixture was placed into a mold, the mold lifted off the clay and the wet brick left to dry in the sun.[13] Some of the bricks of antiquity are of the same size as those of modern times. Larger ones were made as well,[14] and curved ones for barrel roofs.[15] Not considering extremely rare exceptions, burned bricks were unknown in Egypt till Roman times.[16]

There are brick pits in operation in Egypt today which apply the self-same method of manufacture as that employed in ancient times.[17] For this reason we were able to photograph a great number of actual

7. Conference with the author, Luxor, November, 1954.

8. A. Lucas, *Ancient Egyptian Materials and Industries* (London, 1948), p. 61.

9. *Ibid.*, p. 98.

10. *Ibid.*, pp. 66-80.

11. *Ibid.*, p. 62.

12. *Ibid.*

13. R. Engelbach, in *Legacy of Egypt* (Oxford, 1947), p. 127.

14. Lucas, p. 63.

15. Engelbach, p. 128.

16. Lucas, p. 63.

17. *Ibid.*

brick pit scenes in Egypt—in the Faiyum—for the film *The Ten Commandments.*

We are indebted to the ancient Egyptian language for a word in current English usage. That word is *adobe.* Ancient Egypt transmitted it to the Coptic language where the word *toobe* means "brick." The Arabs adopted it from there and brought it with them to Spain. Hence, it reached South and Central America and through Latin-American Spanish entered the English vocabulary.[18]

The same raw material contained in bricks, Nile mud, was employed as a mortar to hold them together. For stones, a mortar made of gypsum was used.[19]

Nile mud was daubed on walls as plaster. A finer plaster was obtained by applying a natural mixture of clay and fine limestone. Sometimes, on top of these, a coat of gypsum plaster was added, which made an excellent base for mural paintings. Gypsum plaster was also used alone.[20]

c) Stone quarrying and working. The quarrying of soft stones was accomplished by digging trenches behind and on each side of the stone to be separated. Finally, a series of wooden wedges were inserted into prepared openings at the bottom, and wetted. By this action the block of stone was pried loose.[21]

The tools handled by these ancient masons to accomplish their tasks were stone, copper and bronze chisels; the typical wooden mallet still in universal use today; and stone hammers,[22] during the wider period in which the picture takes place.

Wetted wedges also formed part of the equipment to detach the hard stones in quarrying. Since copper or bronze chisels are impractical in working hard stone,[23] the designated block was pounded loose by means of a pounding ball made of dolerite.[24] The slots that had to be carved out to admit the wooden wedges were made with the help of a metal tool, perhaps a pick.[25]

Once the stone was separated from the living rock

18. Engelbach,
    p. 129.

19. Lucas,
    pp. 93-94.

20. *Ibid.*,
    pp. 95-96.

21. Engelbach,
    p. 144.

22. Lucas, p. 81.

23. *Ibid.*, p. 85.
24. Engelbach,
    pp. 145-146.

25. *Ibid.*, p. 146.
    See also
    Lucas, p. 83.

it had to be worked to suit its planned purpose. Whether it was destined to form part of a building or to be sculptured into a statue, the tools and methods to accomplish the finished product were the same. They were: pounding stone with stone; rubbing with stones, probably combined with the use of an abrasive powder; cutting with a copper saw with the help of an abrasive; turning tubular drills by hand or with a bow, with the addition of abrasive powder; using crescent-shaped bits of flint (particularly employed for hollowing out stone vessels); drilling with copper or stonepoint drills, with the application of an abrasive agent.[26] Lucas deduces that the abrasive used by the ancient Egyptians was, most likely, finely ground quartz sand.[27]

d) Building methods. The stones were brought from the quarry with ships as close to the building site as possible.[28] They rested on sleds and unlimited manpower pulled them with the help of ropes over rollers and sleepers to the place of work.[29]

It is assumed with good reason that the building blocks were partially cut to fit before being raised to their assigned position on the course. The bedding joint and the two side faces were dressed on the ground. Once placed in their destined positions the top was dressed on the course, while the outside facing was not finished until the whole structure had been completed.[30]

Thorough investigation has convinced archaeologists that the pulley remained unknown in ancient Egypt until Graeco-Roman times.[31] This is undoubtedly true with respect to the lifting of any heavy object. (However, at the Oriental Institute of the University of Chicago there are two small wooden pulleys on exhibit that once formed part of a weaver's loom. Their date is uncertain, but they could be placed within the New Kingdom period.) The manner of raising such heavy materials as stones to the desired building level was accomplished by means of inclines—ramps—con-

26. Lucas, pp. 84-85.

27. *Ibid.*, p. 85.

28. Engelbach, p. 148.

29. Engelbach, in *Introduction to Egyptian Archaeology* (Cairo, 1946), p. 121.

30. *Ibid.*

31. *Ibid.*

structed of brick and rubble. Their size increased in
height and length as the building progressed vertically.
Such a ramp is still standing in connection with an
unfinished pylon within the temple complex of Karnak, at Luxor.[32] As the construction of the biblical
treasure city progresses in the picture, such ramps can
be seen put to practical use.

The stones were rolled up the ramp by the means
already described. With the help of levers they were
eased and pushed from the sled onto the course.[33] A
wooden rocker may have been employed for this purpose as well.[34] Since such heavy blocks could hardly
be pushed onto the course and sided snugly against
the stones next to them, a thin coat of Nile mud was
washed onto the base to act as a lubricant.[35]

In addition to the mason's tools already mentioned
the ancient Egyptians were familiar with plumb rules,
squares, the cord and reel.[36] To establish a horizontal
guide, a small channel was dug into dirt and filled with
water to act as a level.[37] The sighting devices used in
the film are freely adapted from an Egyptian astro-
nomical instrument.[38]

Scaffolding was known in ancient Egypt and used
particularly for buildings of lesser heights.[39] To incise
and paint designs onto pylons men were lowered from
the top with the help of a cradle suspended from
ropes.[40] On the screen this procedure can be clearly
observed.

For Sethi I's jubilee, preparations were made for
the erection of obelisks,[41] and this is of particular
interest to us since one of them is being placed into
its proper position within the framework of the picture *The Ten Commandments*. The practical realization of this scene is derived from the valuable investigations of R. Engelbach.

Fastened onto a sled, the giant obelisk weighing
many tons (Rameses II's obelisk at Luxor is 82 feet high
and weighs 254 tons)[42] was hauled up the ramp toward a sand-filled funnel-shaped pit. Once the obelisk
was in proper position its own weight caused it to tip

32. *Ibid.*

33. *Ibid.*

34. Engelbach,
    Introduction,
    p. 125.

35. Engelbach,
    Legacy,
    p. 150.

36. Engelbach,
    Introduction,
    p. 124.

37. Engelbach,
    Legacy,
    p. 151.

38. Exhibit in
    Oriental In-
    stitute, Uni-
    versity of
    Chicago.

39. Engelbach,
    Introduction,
    p. 122.

40. *Ibid.,* p. 123.

41. Breasted,
    p. 418.

42. Engelbach,
    *Problem of
    the Obelisks*
    (New York,
    1923),
    p. 39.

over and settle in the sand. The sand, in turn, was gradually taken away through openings at the bottom of the pit. In this fashion the obelisk eventually came to rest on its base. Colossal statues probably were set in a similar manner.[43]

Many claims have been made that the ancient Egyptians employed for their remarkable building activities machinery of which we no longer have any knowledge. It is even believed by some that they were able to put mysterious forces to work for this purpose. We wish to quote Engelbach's statement in this regard: "Though modern research robs the Egyptians of the magical powers attributed to them, it makes them more admirable in the eyes of the practical man, as it shows that they could do, with the most primitive tools, feats of engineering which we, with some 3,000 years of mechanical progress behind us, are barely able to copy."[44]

e) Buildings. Two towering pylons flank the gate of Rameses II's walled capital—the biblical Raamses—in the picture *The Ten Commandments.* This follows the pattern of ancient Egyptian cities which usually were encircled by such walls and furnished with gates protected by towers. So it was with the ancient Old Kingdom capital, commonly known as Memphis, whose original descriptive name was "White Wall."[45]

Equally set apart by walls and provided with gates and towers of varying heights were villas or estates, palaces and temples.[46] Such walls and pylons, the latter in the typical shape of truncated pyramids,[47] are still standing and strikingly visible in the Egypt of today.

There is evidence that cities did not always grow into a conglomeration of many buildings, but that some were carefully planned. The "map" of Kahun discloses two distinct sections within the city walls: a residential district containing a palace, estates and housing for servants, and a section where workers lived. Separate gates gave admission to the two districts and each section had its own main street pro-

43. *Ibid.,* pp. 69-74.

44. *Ibid.,* p. 21.

45. Steindorff and Seele, p. 12.

46. E. B. Smith, *Egyptian Architecture* (New York, 1938), Pls. 38-74 *passim.*

47. Steindorff and Seele, p. 161.

48. Erman and
Ranke,
pp. 196-200.

49. J. Capart, in
*Legacy of
Egypt* (Ox-
ford, 1947),
p. 80.

50. Smith,
p. 217.

51. *Ibid.*, Pls.
67, 71. See
also Erman
and Ranke,
pp. 201-211.

52. Smith, Pl. 67.

53. *a*) W. C.
Hayes, in
*Everyday
Life in An-
cient Times*
(Washing-
ton, D.C.,
1951), pp.
110-111.
b) N. M.
Davies, *An-
cient Egyp-
tian Paint-
ings* (Chi-
cago,
1936), I,
Pls. 7, 9,
28, 48.
c) Erman
and Ranke,
pp. 203-211
passim.

54. Erman and
Ranke,
p. 211.

55. *Ibid.*, p. 208.
See also
Davies, II
Pls. 69, 94;
Hayes, pp.
110-111.

56. Erman and
Ranke, pp.
201, 203;
Pl. 13.

57. Smith,
Pl. 71.

58. Erman and
Ranke,
p. 203.

59. Ex. 12:29.

vided with a gutter that ran along the center of it. In the workers' section, side streets branched off the main street at right angles and onto them the modest houses faced. In the residential part of Kahun the gates of the walled estates bordered upon its main street.[48] At El Amarna, Akhnaton's capital, there were "geometrically planned streets"[49] and the "eastern village" which housed the pharaoh's stone cutters was designed within a square.[50]

Temples, palaces and estates held within their walls self-sufficient communities. The palace of a pharaoh or the villa of a noble, for example, consisted of the house of the master and his harem, the quarters for functionaries and servants, and the utility buildings containing kitchens, bakeries, stables and storerooms.[51] We must mention granaries,[52] since one can be seen within the temple precinct on the screen. Were these grain bins of beehive shape a descendant of primitive architecture in vogue before the advent of stone and brick construction, when bent reeds were daubed with Nile mud to give shelter?

Within the walls of palaces and estates grew fruit-bearing trees: sycamore figs, date palms, pomegranates and grape vines; vegetable gardens; and flowering plants such as acacias, oleanders, jasmine, red poppies, corn flowers and dwarf chrysanthemums.[53] Floras exotic to Egypt were brought from afar to enhance the gardens.[54] A rectangular pool, with flowering lotus and stocked with fish, reflected refreshing coolness to those beholding it.[55] There is no evidence that such pools were used for bathing; but bathrooms existed within the house.[56]

An unusual feature existed on Akhnaton's palace grounds: a collection of rare animals was kept—a regular zoo.[57] Sometimes a small chapel stood in the garden for private worship.[58] For dramatic reasons Cecil B. deMille placed such a sanctuary in direct connection with the "Hall of Audience" set, where the idol of Sokar is invoked when Rameses' first-born dies.[59]

These palaces and villas were houses of many man-sions. Some of them contained as many as seventy rooms in buildings two and three stories high.[60] The top floors were sometimes left open to admit air and surrounded by a balustrade, while the roof was supported by pillars.[61] We have adapted this idea in the picture in constructing such a set, where the balcony leads to rooms located in the center of the floor.

A distinctly recognizable feature of ancient Egyptian architecture is its columns. On the screen the spectator can discern columns that are traditional stylizations of papyrus and lotus plants, as well as pillars embodying the palm tree motif. These were adapted from actual examples of Egyptian antiquity.[62]

The village in the land of Goshen[63] represents mud and brick construction, the same manner of building that has prevailed to this day in the villages bordering upon the Nile.

Pyramid architecture plays no part in the picture *The Ten Commandments*. However, since these majestic monuments to man's ingenuity continue to have popular appeal and have become an unofficial trademark of Egypt, we should like to make a few remarks concerning them, to suggest rectifications of possible misconceptions.

It is sometimes claimed that the pyramids were built with Hebrew slave labor. This is wrong. The period of the biblical bondage is that of the New Kingdom. All the well-known pyramids were built during the Old Kingdom, over one thousand years before the age of Moses.

The function of the pyramid was that of a tomb. According to most archaeologists, its design represents a sun emblem.[64] Another scholar considers it to be a symbol of the original mound of creation—the mound of earth emerging through primeval waters, from which a self-created god created all else.[65]

According to scholarly Egyptologists there is no planned mystery embedded in the measurements of the Great Pyramid that would enable man to reconstruct the past history of the world and foretell future

60. Erman and Ranke, pp. 199, 206.

61. *Ibid.*, p. 206.

62. H. Schaefer and W. Andrae, *Kunst des Alten Orients* (Berlin, 1925), pp. 215-323 *passim*. See also Engelbach, *Introduction*, pp. 109-112.

63. Gen. 45:10.

64. Engelbach, *Introduction*, p. 115.

65. H. and H. A. Frankfort, in *Before Philosophy* (Harmondsworth, England, 1951), p. 31.

events by using an arbitrary "pyramid inch" as a guide to interpretation.[66]

f) Tents. Houses of sun-dried brick cannot be carried from camp to camp by a people on the march. Though accustomed to living in them for 430 years[67] in the land of Goshen, the Israelites became a nomadic people again—tent-dwellers as their forefathers had been.[68] The Bible says, among other related passages " . . . Israel shall pitch their tents. . . ."[69]

What did these tents look like in the thirteenth century B.C.? No contemporary description is available to inform us. For the picture *The Ten Commandments* we have patterned the tents of Israel after those still in practical use among the tent-dwellers of Arabia and the wilderness of Sinai.

In spite of recent oilwells and pipelines, which bring cars, airplanes and other conveniences produced by an advanced technology to a few, modes of life do not change much in biblical deserts as the centuries pass by in slow rhythm. As a general rule the nomadic Arab continues to live according to ancient usage and traditions. The sparse grazing grounds in the wilderness are still dotted by his dark tents.

The Arab calls his tent "house of hair."[70] The raw materials used to weave tent cloth are goat hair and sheep wool. Camel hair is never used for this purpose.[71]

The woven strips of material are an average of three fourths of a yard wide and as many as eight of these are stitched together. The over-all length may be 25 feet or, in the case of a very big tent, 70 feet.[72]

This rectangle of black or brown material forms the roof of the tent as well as the two narrow sides of it. It is supported by several poles and two ropes for each pole. The sides are kept taut with ropes.[73] To enclose the two long sides of the tent a piece of material composed of four narrower strips is attached to the rear poles and stretched out lengthwise. This length of material is fastened to the tent with bodkins, and

66. *a*) Engelbach, *Introduction,* p. 120.
   b) E. A. W. Budge, *Dwellers on the Nile* (London, 1926), pp. xix, xxi.
67. Ex. 12:41.
68. Gen. 13:5; 25:27.
69. Num. 1:52.

70. G. W. Murray, *Sons of Ishmael* (London, 1935), p. 80.
71. H. R. P. Dickson, *Arab of the Desert* (London, 1949), p. 66.
72. *Ibid.* Also Murray, p. 80.

73. Dickson, pp. 66-75.

the lower end is buried in the sand to keep it in place, or, if the ground is hard, it is pegged down.[74]

The tents are always located in such a fashion that the long covered rear sides face the prevailing wind.[75] They are usually divided into two compartments by means of curtains—one compartment for the men and the other for the women, where the kitchen section is also to be found. A carpet covers the floor, a type of mattress serves for seating purposes, and a camel saddle and pillows provide backrest.[76]

The tents of Jethro and Moses seen in the picture are arranged according to this general plan.

Sculpture and Painting

a) *General observations.* We, as motion picture makers, have gained a practical knowledge from the surviving expressions of ancient Egyptian painters and sculptors which have helped to make the realization of the picture *The Ten Commandments* possible. Next to written books, both sacred and profane, we have studied their works more than any other. We owe a debt to these remarkable artists of long ago, and to the scientific pursuits of archaeologists who have made their valuable investigations and knowledge available.

The carved or painted hieroglyphs on temple walls and monuments, the sculptures and mural paintings in tombs and palaces, have given us an insight into ancient Egyptian history and into the daily life of royalty and commoner alike.

Through them we can observe the people's occupations in all manner of trades, in agriculture and the arts. We can literally watch a pharaoh holding court or riding in his chariot to victory over his enemies. We become the invited guests to a nobleman's banquet and enjoy the entertainment provided by dancers, musicians and acrobats, while the painted onlookers partake of food and drink. We delight in Egypt's pastimes as unobtrusive witnesses and are fascinated by the elegance of dress and the beauty of jewelry.

Is it not surprising to realize that these people of the

74. *Ibid.*, pp. 70-71.

75. Murray, p. 80.

76. Dickson, pp. 66, 70, 76-77.

Nile valley, whom so many believe to have had a
morbid concern with death and the dead, show us
through their art the everyday activities of life and the
joys and pleasures of living? This is not the attitude
of listless pessimism, but rather the expression of an
optimistic way of life.

Through these means the knowledge of ancient
Egyptian life has become more vivid, more specific
than that of the Israelites of Moses' time. The daily
life of these people has to be drawn by inference and
deduction from the Old Testament and from what is
more concretely known of other people who were their
contemporaries and neighbors in the biblical Near
East. There is no evidence of Hebrew sculptures and
paintings of that time. Such expressions of art were,
as a matter of fact, discouraged by law—unless we take
the specific ordinances relating to the building and fur-
nishing of the Tabernacle into consideration. But
there exists no trace of this shrine, except in the written word. It is also probable that an unsettled nomadic
people, crossing a wilderness over a period of many
years, could not engage nor express itself in sculpture
and painting.

Ancient Egyptian sculpture and painting were
closely related to each other not only because they
were the work of artists and craftsmen, but also because of the fact that the two media were frequently
combined.

In a wider sense the making of bowls, vases, lamps
and jewelry, among many artifacts, should be included
under the heading of sculpture, since these were
carved out of stone or metal; and pottery, whose surfaces were sometimes decorated with patterns, figures
and scenes, is related to painting. In essence, however,
this section is limited to sculptures in the round and
relief and to the painting of murals and statues.

b) Materials and tools. All the stones enumerated for
the construction of buildings found their use in sculpture too. Many more, all native to Egypt, must be

added to these, such as diorite, dolomite, serpentine and steatite.[77]

Ivory from elephants and hippopotami,[78] wood from many lands,[79] gold, silver, copper, bronze and electrum were carved, engraved or embossed. Electrum is a naturally occurring or artificially made alloy of gold and silver, harder than gold and of a pale yellow color. The specimens analyzed by Lucas contained from 20.3 to 29 per cent silver.[80]

Minerals provided the pigments for paint. The colors known were black, blue, white and yellow. Brown was derived from a single pigment or by painting red over black, while green was also produced directly or by mixing blue with yellow. Gray resulted from a mixture of black and white. Pink was a combination of red and white.[81]

The tools handled by sculptors were identical with those of the stone masons in the building craft, though adzes and axes have to be added for the workers in wood.[82]

The painter needed brushes. One method of making them was to double fibrous materials, such as halfa grass or split palm leaves, and to tie these at the doubled end to hold the brush together and to serve as a handle. Another and finer brush was obtained by bruising fibrous wood at one end until the fibres formed bristles. Separate handles were not attached to these brushes.[83]

The surfaces painted when desired were ivory, wood, stone, plaster, papyrus, pottery and, rarely, cloth.[84]

c) Working methods. The designated crude rock was marked to delineate the over-all size of the statue and then cut down to those outlines. At this stage the surfaces were divided into squares to facilitate the drawing of anatomical dimensions upon the stone. Now the statue could be carved to its desired form and finally the fine details and finishing touches shaped. We can assume that wooden statues were executed in the same

77. Lucas, pp. 462-480.

78. *Ibid.*, p. 45.

79. *Ibid.*, pp. 488-508.

80. *Ibid.*, pp. 267-268.

81. *Ibid.*, pp. 391-399.

82. *Ibid.*, p. 509.

83. *Ibid.*, pp. 159-160.

84. *Ibid.*, pp. 45, 403-404.

85. Engelbach,
    Introduc-
    tion, pp.
    130-131.

86. *Ibid.,* p. 131.

87. *Ibid.,* pp.
    134, 141.
88. *Egypt,*
    Unesco
    World Art
    Series
    (Paris,
    1954), Pl.
    14. Also
    Davies, II,
    Pls. 91, 92.
89. Engelbach,
    Introduc-
    tion, p. 134.

90. Lucas,
    pp. 403-404.

91. *Ibid.,* pp.
    401-402,
    406.

fashion and that a like procedure was followed in making reliefs.[85] It is believed that the practice of making preliminary models did not exist in ancient Egypt. Sculptures seem to have been derived directly from drawings.[86]

The many sculptures, whether in the round or in relief, were painted with traditional colors. The skin of men was usually rendered red or brown, while lighter hues, generally yellow[87] and sometimes pink,[88] identified the skin of women. Black served as paint for hair and the pupils of the eyes.[89] Before this took place, however, the stone surfaces were frequently covered with a whitewash to produce a smoother and non-porous painting surface. In the case of sculptures in wood and other wooden objects to be painted, a coat of gypsum plaster mixed with size, perhaps in the form of glue, was applied. The expression for this technique is the Italian word *gesso* derived from the Greek *gyp-sos* via the Latin *gypsum*.[90]

Egyptian painting can be called tempera, though in some instances the pigment was applied dry onto damp plaster. The mixture used to convey the pigments onto the painting surface and to make them adhere was water with gelatin, glue, gum or white of egg. An exception to this general practice was the mixture of pigment with beeswax. To protect them, paintings sometimes were covered with a coating of beeswax. For the same purpose a clear varnish was applied to murals, coffins, pottery and other artifacts.[91]

In some instances eyes, eyelids and eyebrows were inlaid, undoubtedly to create a greater realism. The craftsmanship involved in making artificial eyes serves well to illustrate the care and devotion which these ancient sculptors applied to their work. At their best, artificial eyes contained the following components: the eyeball was usually made of polished opaque quartz, but also of crystalline limestone or alabaster. The cornea, cut of rock crystal, was set into a circular depression drilled into the eyeball and held in place with resin. To create the effect of the iris a disk of dark brown resin was placed behind the transparent cornea. A plug of dark brown or black resin was set into a hole drilled into the cornea to indicate the pupil or else a black spot was painted onto the center of the resin that simulated the iris. Sometimes even the caruncle, the small red spot located at the inner angle where the upper and lower eyelids meet was painted onto the eyeball. Strangely enough, the Egyptians painted these in both corners of each eye.[92]

Eyelids were made of copper, silver, faience, blackened limestone, glass and even gold.[93] Eyebrows evidently were also inlaid as can be observed on Tutankhamon's portrait mask and other works found in that pharaoh's tomb;[94] on some sculptured heads unfilled cavities indicate that provisions were made for them.[95] The eyes of hawks, fish, cobras, leopards, lions and cattle, among others, were inlaid at times.[96]

The process of casting metal was practiced to some degree. Copper weapons and tools were cast into open pottery or stone molds and then additionally hardened by hammering.[97] Bronze was also cast, as witnessed by a hollow cast bronze head of Rameses II.[98] There are numerous small solid gold statuettes that may have been cast.[99]

The art of producing sheet metal to a fineness that in the case of gold can be called leaf, was understood. Copper, gold and silver were hammered into thin sheets of various thicknesses. Gold leaf measuring one five-thousandth of an inch has been found.[100]

Wooden statues were sometimes covered with copper sheeting which was hammered on and fastened with copper nails. Others were sheathed in a similar manner with gold. When foil was used for gilding, the wood was first coated with gesso, upon which the thin gold was glued. With the still thinner gold leaf again gesso was applied to the core and the leaf made to adhere with white of egg. Gold was also hammered onto copper and silver for plating or, when gold leaf was used, it was glued to the underlying surface. Silver, too, was plated onto copper.[101]

92. *Ibid.*, pp. 122-123.

93. *Ibid.*, pp. 122, 132.

94. P. Fox, *Tutankhamun's Treasure* (London, 1951), Pls. 32, 33.

95. *Encyclopédie Photographique de l'Art*, I (Paris, 1936), 76-77, 101.

96. Lucas, pp. 122, 151-154.

97. *Ibid.*, pp. 245-246.

98. *Ibid.*, p. 255.

99. Engelbach, *Introduction*, p. 136.

100. Lucas, p. 264.

101. *Ibid.*, pp. 264-265.

The making of the Golden Calf in the film illustrates to some extent the method of covering a wooden sculpture with gold.

d) Sculptures and paintings. The sculptures of ancient Egypt are both in the round and in relief. An additional type is called incised, which applies particularly to hieroglyphs cut into the stone in outline without any additional modeling of the characters. Sculptures in the round are statues while Egyptian reliefs are of two distinct forms, low and incised reliefs. The difference between these two is that in the former the sculpture projects above the surrounding surface, while in the latter the design is carved below or to that level.[102]

Several examples of these techniques can be seen in the picture *The Ten Commandments.* Incised sculpture can be observed on the obelisk that is being erected in the new treasure-city. Among the statues there is the giant one of Sethi I as it is being pulled over rollers to its destination. Colossi (colossal statues) of Rameses II stand in the palace set. In actuality such sculptures of Rameses II can be seen within the precincts of the temple at Luxor.[103] In typical fashion enormous statues of the seated Rameses II flank the gate to the city of Raamses in the film. Originals representing this king still sit in undiminished grandeur on each side of his rock-temple at Abu Simbel.[104] The famous "colossi of Memnon" (actually representing Amenhotep III of the eighteenth dynasty) formed part of the gate leading to the funerary temple of Akhnaton's father.[105] Towering over the Theban plain they stare blindly toward the east—"God's Land," as the horizon of the rising sun was called by the ancient Egyptians.[106] At the Ramesseum, on the western bank of the Nile opposite Luxor, the broken pieces of a granite colossus of Rameses II lie on sunbaked sand. They inspired Shelley as symbols of shattered self-esteem when he wrote the poem "Ozymandias."[107]

The statue of Khnum, the creator of all living

102. Engelbach, *Introduction*, pp. 130, 139.

103. Steindorff and Seele, p. 263.

104. *Ibid.*, p. 264.

105. *Ibid.*, p. 173.

106. J. A. Wilson, in *Ancient Near Eastern Texts* (Princeton, 1950), p. 29.

107. Wilson, *Burden of Egypt* (Chicago, 1951), p. 253.

Replica of the vulture pectoral worn
by Rameses II on the screen
(Page 153)

(Inset) Pectoral representing the vulture, symbol of Nekhbet, goddess
of Upper Egypt (Cairo Museum). (From Fox, *Tutankhamun's Treasure.*
Courtesy of Oxford University Press.)

Rameses II in his war chariot (Abu Simbel). (From Frankfort, *Kingship and the God*. Courtesy of Oriental Institute, University of Chicago.)

Rameses II, in his chariot, wearing the blue war crown and the armor of divine protection. *(Pages 99, 135, 137)*

Isis conducting Nefretiri to her tomb (Thebes). (From Davies and
Gardiner, *Ancient Egyptian Paintings.* Courtesy of Oriental Institute,
University of Chicago.)

Costume worn by Nefretiri in the film, inspired by murals in that queen's rock tomb. *(Page 133)*

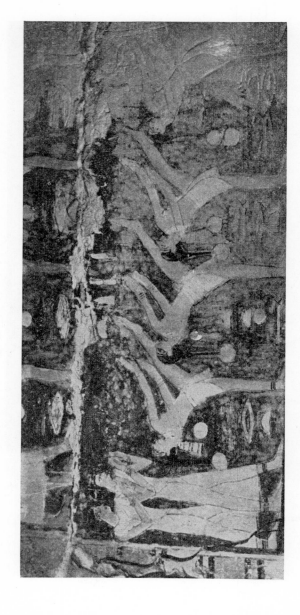

Mural in the tomb of the Vizier Mehou at Saqqarah presenting the performance of a dance. (From *Egypt: Paintings from Tombs and Temples*. Unesco World Art Series. Paris, 1954.)

The ballet performed at Sethi I's court. *(Page 165)*

The delicate necklace copied for the
picture. *(Page 154)*

(Inset) Ancient Egyptian necklace on exhibit at the Metropolitan
Museum in New York. (From Winlock, *Treasure of Three Egyptian
Princesses*. Courtesy of the Metropolitan Museum of Art.)

things[108] and the "lord of the inundation"[109] is also the lord of the river shrine in the picture, where the first plague, the turning of water into blood, becomes manifest. The original sculpture from which our design was derived is exhibited in the Louvre in Paris.[110]

In the set adjoining Rameses "Hall of Audience" the idol of Sokar is the focal point. He, with the head of a hawk and the body of a man was, like Osiris, a god of the nether world.[111] He is the deity whom Rameses implores in vain to restore the life of his and Nefretiri's first-born son.

Prominent in the picture are the sphinxes lining the avenue of approach to the city of Raamses. These imposing creatures of stone with the body of a lion and the head of a pharaoh once symbolized the power and strength of ancient kings.[112] The one standing near the pyramid of Chephren at Giza has impressed mankind with its enigmatic smile for centuries and given rise to the famous "riddle of the sphinx." As told to the author in Egypt it is as follows: What walks on all fours in the morning, on two at noon, and on three in the evening? The answer: It is the life of man, who crawls on all fours as a child, walks on two legs in the full strength of his life, and in old age needs a crutch to support him.

In ancient Egypt, pylons and walls were extensively covered with relief sculptures commemorating, for example, the performance of a religious rite or the pharaoh victorious in battle. Two matching elements of this kind decorate the pylons of the treasure-city set. Facing them, the one on the right tower is copied from a relief on a Karnak temple wall representing Sethi I in his war chariot riding against the Canaanites.[113] The other was adapted from the famous work on Egyptian monuments executed by command of Napoleon I. This source refers the original to the Karnak temple.[114]

The best example of mural painting in the picture can be seen in Nefretiri's bedroom. The ducks in a papyrus thicket are recomposed from several actual

108. J. Cerny, Ancient Egyptian Religion (London, 1952), p. 49.

109. G. Rawlinson, History of Ancient Egypt (Boston 1882), I, 338.

110. Encycl. Phot. de l'Art, I, 111.

111. a) K. Lange, Aegypten (Berlin, 1943), Pl. 53.
b) É. Drioton, in Introduction to Egyptian Archaeology (Cairo, 1946), p. 184.

112. Cerny, p. 73.

113. Schaefer and Andrae, p. 392.

114. Description de l'Égypte (Paris, 1809-), III, Pl. 38.

115. Davies, I,
Pl. 47; II,
Pl. 54. See
also Schae-
fer and
Andrae,
p. 379.

murals[115] in a manner similar to that applied to walls in palaces or villas, as at El Amarna.

Some observations pertaining to Egyptian two-dimensional art must be made. In relief sculpture and mural painting the human figure was practically always shown in profile. Within this method of representation there were some prominent departures that were adhered to dogmatically with few exclusions. Even though the face was shown in profile, the eye and eyebrow were always portrayed as seen from the front—full face. With few exceptions, an identical technique was practiced in depicting both shoulders. The chest appears to be presented in side view. This can be observed best in representations of women where only one breast is shown. Yet jewelry and that part of clothing which covered the shoulders and chest were drawn in full frontal view. The abdominal region was presented in profile, but the navel was displaced sufficiently to be seen fully.[116]

116. Steindorff
and Seele,
p. 179. Also
Engelbach,
Introduction,
pp. 139-140.

In illustrating architectural features, a pond or a bowl filled with flowers, typical conventions were observed. A gate and the plants in the garden to which it led were always shown in front view. But a pond or a body of water were depicted as seen from a point immediately above, while the fish and birds, the boats and plants in, on or by the water were given in profile. Since a bowl of flowers or fruit would hide some from direct view, the Egyptian painter or sculptor would arrange each flower or fruit on top of the container to let the spectator behold a detailed view of the contents.[117] This manner of representing objects is in vogue even today in illustrated maps, where the topography is shown as seen from above, while elements of architecture, of flora and fauna are presented in front view.

117. Steindorff
and Seele,
p. 178. Also
Engelbach,
Introduction,
p. 140.

A peculiar idiosyncrasy indulged in by the ancient Egyptians was their manner of representing hands and feet. They made no distinction between right and left. To illustrate the point, this means that if the left hand and the left foot were in the forefront of the scene, i.e. closest to the viewer, they showed the left thumb and the big toe of the left foot first, instead of the little finger and the little toe.[118] Exceptions to this convention can be noted on works of art pertaining to the period of Akhnaton. There, the short-lived religious revolution temporarily brought about a trend toward realism in art.

Two-dimensional art of the ancients does not create the illusion of distance, of depth in space. Nevertheless the Egyptians had developed a convention which conveyed these ideas to them. Generally speaking, the effect of distance was established by depicting the foreground in the lowest horizontal section of the plane. Progressing upward, the element most distant was placed on a horizontal line in the uppermost part of the picture,[119] without, however, considering any perspective diminution of the object's size.

Important persons were drawn larger than other people. In some instances this also applies to sculptures in the round. For example, the colossi of Rameses II at Abu Simbel also represent his queen Nefretiri and other members of his family but their full figures do not even reach his knee.[120]

It is believed with good reason that Egyptian statues were not planned to be free-standing but to form an integral part with the architecture against which they were placed. Thus, they could be seen only from the front or in profile.[121] Of course, there are exceptions to this observation too. Among these are the statuettes for domestic and funerary use, as well as the sphinxes which still can be seen free-standing, lining the approach to the temple of Karnak.

Did ancient Egyptian portraiture convey any likeness of the individual it represented? The stylized form which limited exact portraiture, the uniformity of traditional poses, and to some extent the similarity in dress lead many people to imagine that ancient Egyptians looked more or less alike. The superficial impression thus gained is the same as that created by watching a company of uniformed men marching in

118. Steindorff and Seele, p. 179 (re feet only).

119. Engelbach, *Introduction*, p. 140.

120. K. Baedeker, *Egypt and the Sudan* (Leipzig, 1914), p. 405.

121. Wilson, *Burden*, p. 53.

unison without apparent individual distinction. Upon examination of facial characteristics on sculptures and paintings the individuality of the person represented can frequently be recognized. Not only that, but the typical features generally remain alike in different works of art showing the same individual.[122] The variations in anatomical design between various representations of one and the same person were, perhaps, caused by the same factor that brings about differences in more recent works of art. After all, each artist sees the object with his own set of eyes, however formalized the art style may be. Compare the many portraits of George Washington done by different artists, for example!

There are people to whom "real" art does not begin till the advent of the great Greek masters. It is impossible to say how much or how little Greek artists owed either directly or indirectly to their Egyptian predecessors, with whom their forefathers and a few contemporaries were in contact. Engelbach writes: "It should be borne in mind, that the time which elapsed between the fashioning of the diorite statue of King Chephren [builder of the second pyramid at Giza] and that of the Venus de Milo, is greater than that between . . . the Venus de Milo and the present day!"[123]

Whether one admires Egyptian art or not is beside the point. What is impressive about it is its symmetry and its motionless quality. It creates in the viewer the feeling that man, beast and flower were meant to stay in that stony pose eternally, suspended in time in an attitude sufficient to itself.[124] One dare not even imagine that the colossus of Rameses II standing in the Luxor temple might ever move one foot before the other in an undignified moment; nor that this pharaoh would want to rise from his rocky seat at Abu Simbel. The raised arms of Sethi I, pulling his bow, belong up in the air never to come down. Befitting the god-kings they were, the curious smile on the sculptured faces of pharaohs is expressive of all the wisdom of

122. Ibid., p. 54. Also Engelbach, Introduction, pp. 134-135.

123. Engelbach, Introduction, p. 138.

124. Cf. Wilson, Burden, pp. 53-55.

life; their unblinking eyes behold eternity. Even Rameses' severed head—once belonging to the broken statue about which Shelley wrote his poem—still sees with its granite eyes no beginning and no end, but everlastingness.

Furniture

Whether it be metal or stone, leather or fibre, gem or bone, all of these materials contributed to the making of furniture. There were chairs with embossed gold panels, thrones encrusted with gems and glazes, beds standing on legs of ivory, seat cushions covered with leather and bedsprings made of finely plaited linen. The essential component of furniture, however, was wood.

Egypt had timber of its own—acacias and willows; the almond, carob and persea tree; the sidder, sycamore fig and tamarisk; the dom and date palm. The raw material derived from these trees was not always entirely satisfactory or suitable for the many uses to which wood was put and foreign timber had to be imported. Such timber was not only of better quality but of larger size. Among these importations we find ash, beech, cedar, cypress, elm, juniper, oak, pine, yew and ebony. This last word is of linguistic interest since it derives from the ancient Egyptian *hebeny* to become *ebony* in our language, according to A. Lucas.[125]

125. Lucas, pp. 488-508.

The woodworking tools were the same as those already enumerated in other sections of this chapter. Considering the fine work that was accomplished the absence of two tools is notable; they are the plane and the lathe. Wooden surfaces were smoothed by rubbing with fine-grained sandstone. There are some scholars who believe the lathe existed at this early age; but to others it appears that such suspected components of furniture were filed rather than turned.[126]

126. *Ibid.*, pp. 508-511.

The art of making plywood was known; for example, parts of a six-ply coffin belonging to the Old Kingdom have been found, each layer measuring about 0.16

inch. As in modern plywood, the individual sheets were put together with the grain alternating. Fine veneer was also applied and held on by means of small wooden pegs or glue. The craft of inlaying was widely practised. Not only was wood such as ebony used for this purpose, but ivory, stones, faience and opaque glass as well.

Dowels of wood and ivory were used for joining wood together; dovetailed, mitred, and mortise and tenon joints had been developed.[127]

127. *Ibid.*, pp. 512-513.

The craftsmanship of these ancient furniture and cabinet makers is still practiced in Egypt today by specially trained artisans. For use in the picture *The Ten Commandments* several replicas of original pieces were made for us in Cairo, such as chairs, bedsteads, boxes and chests.[128] The workmanship is so excellent that if a comparison were to be made between them and the originals on exhibit at the Egyptian Museum in Cairo it would take an expert to note the distinction.

128. See Fox, Pls. 9 and 60, for example.

The ancient Egyptian bed consisted of a frame standing on legs usually carved in the likeness of lion or cattle legs; the footboard was frequently decorated with symbolic designs. In place of springs a network of plaited linen thread or leather was stretched between and fastened to the frame. The beds seem to have been padded for comfort but the head reposed on a concave surface supported by a stand, similar to the ones still used in Japan today. Pillows made of leather stuffed with feathers helped to soften this hard headrest.[129] Tutankhamon was the owner of a folding camp bed, for travel purposes.[130]

129. *a*) Erman and Ranke, pp. 212-213.
b) M. A. Murray, *Splendour that was Egypt* (New York, 1949), pp. 113-114.

Every variety of chair could be found in ancient Egypt, from low stools, folding camp stools and backless seats to regular and armchairs. To facilitate pleasant conversation there were loveseats, and a person of note would rest his feet on a footstool.[131]

130. Fox, Pl. 59.

131. Erman and Ranke, pp. 213-214. Also M. A. Murray, pp. 113-114.

Clothing and household linens were kept in chests, while a great variety of boxes were used to keep all manner of belongings in order. Long tables were not known; but food was served on a stand holding a tray to be placed in front of the eater,[132] just as our present generation partakes of food, at times, while watching television.

Beautifully carved lamps, filled with oil and a floating wick, brought light to festive rooms at night.[133] Less elaborate lamps existed as well, and from Herodotus we learn that the receptacle was filled with salt and the oil soaked into it to prevent its spilling.[134] Flat braziers held fire to provide heat when required.[135]

Akhnaton sent beds and chairs as presents to Babylonian kings, and a king from the island of Cyprus requested a gilt bed as a favor.[136] It may have been because of the rarity of beds and chairs elsewhere at that time, but in any event these items of comfort evidently represented a welcome and extraordinary gift to these foreigners. Sinuhe, returning from his exile in western Asia, expressed his joy at resting in a bed again after the many years of sleeping on hard ground.[137]

If a people were to be appraised by nothing else but their furniture, a fairly good picture of their cultural state could be gained. A highly developed culture reflects itself in the material refinements of everyday living as much as in others. In ancient Egypt these particular refinements become apparent not only in the variety of functional furniture, but in the basic elegance of their design and quality of construction. The popular availability of the chair, which up to the Middle Kingdom had been reserved for the pharaoh and his nobles only,[138] is in itself a cultural achievement. True, the chairs of the royal palace and noble villas were made of costlier stuff than the ones on which common people sat; nevertheless, it is of symbolic significance that the whole Egyptian nation of some 3,000 years ago had raised itself off the floor to sit on chairs.

132. Erman and Ranke, pp. 215-216; M. A. Murray, pp. 113-114.

133. Fox, Pls. 19, 20.

134. *Herodotus*, trans. G. Rawlinson (London, 1862), II, 90.

135. Erman and Ranke, p. 217.

136. *Ibid.*, pp. 213, 619.

137. *Ibid.*, p. 212.

138. *Ibid.*, p. 214.

COSTUMES AND ADORNMENTS

Egyptian Materials and Costumes

a) Materials. At a very early stage in ancient Egypt the raw materials for weaving were grass, reeds and hemp.[1] However, throughout the period of its ancient history, the predominant textile in this land of the Nile was linen until it was supplanted by cotton, after the seventh century A.D.[2] The textures achieved with linen are of an amazing variety: from the roughest weaves to silk-like gauze, from plain materials to looped and patterned products of the loom.[3] In comparison to a modern linen handkerchief containing approximately 100 threads per inch, linen has been found in tombs measuring 160 threads in the warp and 120 in the weft per square inch.[4]

The use of wool by ancient Egyptians is generally looked upon with disdain. Elizabeth Riefstahl points out that the word "wool" was unknown during the pharaonic period, though a word of semitic origin "of the time of Ramses II . . . refers to an article of commerce" as "wool." A reference to "Syrian" cloth makes this word synonymous with "wool."[5] It is of interest to note that during the eighteenth dynasty Syrian captives were employed as weavers in temples and that Asiatic materials, i.e. woolen materials, came to Egypt as loot and tribute.[6]

1. A. Lucas, *Ancient Egyptian Materials and Industries* (London, 1948), pp. 166-171.

2. *Ibid.*, p. 170.

3. *a) Ibid.*, p. 166.

b) E. Riefstahl, *Patterned Textiles in Pharaonic Egypt* (Brooklyn, 1944), pp. 1, 2.

c) A. Erman and H. Ranke, *Aegypten* (Tübingen, 1923), p. 535.

4. Riefstahl, p. 1.

5. *Ibid.*, pp. 29, 30.

6. *Ibid.*, p. 31.

Though the woolen materials found in early tombs may be of a late date, Lucas nevertheless states that wool was "probably always used for clothing to at least some extent" and "there cannot be any doubt that the Egyptians, who possessed large flocks of sheep, made use of wool as a covering."[7] According to Elizabeth Riefstahl fleece-bearing sheep were im-- ported into Egypt from Asia during the New King- dom; the native Egyptian sheep was a hair-bearing animal.[8]

Herodotus (fifth century B.C.) describes Egyptians wearing white woolen garments over their linen attire, remarking that wool was considered unclean for use in the temple or for burial of the dead.[9] This state- ment by the Greek historian might explain the paucity of woolen finds, since the overwhelming number of discoveries made in Egypt are those of temples and tombs.

The first mention of silk in Egypt occurs in a text of the first century A.D. describing Cleopatra.[10] In the picture *The Ten Commandments* the ambassador from Troy presents Rameses and Nefretiri with a piece of silk. Sanskrit texts indicate the possible existence of a silk industry in India as early as 4000 B.C.[11] Troy lay at the crossroads of international trade in the pe- riod with which we are concerned. A piece of this rare and strange material might have reached the court of Troy and from there been sent as a worthy gift to Egypt.

Another material spoken of in the picture is the Sammur gown. It refers to a unique woven material whose threads are gained from "a large mollusk called Pinna marina, a genus of bivalve mollusks having a silk byssus or beard." The Arabs called it "sea-wool." At one time it was known as "fishdown" in Egypt. The name *sammur,* meaning "sable," is taken from an old text describing the manufacture of this material in medieval Spain. This woven product was of a golden color with varied shadings.[12]

Animal skins, undoubtedly an element of clothing in

7. Lucas, pp. 166, 168.

8. Riefstahl, p. 29.

9. *Herodotus,* trans. G. Rawlinson (London, 1862), II, 114.

10. Lucas, p. 170.

11. *Encyclopae- dia Britan- nica* (New York, 1936), XX, 665.

12. R. B. Ser- jeant, *Ars Islamica,* XV-XVI (1951), 60-61.

prehistoric Egypt, remained as ceremonial adjuncts to costume.[13] There is the animal tail that the pharaoh is sometimes shown with; and the traditional leopard skin, an insignia of the higher priesthood, of which the pharaoh was high priest and his sons were members.[14] Kilts, loincloths and tunics were sometimes made of leather.[15] For protection against excessive wear some soldiers and laborers are shown wearing leather netting over the seat of their kilts.[16] Leather was also used in applique work for decorative purposes.[17] Scalloped leather platelets were sewn onto tunics.[18]

Materials with a decorative feather pattern indicate that actual feathers were used at one time.[19]

Aside from pattern and tapestry weaving, which received stimulation by the introduction of the upright loom through the Asiatic Hyksos (1730-1570 B.C.),[20] embroidery was also practiced.[21] Beads were woven into materials or sewn onto them, as well as sequins of gold and faience;[22] or they were incorporated into a network covering the actual garment.[23]

b) Colored materials. What is known about ancient Egyptian costumes is derived mostly from the study of sculptures and tomb paintings and stated in the form of deduction and interpretation. The findings of actual garments or textiles have been very limited, though the discoveries in the tomb of Tutankhamon of a great variety of costumes and materials have thrown new light on this subject.

Various scholars have written about costumes and materials, but Elizabeth Riefstahl, whose outstanding work is extensively referred to here, remarks that the "scanty modern literature on weaving and costume . . . presents many conflicting statements . . . and often draws conclusions which are inadequate or wholly unsupported by evidence."[24] The Tutankhamon discoveries (and others) present some evidence to the effect that what was painted, incised and sculptured by these artists of long ago does not altogether repre-

13. Erman and Ranke, pp. 232, 538.

14. *a) Ibid.,* pp. 232, 233.
b) G. Steindorff and K. C. Seele, *When Egypt Ruled the East* (Chicago, 1947), p. 85.

15. Riefstahl, pp. 9, 10, 40, 41.

16. *Ibid.,* p. 41 See also Erman and Ranke, p. 240.

17. Lucas, p. 46.

18. R. Engelbach, in *Introduction to Egyptian Archaeology* (Cairo, 1946), p. 152.

19. Riefstahl, pp. 12, 13.

20. Lucas, p. 166.

21. *a)* Riefstahl, p. 2.
b) G. M. Crowfoot and N. de G. Davies, *Journal of Egyptian Archaeology,* XXVII (1941), 113, 115.

22. Riefstahl, p. 11. See also Crowfoot and Davies, p. 116.

23. Riefstahl, p. 11.

24. *Ibid.,* p. 2.

sent what the Egyptians of old wore. It seems that these artistic representations in tomb and temple followed an established tradition adhered to in spite of changes that had, and might have, taken place in everyday life. At a casual glance, all the artistic expressions of ancient Egypt do have that enormously static, unchanging quality. It is only upon closer inspection that changes in style become apparent in the passing of centuries. (The short interlude of Akhnaton's time, with its artistic realism, is the prominent exception to this observation.) It is also possible that the costumes so shown on these monuments of antiquity were those worn for ceremonial-religious functions only.[25]

25. *Ibid.*

The existing examples in monument and tomb art from which costumes can be studied establish an almost exclusive predominance of plain white textiles for Egyptians.[26] Foreigners, on the other hand, are shown in multicolored and patterned attire.[27] One would, therefore, be led to believe the apparent evidence that Egyptians wore, in the main, nothing but plain white dress. Indeed, most modern reproductions of ancient Egyptians depict them in this fashion. The cautious statement has been made that such evidence could be misleading.[28]

26. *Ibid.*

27. N. M. Davies, *Ancient Egyptian Paintings* (Chicago, 1936), I, Pls. 24, 42; II, Pl. 60, for example.

28. Riefstahl, p. 46.

In designing and making the many costumes required for the picture, deviations from these long-held traditional views were made at times. When they were made, they were governed by the expressed doubts of actual knowledge (indicated in the previous paragraphs) or by factual information, or they were undertaken for technical and dramatic reasons. The factual information in behalf of materials other than white is, in part, as follows:

During the Old Kingdom, unicolored costumes were worn in either red, yellow, blue or blue-green.

Deities and royalty of the New Kingdom are sometimes shown in colored dress.

29. *Ibid.,* p. 1.

Colored cloth samples have been found in tombs.[29]

In written lists of offerings to the dead, colored

materials are included throughout the many periods of ancient Egyptian history. The translation into English of the Egyptian words is not certain in this case, but the colors may have been white, green, blue, and light and dark red.[30]

A hunter of the Old Kingdom is shown in a tunic of many colored stripes sewn together. The material appears to be leather.[31] This costume was adapted in the film for prince Moses.

Cloaks with horizontal, multicolored stripes were worn during the Middle Kingdom. The particular cloak Elizabeth Riefstahl refers to may have been made of leather, or woven reeds.[32]

Gold cloth is indicated in a kilt,[33] and in the picture prince Rameses wears a similar one.

During the New Kingdom, contact with Asia, its people and culture, became more pronounced. The Asiatics wore colorful attire, as can be observed time and again in Egyptian art, when these Semites appear before a pharaoh or some notable, paying obeisance and tribute.[34]

The textual evidence of Syrian cloth and Syrian weavers in Egypt has already been indicated. It is worth repeating that the discoveries in the tomb of Tutankhamon proved that there was more to the available choice of dress than the evidence of paintings and sculptures had led archaeologists to believe up to that time. In some of the colored pattern or tapestry weaves Asiatic design has been recognized.[35]

Tutankhamon's famous tunic with its intricate colored patterns ornamenting the collar and ending in a cross-design on the chest[36] inspired the costume Sethi I wears on his death bed in the picture. This tunic has been compared with a "dalmatic" and is considered a precursor of those in use to this day in Christian rites.[37]

We read again that monochrome linens in rose, yellow, red-brown, blue or blue-green existed in the New Kingdom,[38] its nineteenth dynasty being the period of Moses, Sethi I and Rameses II.

30. *Ibid.,* pp. 1-2.

31. *Ibid.,* pp. 9, 10.

32. *Ibid.,* pp. 7, 8.

33. Erman and Ranke, p. 235.

34. N. M. Davies, I, Pls. 24, 42; II, Pl. 60. See also Riefstahl, p. 18.

35. Riefstahl, p. 32. Also Crowfoot and Davies, p. 127.

36. Crowfoot and Davies, Pl. 14.

37. *Ibid.,* p. 117.

38. Riefstahl, p. 46.

Mrs. Crowfoot describes "a robe in yellow linen with narrow stripes in green and dark brown and bands with flying ducks in green" and two other robes "with stripes in brown and green bands" and "bands alternately in black and red."[39]

The use of metals and beads to form designs on textiles has already been indicated. Aside from abstract designs, hieroglyphs and elements copied from nature were woven or embroidered into the material.

A variety of patterns, some of them intricate, were accomplished in ancient Egypt from very early times by means of pleating.[40] Such effects were successfully adapted in several costumes made for the actors.

Not every archaeologist will subscribe readily to all the choices of textile colors made by Cecil B. deMille and the costume designers. Yet the selections made are based on actuality or within probability of actuality. In some cases, where the scholar is likely to disagree, the colors were chosen for technical reasons of photography. The delicate hues of textiles would disappear rather rapidly from what the camera can see and impress upon the photographic negative in the brilliant sunlight of Egypt, burning upon the arid desert. For example, the uniforms of the charioteers had to be designed in more light-absorbing colors, i.e. darker colors, or they would have faded from view far too rapidly. The creation of dramatic mood is often greatly dependent upon color. Certain traditional concepts exist in the modern western mind with regard to color and costume, which the ancient Egyptian luckily did not have to consider. This consideration influenced decisions in a few cases.

c) Dyes. Colored textiles having just been dealt with, something needs to be said about the art of dyeing in ancient Egypt. It has been stated that it is relatively easy to dye materials derived from animals, such as wool. Wool contains a natural agent which facilitates adherence of the coloring matter. On the other hand vegetable fibres, such as linen, cannot be

39. Crowfoot and Davies, p. 116.

40. Riefstahl, p. 8.

made color-fast without a mordant (an agent that fixes the dye). Without such a mordant the colors would gradually fade. Elizabeth Riefstahl calls particular attention to the fact that madder (a red dye used by the Egyptians) "would wash out in hot water unless a mordant were used to fix it."[41] It appears almost certain that the ancient Egyptians did their laundry in very much the same fashion as modern Egyptian villagers do today, namely, along the banks of the Nile and in its unheated water. That laundry was done in such a fashion is indicated by Erman and Ranke.[42]

The earliest actual description of the use of mordants dates from the first century, A.D., and is by Pliny.[43] The fact that in the most ancient times matting, which is made of vegetable fibre, had been dyed, is substantiated.[44] The existence of textiles dyed in different colors has been established in previous paragraphs. The investigation of the many colored threads composing the collar decoration of Tutankhamon's tunic shows them to be of dyed linen.[45] There is no need to argue whether or not mordants existed in Egypt before Pliny. The fact that materials made of vegetable fibres were dyed exists beyond any doubt.

d) Costumes. In spite of the impressive evidence of costumes found in temples and tombs, in sculptures and paintings and in a few actual examples, the precise manner in which the materials were cut and draped cannot always be ascertained.[46] Generally speaking, Egyptian costumes were draped and not tailored.[47]

1. MEN'S COSTUMES. The primary element of an ancient Egyptian's costume was the kilt,[48] which was draped around the hips. In the long history of its use it underwent many changes, both as to length and width, the application of patterns by means of pleating, the rounding of the corners, and so forth.[49] The manner of draping at one time ran clockwise and at another counterclockwise.[50] At still another period two

41. *Ibid.,* p. 29.

42. Erman and Ranke, pp. 244-245.

43. Lucas, p. 176.

44. *Ibid.,* p. 172.

45. Crowfoot and Davies, p. 113.

46. Riefstahl, p. 2.

47. *Ibid.,* p. 3.

48. Erman and Ranke, p. 233.

49. *Ibid.,* pp. 232-237.

50. Engelbach, pp. 149-151.

51. Erman and
Ranke,
pp. 235-237.
52. Riefstahl,
p. 4.
53. Engelbach,
p. 149.

54. Erman and
Ranke, pp.
233-234.
55. Riefstahl,
p. 3.

56. Engelbach,
pp. 145-150.

57. Ibid., pp.
149-150.

58. Riefstahl,
p. 5.

59. Ibid., p. 3.
See also
Crowfoot
and Davies,
p. 115.
60. Engelbach,
p. 151. Also
Erman and
Ranke, pp.
236, 238.
61. Riefstahl,
p. 5.

62. Ibid. Also
Engelbach,
p. 152; Er-
man and
Ranke,
p. 241.

kilts were worn, a longer one above a shorter one,[51] and vice-versa.[52] This kilt was held in place by tucking in the outside corner of the upper edge, while the inside corner was pulled up and twisted.[53] Belts were also used, often decorated with the name of the owner.[54] Riefstahl, who also mentions belts (girdles), writes that the upper corners of the kilt were tied or that attached ties served this purpose.[55] What frequently appears to be a knot slung through the belt is explained by Engelbach as a "peculiarly-tied bow, with the ends tucked out of sight as a general rule."[56] The same author makes a distinction between the kilt and the loincloth, implying that the latter developed into the long apron.[57]

Two additional items of clothing were basic, the shirt or tunic, and the cloak or mantle.

The shirt or tunic also underwent changes. It was held in place by being tied over the left shoulder, leaving the right shoulder free—or else shoulder straps functioned to hold the garment up.[58] Another type of shirt or tunic was made by doubling a length of material, sewing it up along the sides, and leaving openings for the arms. Where the material was folded over, an opening was cut to permit the head to pass through. To the tunic of Tutankhamon a pair of tailored sleeves were attached.[59]

Cloaks or mantles are in evidence in ancient representations.[60] From them it can be learned that a piece of cloth was wrapped in such a fashion around the body that it either covered both arms or left one arm free.[61] Such cloaks were used widely in the picture *The Ten Commandments.*

2. WOMEN'S COSTUMES. The basic costume for women consisted of a tube of material, which was supported by two bands, i.e. shoulder straps. These bands covered the breasts.[62]

A cloak or mantle was also worn by women. During the New Kingdom, such cloaks appear to have been made from diaphonous materials and have the quality of a flowing robe.[63] Frequently the waistline was accented by the addition of a belt or sash, its two ends gracefully trailing to below the knees.[64] What appears to be a short cape, or a shawl, to cover the shoulders is indicated by Erman and Ranke.[65]

As it was done with the costumes of men in the film, so it is with the dresses the "Egyptian" women wear: The delineation discernible in sculptures and paintings provided the pattern.

The tomb of Nefretiri in the Valley of the Queens at the necropolis of ancient Thebes was, among others, visited by us. The life-size representations of this beautiful queen who had been a wife to Rameses II provided us with designs for the costumes her counterpart wears in the picture.[66]

In the Louvre Museum in Paris stands a statue of a queen of the twenty-second dynasty. She is dressed in an elaborate costume in which the protective wings of a deity envelop the body. It is patterned in gold, silver and electrum.[67] We read in Riefstahl's text that such a costume "may have been . . . merely of the imagination of the artist." She continues to state, however, that there are Egyptologists who believe them to be "reproductions of actual garments, and indeed, we know that in the time of Tutankhamun not only the feather-patterned cloths . . . but also headdresses of cloth and sequins, made in the semblance of hawks with outstretched wings were woven in colored linen threads."[68] This costume was copied, in gold cloth, for Nefretiri to wear in the picture. The headdress she wears with it is depicted in that queen's tomb.

e) Royal costumes. In essence, the pharaoh's attire was made up of the same basic components as that of any other man: the kilt, the tunic or shirt, the cloak or mantle. On some of the monuments, particularly of earlier dynasties, the accent on the royal costume is one of great simplicity.[69] In these instances, only the insignia of his high position make the pharaoh readily distinguishable from those he rules (unless the hiero-

63. Riefstahl, pp. 5, 6; Erman and Ranke, pp. 242-244.

64. Riefstahl, p. 6.

65. Erman and Ranke, p. 242.

66. *Temples et Trésors de l'Égypte,* Art et Style 20 (Paris, n.d.), Pl. 18. See also N. M. Davies, II, Pls. 91, 92.

67. *Encyclo- pédie Photo- graphique de l'Art,* I (Paris, 1936), 105.

68. Riefstahl, p. 45 and Pl. 56.

69. Erman and Ranke, p. 64.

70. a) Encycl.
Phot. de
l'Art, I, 47,
52.
  b) Encyclo-
pédie Photo-
graphique de
l'Art, Musée
du Caire
(Paris,
1949), Pls.
8, 11, 52,
79, 82, 96.

71. Steindorff
and Seele,
p. 114.

72. a) Erman
and Ranke,
p. 66.
  b) H. Schae-
fer and W.
Andrae,
Kunst des
alten Orients
(Berlin,
1925), Pls.
345, 357,
397.

73. Riefstahl,
p. 37.

74. Engelbach,
p. 152.

75. Erman and
Ranke, p.
652.

76. Riefstahl, p.
37.

77. Ibid., pp.
12, 36.

78. Ibid., p. 37.

79. Lucas, p.
265.

80. Epigraphic
Survey:
Medinet
Habu, I
(Chicago,
1930), Pls.
19, 25-B.
See also
N. M. Davies,
II, Pl. 103;
III, 199.

glyphic texts carved into his statues are taken into consideration), for he is represented standing, or else sitting on a simple throne, dressed in a regal kilt only and wearing a royal headdress.[70]

New modes established themselves during the New Kingdom with its active international relations.[71] The costumes of the pharaoh and the nobles become more elaborate and varied. While the king continues to wear his traditional costumes of old and to bear the insignia of his exalted rank, he frequently wears a tunic or robe which reaches to his ankles.[72] For war purposes the pharaoh owns a coat of mail,[73] made of platelets sewn onto a tunic. The one found in Tutankhamon's tomb bears leather platelets.[74] The use of bronze scales is also established.[75] One made of iron dates of the tenth century B.C.,[76] some three hundred years too late for the era of Sethi I, Rameses II and Moses. It is entirely probable that similar protective clothing was worn by certain men in the service of the pharaoh.

These designs, which were also adapted to other materials, have their origin in the plumage of birds. The war-god Montu is shown with such an element of clothing, made of feathers.[77] Another design, related to the one just discussed, can be seen in a "corselet" found in the tomb of Tutankhamon now in the Cairo Museum.[78] It is made of gold, silver, carnelian and faience.

The knowledge that gold was readily available in ancient Egypt and that gold plating was known[79] caused us to make such a feather pattern coat of mail for the royal prince Rameses.

At Medinet Habu, near Luxor in Upper Egypt, where the University of Chicago maintains a staff of archaeologists, and in the Theban Valley of the Queens, there are two representations of Rameses III,[80] which gave rise to two costumes: one for the victorious prince Moses as the commander of the Egyptian host; the other for Pharaoh, Rameses II, to wear during his pursuit of the Israelites to the Red Sea.

One costume detail these artists of long ago incised and painted is of particular interest to us. It depicts a design of falcons. Their outspread wings cover the chest and back of the king, emblematic of Horus and a "symbol of divine protection."[81]

A similar use of such an element of divine protection was made of the vulture, symbol of Nekhbet, tutelary goddess of Upper Egypt.[82] We have alluded to this with the statue of a twenty-second dynasty queen. This protective design occurs elsewhere as well—for example, on Tutankhamon's second coffin[83] and on a miniature coffin found in that pharaoh's tomb.[84] The over-all design of these coffins appears to be in the form of a stylized cloak. This pattern, as well as the protective wings, was adapted to create the royal robe worn by Rameses II in the picture *The Ten Commandments.*

The particular apron the pharaoh wore, suspended from his belt, was elaborately executed.[85] The cobra (usually called "uraeus"), symbol of Lower Egypt,[86] formed part of its design. Steindorff and Seele describe it as a piece of "stiffened material, decorated with fine embroidery and ending in . . . uraeus serpents."[87] Riefstahl states that these aprons were sometimes made of beads, "sometimes apparently of metal inlaid with glass paste or semiprecious stones."[88] It is not unlikely that the basic material was leather adorned with gold, faience and jewels—or, perhaps, the decorations were partly painted, in a fashion similar to the pharaoh's headcloth (to be described later). In the picture both Sethi I and Rameses II wear richly adorned royal aprons. This apron seems to have had its origin in prehistory where it probably was the only covering a man wore.[89] A less decorative form of apron was worn by other men as well. A scribe and a high priest under Sethi I are shown with them.[90] Soldiers can be seen wearing a variation of it, undoubtedly for protection.[91]

f) Royal insignia. Before we describe royal insignia

81. *Epigraphic Survey,* I, 7.

82. *a)* Steindorff and Seele, p. 134. *b)* P. Fox, *Tutankhamun's Treasure* (London, 1951), pp. 23, 25.

83. Cairo Museum Exhibit No. 222. See also Fox, Pl. 29.

84. Cairo Museum Exhibit No. 452. Also Fox, Pl. 46.

85. N. M. Davies, I, Pl. 12; II, Pls. 100-103.

86. Engelbach, pp. 147-148.

87. Steindorff and Seele, p. 84.

88. Riefstahl, pp. 4, 5.

89. *Ibid.,* p. 4.

90. N. M. Davies, II, Pls. 67, 88.

91. *Epigraphic Survey,* I, Pls. 37, 41.

applied to costume, to crowns and scepters, we must indicate some heraldic concepts derived from Egypt's ancient religion.

Horus, son of Osiris and Isis, was at one time the national god of Egypt and at all times the pharaoh was considered his incarnation.[92] Horus was identified with the falcon or sparrow-hawk,[93] who could soar so effortlessly towards the sun. He was the patron deity of both Upper and Lower Egypt and as falcon (or hawk) symbolized royalty.[94] We have seen earlier how the falcon's wings, i.e. Horus, enveloped the pharaoh's body protectively.

Nekhbet, the goddess of El-Kab, once the capital of Upper Egypt, was represented by the vulture.[95] We have already described this divine symbol enfolding the pharaoh within its wings in referring to Tutankhamon's coffins and how we applied this idea to the royal robe of Rameses II. The head of the vulture, frequently modeled in gold, appears on the persons of the pharaoh and his royal family as a regal emblem to be worn on the head, or as a pectoral.[96]

The cobra, i.e. "uraeus," serves an identical purpose. It symbolizes Lower Egypt and is derived from the goddess of Buto, once the capital of that land.[97] When we see this insignia on the king, or worn by members of his family, it is not only representing the royalty of Lower Egypt but "coiled itself on the forehead of the king in order to destroy all his enemies, just as it had once annihilated the adversaries of the sun-god Re."[98] Frequently, the uraeus and the vulture emblems are seen together.[99]

There were many emblematic headdresses which identified the wearer as pharaoh.

Headcloths were worn by men and women;[100] but the one of the king was of a special shape. This particular shape perhaps derived from being worn over a bulky wig. It ended, in front, in two lapels falling upon the chest.[101] At times it appears as if these lapels were pleated. In any event, horizontal stripes are frequently accented. This headcloth was called "nemes."

92. Steindorff and Seele, pp. 134, 142.

93. *Ibid.*, p. 137.

94. J. H. Breasted, *History of Egypt* (New York, 1921), pp. 34, 38.

95. Steindorff and Seele, p. 137. See also Breasted, p. 38.

96. Fox, Pl. 36. See also n. 99 below.

97. Steindorff and Seele, p. 137. Also Breasted, p. 38.

98. Steindorff and Seele, p. 83. Also Fox, Pls. 8, 10, 11, 23, *et passim.*

99. Fox, Pls. 28, 30, 33-35, *et passim.*

100. Engelbach, p. 145.

101. Steindorff and Seele, p. 84. Also Erman and Ranke, p. 64.

Executed in a variety of colors, it is quite possible that it was made of leather and painted.[102] Among others, the mask of Tutankhamon shows such a headcloth. To the headband the vulture and uraeus are affixed.[103] Another one is shown on a contemporary painting of Rameses III, in blue and gold.[104] Frequently the uraeus emblem appears alone.[105] Such headcloths are worn in the picture by Rameses I, Sethi I and Rameses II.

A variety of crowns functioned symbolically as head covering for the pharaoh to be worn on ceremonial occasions. There was the white crown of Upper Egypt, called "hedjet," of a conical shape not unlike a modern bowling pin.[106] The crown of Lower Egypt was red and cylindrical, with a piece rising high in diminishing shape in the back. Its name was "deshert."[107] It is not known of what material these crowns were made. Usually the pharaohs wore a combination of the two crowns, named "sekhemti,"[108] the white crown sitting, so to speak, in the open cylinder of the red one. This crown, visibly showing the union of Upper and Lower Egypt, can be seen on the screen. Another crown which came about during the New Kingdom is worn by Rameses II in the picture. Its ancient name is "khepresh." Modernly it is called "war crown" or "blue crown" because of its basic color. Sometimes it seems to have been decorated with metal studding and it has the "uraeus" affixed in front. It may have been made of leather.[109] The many different crowns worn by deities were occasionally worn by the pharaoh for particular religious rites.[110]

Another royal insignia is the animal tail affixed to the pharaoh's costume.[111] We did not use this in the picture (nor did we use the artificial beard with which the pharaoh and others are sometimes depicted). This instance serves as illustration to the effect that in making a motion picture one has to eliminate such elements of clothing as might make a serious character appear ludicrous to modern eyes, unless it is of dramatic consequence to the part the actor has to portray.

102. Engelbach, pp. 145-146.

103. Fox, Pls. 32, 33.

104. *Epigraphic Survey*, IV (Chicago, 1940), Pl. 219.

105. *Encycl. Phot. Musée du Caire*, Pls. 9, 80.

106. Engelbach, p. 147. Also Fox, Pl. 56.

107. Engelbach, p. 147; Fox, Pl. 57.

108. *a*) Engelbach, p. 147. *b*) *Art of Ancient Egypt* (Vienna, 1936), Pl. 178.

109. Engelbach, pp. 146-147; *Art of Ancient Egypt*, Pls. 158, 160.

110. Engelbach, p. 147.

111. *Ibid.*, p. 149.

Among the scepters—insignia of the pharaoh's might
—there are the following that can be seen in the film
The Ten Commandments: The "crook," the hieroglyph
of which means "ruler," [112] has the name "hekat" and
is derived, prehistorically, from the shepherd's crook.[113]
In conjunction with this scepter the pharaoh is usually seen holding another one in paintings and on statues. The name "flail" has been given it, though it appears to be a misnomer. It is not a symbolized whip as
has been thought, but, according to some, it represents
a fly-switch.[114] Others believe it to be related to a
peculiar instrument still in use among shepherds in
Arab countries. With this "flail" they collect ladanum,
a prized ingredient for the making of perfumes. This
ingredient attaches itself to the three whiplike appen-
dices as they are brought in contact with the foliage
of the plant.[115]

Another scepter is identified with authority. It consists of a handle, to which a narrow rectangle is attached; its long edges are concave. It seems that this
object once was a weapon in primitive times, carried
by tribal chiefs, and used like a club. This same scepter is also seen carried by men of lower station than
the pharaoh. It indicates a position of command.[116]

g) Costume accessories. Perhaps the majority of the
ancient Egyptian people preferred to walk barefoot
most of the time. It was only during the New Kingdom
that the wearing of sandals became more customary.
Basically, the design of sandals remained the same
throughout the many centuries. Sandals could be made
of papyrus, palm fibres or rush, as well as leather.[117]
One of the highly ornate sandals exhibited in the Cairo
Museum had an undersole of leather (now decayed),
which had been lined with a sole made of rush.[118] A
thong attached to the sole and arising from between
the big toe and the others, connected to a strap crossing over the instep to hold the sandal in place. At times
a connecting ankle-strap held the sandal onto the foot
more securely.[119]

112. Erman and Ranke, p. 63.
113. W. C. Hayes, *Scepter of Egypt*, Part I (New York, 1953), p. 286.
114. Erman and Ranke, p. 63. Also Fox, Pl. 28.
115. Hayes, pp. 286-287.
116. *Ibid.*, p. 287. Also Fox, Pl. 67.
117. Erman and Ranke, p. 253.
118. Fox, Pl. 16.
119. Hayes, p. 240; Fox, Pl. 16.

Another item related to footwear must be mentioned here, greaves. In the picture we show them used for military purposes. The authority cited is the only one we could find on this subject.[120]

Gloves were in use, perhaps for archery as well as to protect the hands from the strain of chariot reins.[121]

A great number of different staves or canes are exhibited in the Cairo Museum. Some of them had a ceremonial significance, while others evidently served both for walking and protection.[122]

An elegant fan made of ostrich feathers with a finely carved ivory handle which contains colored inlays and the cartouche framing her name was made for Nefretiri to use in the picture. It was copied from an original in the Egyptian Museum at Cairo.[123]

Sometimes a folded piece of material can be observed in the hand of a sculptured or painted Egyptian. William Hayes believes that these may have been handkerchiefs, though the articles so held could have been fly-switches.[124] We have assumed that these folded pieces of material were handkerchiefs.

The problem of designing and making the many costumes for the picture *The Ten Commandments* was a serious one indeed. It taxed the responsibility of Cecil B. deMille and that of all those of his staff concerned with realizing into actuality what to a great extent only exists in the sculptures and murals of ancient Egypt and in the deductions and interpretations of a few modern scholars.

On a foregoing page we have stated that the ancient Egyptian luckily did not have to face this problem. He wore the clothes of his day, unaware that people would become interested in what they were made of and how they were worn some 3,000 years later.

Hebrew Materials and Costumes

a) Materials. The materials available to the Hebrews for clothing were no different from those in general use throughout the ancient Near East. In earliest times these were the skins of animals, but later, wool and

120. Erman and Ranke, pp. 237, 253.

121. Erman and Ranke, p. 234. Also Engelbach, p. 152.

122. Hayes, pp. 284-285; Fox, Pls. 14, 17, 23.

123. Fox, Pl. 51.

124. Hayes, p. 91, *et passim.*

linen became dominant. Leather was also known and the hair of goats and camels was spun into thread and woven into textiles.[125]

b) General observations. One cannot talk of an exclusive Hebrew costume in this general era of history. Certain elements of clothing are named in the Old Testament, such as "coat," "skirt," "mantle," "girdle" (i.e. a loincloth) or "shoes,"[126] but there is nothing that would indicate special clothing worn by Israelites only, to the exclusion of others. What the ancient Hebrews wore, or the Israelites of Moses' time, is only known in generalities that can be gleaned from the biblical text as indicated above. The commandment of Deuteronomy 22:12, "thou shalt make thee fringes upon the four quarters of thy vesture," cannot be considered too seriously as indicating an identifying mark in clothing of that time, for ancient Egyptian and Asiatic costumes also show fringes. The detailed description of priestly garments given in Exodus 28, etc., is an exception, but we can recognize that this is a special garment not worn by Israelites at large.

In existing records of ancient ages, the name Israel occurs for the first time on the stela of pharaoh Merneptah (1225 B.C.).[127] Before that time the name of this people or nation was apparently unknown to the Egyptians. We must assume that the Israelite tribes (which were to form a nation later) were listed by the Nile dwellers under the general category of Asiatics and, perhaps, Syrians or Sand-Dwellers, a term probably meaning Palestineans.[128] Such Semite people as the Asiatics or Syrians are represented in ancient Egyptian art and thus we can observe the colorful costumes they wore.

These costumes consist of a gaily patterned piece of material wrapped around the body to cover the loins—or else, it is a richly embroidered or pattern-woven dress.[129] Such dresses are very narrow and we can easily imagine that they would hinder the motions of the body, particularly those of the legs. The sug-

125. *Dictionary of the Bible,* ed. J. Hastings (New York, 1954), p. 196.

126. *Ibid.,* pp. 196-197. See also Gen. 37:3; Deut. 27:20; Judg. 4:18; II Kings 1:8; Ex. 3:5.

127. J. A. Wilson, *Burden of Egypt* (Chicago, 1951), p. 255.

128. Wilson, in *Ancient Near Eastern Texts* (Princeton, 1950), pp. 227, 228, 248.

129. N. M. Davies, I, Pls. 10, 11, 26, 42; II, Pls. 58, 60.

gestion lies at hand that these costumes represent the best finery fit for a royal reception. We read that such tight costumes were worn by Semitic city dwellers.[130]

In the picture *The Ten Commandments* we do not deal with Semitic city-dwellers. We represent the Hebrews who live in hard bondage in pharaonic Egypt—we represent them as nomads on the Exodus, crossing the Sinai Peninsula until, after years of wandering, they reach the river Jordan, the borders of the Promised Land.

It should not need stressing that such richly embroidered, formal attire as is depicted on the monuments is not for wear in the brickpits and is unsuitable for the strenuous life of a nomad in barren lands.

c) Men's costumes. The earliest garment was the apron,[131] loin- or waist-cloth,[132] which developed into the tunic, generally translated "coat" in the English Version of the Bible.[133] This coat or tunic was held together by a girdle (i.e. belt) made of cloth or leather.[134] Working clothes consisted of the apron or the tunic.[135]

A cloak was worn over the tunic and this item of costuming seems to be identical with the "aba" (cloak or mantle) worn by desert Arabs today. This cloak is described as consisting of woolen material sewn together in such a fashion that the front is left open and openings provided for the arms.[136]

We have described a striped material in discussing Egyptian costumes. The source used states this material to be "similar to the striped woolen mantles worn by Bedouins today."[137] It is reasonable to assume that similar striped textiles were worn by the "Sand-Dwellers" of antiquity and we have made use of them in the film. Moses, Aaron and other Hebrews wear such materials. The choice of colors for the dress was, at telling instances, derived from a tradition which ascribes specific colors to each of the twelve tribes. They are as follows:

130. *Dict. of the Bible,* p. 196.

131. *Jewish Encyclopedia,* IV (New York, 1907), 293.

132. *Dict. of the Bible,* p. 196.

133. *Ibid.*

134. *Jewish Encycl.,* IV, 293.

135. *Ibid.*

136. *a) Ibid.*
b) H. R. P. Dickson, *Arab of the Desert* (London, 1949), p. 93.
c) G. W. Murray, *Sons of Ishmael* (London, 1935), p. 71.

137. Riefstahl, pp. 7, 8.

Reuben . . . . Red
Simeon . . . . Green
Levi . . . . White, black and red
Judah . . . . Sky-blue
Issachar . . . . Black
Zebulun . . . . White
Dan . . . . Blue
Gad . . . . Gray
Naphtali . . . . Wine-colored
Asher . . . . Pearl-colored
Joseph . . . . Black
Benjamin . . . . All colors combined[138]

Special emphasis is made in the picture regarding Moses' robe (cloak) made of "Levite cloth."

d) Head coverings. The Old Testament has very little to say about head coverings. There is the instance of ropes being put upon the head[139] and helmets are spoken of in I Samuel 17:5, for example. In the detailed description of the priests' clothing a specific ordinance prescribes a miter for Aaron the high priest, and bonnets for his sons,[140] but these are not for the people at large. Compared to the customs of the period in which the picture *The Ten Commandments* unrolls itself (thirteenth century B.C.), that of men covering their heads is of a relatively late date. Indeed, our source states that "bareheadedness was customary among men in Biblical times."[141] There are some outstanding illustrations in this regard in the case of Samson[142] and Absalom.[143]

The paintings in Egyptian tombs present Semites without any head covering and portrayals of Syrians clearly show a headband only, i.e. a fillet, tied around the hair and forehead.[144] It has been assumed by some that the Israelites sooner or later adapted the headcloth held in place by a rope or band that is still in use among Arabs of today.[145] Ancient Egyptian art further suggests a tight-fitting skull cap, perhaps made of fabric or leather, worn by commoners.[146] This skull

138. *a) Jewish Encycl.,* V (New York, 1907), 405.
b) Midrash Rabbah, V, trans. J. J. Slotki (London, 1939), 29–30.

139. I Kings 20:32.

140. Ex. 28:4, 37, 40.

141. *Jewish Encycl.,* II (New York, 1903), 531.

142. Judg. 13–16.

143. II Sam. 14:25, 26; 18:9.

144. N. M. Davies, I, Pls. 11, 21, 42. II, Pls. 58, 60.

145. *Jewish Encycl.,* IV, 294.

146. N. M. Davies, I, Pl. 49; II, Pls. 67, 71.

cap, too, is in wide usage throughout the Near East at the present time. At times certain actors in the picture wear headcloths or skull caps. It may be surprising to some that we show Moses bareheaded, once he has reached the stature of prophet and lawgiver. We have already indicated the justification for this in the preceding paragraph.

Another reason may again come as a surprise to some readers: The custom of Jewish men to keep the head covered is not described in the Old Testament. The general custom of wearing a head covering in everyday life had its start perhaps as late as the early centuries of the current era. We do not know of what date the Midrash is which forbade the reciting of certain prayers and reading aloud from the Torah without the head being covered. In the thirteenth century A.D., it was observed that the Jews of Spain covered their heads during prayer, while those of France did not follow that custom. Jewish regulations of the Middle Ages generally, but not exclusively, prescribe that the head should be covered. However, an observation made in the sixteenth century A.D. clearly states this to be a custom, not a law. It was not until the seventeenth century A.D. that what had been a custom became religious law to the followers of the Jewish faith.[147] It is of interest that among the adherents of the modern reform movement of Judaism, the head is not covered during religious services.

147. *Jewish Encycl.*, II, 531-532.

In early Old Testament times the wearing of veils among women (as head covering and not to be understood as a covering for the face) was not universal.[148] In some instances it must have been a large piece of cloth which not only covered the head, but enveloped the body as well.[149] It is outside the Old Testament text that regulations appear which demand that a woman should not be seen in the street with her head uncovered.[150]

148. *Ibid.*, p. 530.

149. *Dict. of the Bible*, p. 198. Cf. Gen. 24:65.

150 *Jewish Encycl.*, II, 530.

e) Women's costumes. The costume of women barely differed from that of men. They wore the tunic as well as the coat or cloak (see: veil, above). It is believed, however, that the dresses of women, though of the same basic design as those of men, were longer and wider.[151]

The Semitic women depicted on Egyptian tomb walls wear a many-colored patterned dress of simple cut, leaving the right shoulder bare.[152]

To those who like curios, it may be of interest to know that Thomas De Quincey (1785-1859) wrote an essay, "Toilette of the Hebrew Lady," in which he describes the costumes of Hebrew women.

f) Footwear. Though a "shoe-latchet" is mentioned as early as Genesis 14:23, and shoes in the revelation of the Burning Bush,[153] the wearing of them probably was not very general. We have to refer again to the actual documentation of contemporary Egyptian monuments to observe that one group of Semitic women and a boy are all attired with ankle-high boots. Elsewhere, a man is shown shod with sandals.[154]

Hair Styles

a) Hair styles in Egypt. When one looks upon the statues, reliefs and paintings depicting the great and the small of ancient Egypt one becomes aware of a great many hair fashions.

Among men, in some cases, such fashions look uncomfortably pompous by the sheer mass of hair they contain.[155] Others appear to the modern eye like "page cuts" or "bobs."[156] We can also observe short haircuts and bald heads; both are frequently implied by the tightfitting skull caps men were wont to wear and the latter may have been brought about by natural causes or else the heads were shaved.[157]

During the Old Kingdom men sometimes wore dapper moustaches and natural beards.[158] But these external signs of masculinity soon disappeared and instead—first only by the pharaoh and then by others as well—an artificial beard was worn. This custom was no longer predominant in the period of the film. We

151. *Jewish Encycl.*, IV, 293.

152. N. M. Davies, I, Pl. 10.

153. Ex. 3:5.
154. N. M. Davies, I, Pls. 10, 11.

155. *Encycl. Phot. Musée du Caire,* Pls. 82, 142, 145, 146. See also *Encycl. Phot. de l'Art,* I, 66, 67, 103A.

156. *Encycl. Phot. Musée du Caire,* Pls. 30, 41. Also *Encycl. Phot. de l'Art,* I, 36, 108; N. M. Davies, I, Pls. 7, 34, 44, 48.

157. a) *Encycl. Phot. Musée du Caire,* Pls. 12, 43.
b) *Encycl. Phot. de l'Art,* I, 12, 18, 21, 29, 37, 81.
c) A. Mekhitarian, *Egyptian Painting* (Geneva, 1954), p. 125.
d) Erman and Ranke, pp. 247, 262.
e) N. M. Davies, I, Pls. 7, 8, 49; II, Pl. 54.

158. Erman and Ranke, pp. 247, 252. See also *Encl. Phot. Musée du Caire,* Pls. 5, 6, 12; Engelbach, p. 151.

dispensed with it altogether, for even at its best it was a clumsy affair held onto the chin by means of bands attached to the headdress.[159]

A rather startling full-length portrait of Rameses II shows this pharaoh unshaven, even though he is attired in full regalia. The stubble on his face looks no different from that of some commoner who could never make any aspiration to regal grandeur.[160]

While there is no doubt that priests shaved their heads,[161] there is no unanimity of opinion as to whether the pharaoh and other men did the same, or merely cropped their hair close to the head.[162] It is an "either —or" proposition. We show Pharaoh as well as prince Rameses with shaved heads on the screen, reasoning that since both of them were priests by tradition, they followed this priestly custom. Moses, as prince of Egypt and commander of Pharaoh's host, wears his hair cut short.

Young boys had their heads shaved except for a strand of hair.[163] We assume that this sign of youth was no longer adhered to when manhood was reached. It remained, however, as a telling identification for the sons of the pharaoh, who continued to wear this lock of youth even as grown men. In the picture, Moses and Rameses—and later also the son of Rameses and Nefretiri—are shown with this lock while they are princes of Egypt. This princely lock changed in appearance from time to time. Sometimes it looks braided or it is a strand of hair held together by some jeweled band of gold; and yet another style shows a blue material enveloping or simulating the lock.[164]

Professional barbers plied their trade in open-air shops, as it is done in villages of the Near East to this day.[165]

For women the choice of coiffures was equally great. They wore their hair short or long, in plaits and curls, plain or artfully waved. Sometimes the long combed hair fell in massive strands down the back and below the right and left shoulders in front. Hair ornamentations were frequently used, such as a decorated band,

159. Erman and Ranke, p. 252. Also N. M. Davies, I, Pl. 12.

160. N. M. Davies, II, Pl. 100. Also Erman and Ranke, p. 262 (Pl. 102).

161. Erman and Ranke, p. 246. Also Encycl. Phot. Musée du Caire, p. 148.

162. Erman and Ranke, p. 246; Engelbach, p. 151.

163. Erman and Ranke, p. 89.

164. a) Ibid.
b) N. M. Davies, II, Pl. 103.
c) Epigraphic Survey, IV, 198.

165. Erman and Ranke, p. 246, Pls. 20, 21.

166. N. M. Davies,
I, Pls. 26,
35, 36, 37,
52; II, Pls.
54, 61, 70,
72, 87, 89,
91, 92. See
also *Encycl.
Phot. Musée
du Caire*,
Pls. 12, 32,
51, 58, 59,
82, 88; Er-
man and
Ranke, pp.
249-251.

167. *a*) H. E.
Winlock,
*Treasure of
El Lahun*
(New York,
1934), Pls.
2, 3.
b) Winlock,
*Treasure of
Three Egyp-
tian
Princesses*
(New York,
1948), Pl. 3.
c) Schaefer
and Andrae,
p. 307.

168. Erman and
Ranke, pp.
246-250.
Also Engel-
bach, p. 151;
Lucas, pp.
41-42.

169. Lucas, pp.
42-43.

170. *Ibid.*, p. 383.

or a lotus blossom was set into it.[166] Ladies of rank, particularly those of royalty, used attractive gold decorations to enhance their beauty—for example, in the form of small tubes through which strands of hair were pulled or of gold wire delicately shaped into a circlet, placed upon the head with gold rosettes set into the hair. Another head ornament, which barely permitted the hair to show, was composed of gold bands linked solidly together and decorated with a prolific rosette design.[167]

These elaborate styles for men and women, in the main, were accomplished with the help of "switches" or complete wigs.[168] A number of these have been found. Those exhibited in the Cairo Museum have been microscopically examined and carefully analyzed by Lucas. According to his reliable report the opinion that wigs were, at times, made of wool or horsehair has to be discarded. They were always made of human hair, though sometimes a filler was inserted consisting of reddish-brown fibres of the date palm. When first examined such human hair appeared to be black. Upon cleaning, the natural colors were found to vary from light brown to brown to dark brown. The darkening of the color undoubtedly had come about by an accumulation of foreign matter over the millenia—and beeswax. Beeswax was applied to keep the hair in order, to set it in manifold patterns.[169] On mural paintings the ancient Egyptians generally depicted the hair of their own people in black.

With all these customs of wearing elaborate wigs, cropping the hair short or shaving it, it is amusing to find that the ancient Egyptians had vanities similar to modern men and women. Prescriptions to promote the growth of hair have been deciphered. One ointment was composed of the fats of the gazelle, serpent, crocodile and hippopotamus. The other prescribed a combination of the fats of the lion, hippopotamus, crocodile, cat, serpent and goat.[170] To prevent hair from turning gray or white, it was suggested that the blood of a black calf or that of a bull's horn be cooked in oil and applied.[171] We cannot vouch for positive results.

b) Hair styles among Hebrews. When we deal with some physical characteristics of the Israelites in certain Bible periods, such as the era of Moses, we are confronted with a lack of specific and detailed description, the existence of which would be most desirable for the making of a motion picture such as *The Ten Commandments.* The same paucity of data exists on the subject of hair as it does with Hebrew costumes.

The Bible does have some hints describing the color of hair as black,[172] red[173] or ruddy,[174] if the general appearance of Esau and David can be applied to hair in the last two references.

Some specific instructions, though of a date later than the Exodus, tell how hair is to be worn. An ordinance prescribes that the corners of the head not be rounded nor the corners of the beard marred;[175] that the head not be shaved, but the hair polled and no long locks worn.[176] The priests are commanded not to shave their heads as a sign of mourning,[177] which does imply that the lay people followed a custom of shaving their heads.

Hair was considered sacred among some ancient people and thought of as the seat of life.[178] This concept may well apply to the story of Samson, whose strength left him when Delilah caused a man "to shave off the seven locks of his head."[179] The Nazarites, of whom Samson was one, when putting themselves under the obligation of a vow, were forbidden to have a razor "come upon [their heads]."[180] When their vow was fulfilled the hair was shaved off and placed into the "fire which is under the sacrifice of the peace offerings."[181]

While we cannot pinpoint a specific Israelite hairdress for the general era of the picture, we can again rely to some extent on the monuments of antiquity, which show us Semitic men and women.

These Semitic men wear the hair of their heads

171. Erman and Ranke, p. 261.

172. Cant. 5:11.
173. Gen. 25:25.
174. I Sam. 16:12.

175. Lev. 19:27.

176. Ezek. 44:20.
177. Lev. 21:5.

178. *Encyclopaedia of Religion and Ethics,* ed. J. Hastings, VI (New York, 1922), 474.
179. Judg. 16:19.

180. Num. 6:5.

181. Num. 6:18.

usually, but not always, in a length that leaves the neck free. They are always bearded. The beard thinly outlines the upper part of the jawbone and becomes fuller as it proceeds towards the chin, where it ends in a point. In the particular document we refer to, each man is without a moustache.[182] The period is the late twentieth century B.C., or roughly the era of Abraham. Semitic war prisoners of the fourteenth century B.C. present slightly longer hair, a fuller beard, and moustaches. A few centuries later the curled and highly ornate beard of Assyrians does not appear in this fashion on their Jewish war prisoners.[183]

The pictures of Semitic women studied by us show the hair to be very full and falling below their shoulders. The likeness to certain Egyptian hair styles is literal.[184]

While searching for information on Hebrew hair fashions for the picture *The Ten Commandments* we discovered some information not related to the Bible. We found the description of a custom adopted by married Jewish women which was of non-Jewish origin. The clipping of hair that certain orthodox Jewish women performed upon marriage derived from Slavonic customs. This was taken over by the Jews of Poland in the sixteenth century A.D., from where it spread to other countries. The cropped head was covered by a cap, and later a wig was worn over the owner's hair.[185]

Perfume, Incense and Cosmetics

Make-up played an important part in the lives of the ancient Egyptians. Cosmetics for the eyes, lips and cheeks, oils and ointments for the hair and body were extensively used.

Related to these are many artifacts made for their use. Among them are artfully carved containers to hold perfumes and decorated mirrors made of polished metal. The desire to be and feel clean caused men to shave with straight-edged razors.

The most widely used eye-paints were malachite (a

182. *Jewish People: Past and Present*, I (New York, 1946), Plate facing p. 36.

183. *Ibid.*, pp. 12-15.

184. *Ibid.*, Plate facing p. 36.

185. *Jewish Encycl.*, II, 531.

green ore of copper) and an ore of lead called galena. Both of them are referred to as "kohl."[186] The green color derived from malachite was applied to the lower eyelids, while the black of galena was painted upon eyebrows and upper eyelids from where it was drawn out in an elongated line to give Egyptian eyes such a startling appearance.[187]

Egyptian women liked to color their cheeks. The ingredient applied seems to have been powdered red ochre.[188] There is an ancient sketch showing a woman putting rouge upon her lips with a special applicator[189] that looks not unlike a modern orange stick.

Whether rich or poor, Egyptians loved to have their bodies rubbed with oil. Such treatment not only brought forth a feeling of well-being but, considering the climatic conditions in which these people lived, it was a necessity as well.[190]

Since the process of distillation was still unknown at that time, a variety of perfumes was obtained by soaking flowers and other fragrant substances in oil and fat. Such oils and ointments were also imported, but in ancient Greece Egyptian perfumes were considered the best. Aside from fats and oils some of the ingredients to make perfume were cinnamon, myrrh, cardamon, sweet rush, bitter almonds, root of iris, honey, wine, resin, cassia, balsamum and fruit extracts.[191]

Incense was burned for personal as well as ritual use. It may interest the reader to compare the words *incense* and *perfume*. They have a close identity in their original meaning and usage. The former is derived from the Latin *incendere,* i.e. "to burn," and the latter from *per fumum,* which means "through smoke."[192]

There are two formulas in the Book of Exodus prescribing the ingredients and amounts for the admixture of an "oil of holy ointment"[193] and "a perfume . . . pure and holy."[194] To make the ointment, the following measures are given: ". . . of pure myrrh five hundred shekels, and of sweet cinnamon half so much . . .

186. Lucas, pp. 99-104.

187. Erman and Ranke, p. 257.

188. Lucas, p. 104.

189. Erman and Ranke, p. 258.

190. *Ibid.,* p. 259.

191. Lucas, pp. 105-110.

192. *Ibid.,* p. 110.

193. Ex. 30:25.

194. Ex. 30:35.

195. Ex. 30:23-
24.

196. *Dict. of the
Bible*, pp.
970-971.

197. Ex. 30:35.

198. Ex. 30:34.

199. Ex. 30:32,
38.

200. Ps. 45:8;
Prov. 7:17;
Cant. 1:12-
14; 3:6;
4:10.

201. *Dict. of the
Bible*, p.
700.

and of sweet calamus two hundred and fifty shekels, And of cassia five hundred shekels . . . and of olive oil an hin. . . ."[195] The measure of the Temple shekel was 224.2 grains Troy, while the sacred hin amounted to eight or nine pints.[196]

To compound the perfume, "a confection after the art of the apothecary,"[197] "Take unto thee sweet spices, stacte and onycha, and galbanum . . . with pure frankincense: of each shall there be a like weight."[198] But a severe ordinance was issued in conjunction with these prescriptions: "Upon man's flesh shall it not be poured, neither shall ye make any other like it. . . . Whosoever shall make like unto that . . . shall even be cut off from his people."[199] The implication of these verses is that ointments and perfumes were cherished by the ancient Israelites, of which there is evidence elsewhere in the Bible.[200] Some Bible scholars interpret the passage in Nehemiah 3:8, "Hananiah the son of one of the apothecaries," to suggest the existence of a guild of perfumers.[201]

Egyptian Jewelry

a) General observations. The Museum at Cairo and the Metropolitan Museum in New York, to mention but these two, exhibit magnificent examples of the ancient Egyptian jeweler's art. Much can be seen there to inspire a modern craftsman.

When we speak of jewelry here, we refer to it in a broad sense, combining jewelry as ornamentation with amulets which had magical values.

So far it has been impossible to determine with certainty what primary concept ancient man gave to jewelry. Were bones or stones—or whatever material— a delight to man as an accessory for adornment? Or did he confer into them a religious symbolism? Did they contain the power of magic to prevent evil? Whether they be jewelry or magic, both were and are extensively employed throughout the world.

In everyday English of today the words *amulet, charm* and *talisman* are interchangeable, but we should define their meaning for clarification. The word *amulet,* according to J. T. Shipley, derives from the Latin *amolire letum,* i.e. "to turn away death."[202] The amulet is an object worn on or carried by the person as a preventative, to protect from something that is feared.[203]

Originally a charm was an incantation, a formula chanted to bring about a desired effect. Amulets were "charmed" in this fashion at times. They were also issued in written form.[204]

A talisman's magic function is to ensure good luck or to bring about beneficial qualities.[205]

The modern fad for charm bracelets is as new as ancient Egypt. H. E. Winlock in describing an unearthed treasure pertaining to three princesses states that "each of the three ladies had some eight strings with one or more amulets" which were worn around the neck or arm.[206]

b) Materials. The raw materials for making jewelry in ancient Egypt were of a wide variety. Among them we find animal products such as bones, teeth, shells and even ostrich egg-shell. The vegetable world provided resins, seeds, straw and wood. Pebbles, faience, glass, gold, silver, electrum, copper and precious and semiprecious stones derived from the realm of minerals.[207] A small number of beads made of meteoric iron and pertaining to the predynastic age of Egypt have been found.[208]

Among the precious and semiprecious stones there were those known in the general era which the picture *The Ten Commandments* portrays. Others did not make their appearance till a later date, or were never known in the Egypt of antiquity. We shall list them in the order indicated. The stones employed were the agate, onyx, amethyst, alabaster, carnelian, sard, chalcedony, chrysoprase, green felspar (Amazon stone), garnet, jasper, lapis lazuli, malachite, peridot (olivine), quartz (rock crystal) and turquoise.[209]

Sardonyx is one of the stones not known in the

202. *Dictionary of Word Origins* (Ames, Iowa, 1955), p. 21.

203. *Encycl. of Rel. and Ethics,* III, 392-393.

204. *Ibid.,* p. 393.

205. *Ibid.*

206. Winlock, *Three Princesses,* p. 25.

207. Lucas, pp. 52-53, 442.

208. *Ibid.,* p. 270.

209. *Ibid.,* pp. 442-461.

broader period of the picture. Jadeite may have been worked into gems, but not true jade. Pearls did not make their appearance until about the third century A.D., but mother-of-pearl was known. Only the green beryl was used in the Egypt of old, while the blue aquamârine or the yellow and white beryl remained unknown. Similarly, the finest quality of beryl, the emerald, has not been found among the many precious discoveries.[210]

The gems that were never used in the long history of ancient Egypt were the diamond, opal, ruby and sapphire.[211]

In this context we must mention that the art of glazing was practiced.[212] To cement inlays into their setting resin alone was used, or else it was mixed with powdered limestone. Such cements were frequently colored to enhance the stone to be set.[213] Silver, perhaps, was used as a solder in combining the various metallic elements to make jewelry.[214]

c) Jewelry. The single components that made the finished product were manifold. Of these no other has been employed so predominantly as the bead. It was shaped into the most diversified forms, somewhat depending on the raw material used for this purpose. In the most ancient times the bead was worn as found in its natural state—such as a pebble. The shapes produced by Egypt's craftsmen were extremely diversified. The ancient tombs have disclosed to us spheres, tubes, rings, discs, drop- and barrel-shaped beads, rhomboids, squares, spirals, and some beads in the form of acacia seeds. Their sizes, too, vary greatly. There are some gold beads, for example, that are 0.078 inches in diameter, with walls less than 0.039 inches thick.[215]

Beads were strung on hair,[216] leather, linen thread[217] and gold wire.[218] They were linked to jewelry by other means as well. In the film there is a scene where Bithiah, Moses' foster mother, is stringing some beads on wire. The frame on which the stringing takes place

210. *Ibid.*

211. Lucas, p. 442.

212. *Ibid.*, pp. 178 ff.

213. *Ibid.*, p. 13.

214. *Ibid.*, p. 248.

215. *Ibid.*, pp. 55-58. See also Winlock, *Three Princesses,* p. 48, and *El Lahun,* pp. 30, 37, 43, 44; Hayes, pp. 229-233.

216. Lucas, p. 43.

217. Hayes, p. 229.

218. Winlock, *Three Princesses,* p. 42.

is our invention, though it contains ancient Egyptian
elements of design.

The many precious and semiprecious stones were
cut to size for inlay work and set into a frame of gold,
called a "cloison."[219] Such cloisons were often soldered
to a base of precious metal. Sometimes the reverse of
the base showed a replica of the obverse in beautifully
executed engraving.[220]

During the New Kingdom the employment of glass
became more pronounced, for it was easier to cut to
the needed size than the hard stones and could imi-
tate the actual gem quite successfully.[221]

Other methods were applied to obtain the diversified shapes used as components in the making of
jewelry. These were, among others, modeling, beating
of gold against a die,[222] moulding,[223] embossing and
engraving,[224] and carving.[225]

In some instances nature suggested the many designs. They also represented symbols such as hieroglyphs which expressed meanings like "eternity," "joy,"
"protection and life."[226] In other examples an engraved
or inlaid text contained a good wish, or the name of
the wearer or donor.[227]

All these elements were used to make bracelets,
armlets, anklets, necklaces, pectorals, broad collars,
rings, earrings (which were unknown in Egypt before
the New Kingdom)[228] and ornaments for the hair and
head. All of these were made and are shown to great
advantage on the screen. Some of them represent exact
replicas of the originals found by archaeologists among
the treasures in the tombs of Egypt. Among them are
two pectorals found in the tomb of Tutankhamon now
on exhibit at the Cairo Museum. One represents the
traditional vulture symbol of the goddess of Upper
Egypt, Nekhbet;[229] the other delineates the "Birth of
the Rising Sun," in which the scarab motif predomi-
nates.[230] In the description of another pectoral we read
that "three hundred and seventy-two fashioned bits
of hard stone were cemented into place," i.e. into gold
cloisons; yet, the over-all size of the design is only 3.198

219. Engelbach, p. 154.

220. Winlock, *El Lahun*, p. 31. See also Fox, Pl. 36.

221. Engelbach, p. 155.

222. Winlock, *Three Princesses*, pp. 17, 23.

223. Engelbach, p. 155.

224. Hayes, pp. 230, 233.

225. Fox, Pl. 48.

226. Winlock, *El Lahun*, p. 52.

227. Engelbach, p. 253. Also Hayes, p. 235.

228. Erman and Ranke, p. 254.

229. Fox, Pl. 36.

230. *Ibid.*, Pl. 47.

231. Winlock, *El Lahun*, p. 31.

232. *Ibid.*, pp. 32-33.

233. Fox, Pls. 36, 47. Also Hayes, p. 231.

234. Erman and Ranke, p. 254.

235. Fox, Pl. 36.

236. Winlock, *El Lahun*, pp. 44, 47; *Three Princesses*, Pls. 10, 11, 15, 18.

237. Winlock, *Three Princesses*, Pl. 11.

238. *Ibid.*, p. 28.

by 1.755 inches. Each stone was accurately fitted to enhance the perfection of the finished design.[231]

Pectorals are pendants hanging from a necklace and reaching just about to the breastbone. Perhaps they developed from the plain amulet worn by ancient man, suspended from the neck, into this typical ancient Egyptian jewel of symbolic design.[232]

Frequently the clasp that held the necklace around the neck was of an elaborate design also.[233] Since the pectoral was heavy, this clasp acted as a counterweight in back.[234] Such clasps locked by means of a tongue fitting into a slot.[235] Other methods of fastening jewelry to the body were as simple as a cord to be tied or a pin inserted through catches fixed at each end of the loose wristlet, and as complex as a separate decorated panel which slid into the grooved ends of a bracelet. Tongue and groove again were used to fasten anklets.[236]

Another replica made for the picture was copied from an original on view in the Metropolitan Museum in New York. It is a necklace composed of a delicate and attractive network of beads of various kinds and inlaid drop designs.[237]

The broad collars worn by the actors are all derived from the antiquities of Egypt. We would like to point out one, worn by Sethi I in the picture, in which a particular symbol is applied. This symbol is popularly called the "Eyes of Horus," whose amuletic value was that of protection for both the living and the dead.[238]

One of the symbols that appears frequently on Egyptian jewelry and particularly on rings is the scarab. The tourist who travels in modern Egypt is always tempted to buy such a scarab as a memento; it usually turns out to be an imitation. The scarab symbol was derived from an insect called the sacred beetle. It was one of the symbols of the sun-god and named "khepri." On objects other than seal rings it is frequently shown rolling the sun-disk with its legs—a direct copy from nature, where the actual insect rolls the ball containing the unhatched eggs with its legs.

The verb of *khepri* is *khoper,* which means "to come into existence." Just as the sun came into existence by itself, so the beetles appeared to the ancient Egyptians to come into existence by themselves out of the ball pushed by the parent beetle.[239] Such scarabs frequently contained the name of a pharaoh or a person of lesser rank engraved on the underside. They were a popular form of gift. In other instances such scarabs carry the record of an event or a wish for good luck.[240]

The insignia of the pharaoh also are jewelry. They, as well as some hair ornaments, have been described under the titles "Costumes" and "Hair Styles," respectively.

The impression created by ancient Egyptian jewelry is expressed perfectly by H. E. Winlock: "All is inspired by a very vital love of beauty and a very living vanity."[241]

Hebrew Jewelry

a) General remarks. It is but natural that the early Hebrews and Israelites were no different from the people among whom they lived in wearing amulets and charms.[242] We learn that the jewelry known to them was that generally worn by the people of the nations surrounding them, such as Egypt.[243]

In actuality the problem of Hebrew jewelry did not arise in the making of the picture *The Ten Commandments.* The obvious assumption is that an enslaved people working in hard bondage could not possess this kind of wealth. The jewelry given the Israelites upon their departure from Egypt was, as stated in the Bible, Egyptian.[244]

b) The breastplate of the high priest. On a previous page we have described the pectoral as a breast ornament. In this sense there is an affinity between the Egyptian breast ornament and the breastplate of Israel's high priest. This breastplate was not needed in the film. Nevertheless, the jewels set into it present an interesting problem. As translated in the Authorized

239. J. Cerny, *Ancient Egyptian Religion* (London, 1952), p. 50. See also Engelbach, pp. 252-254.

240. Engelbach, p. 253.

241. Winlock, *El Lahun,* p. 24.

242. *Jewish Encycl.,* I (New York, 1906), 546.

243. *Jewish Encycl.,* V, 593.

244. Ex. 12:35.

Version of the Bible, they are sardius, topaz, carbuncle, emerald, sapphire, diamond, ligure, agate, amethyst, beryl, onyx and jasper.[245] We have indicated earlier that some of these stones were unknown in ancient Egypt. Gems did not naturally occur in Canaan but were imported, for example, by Solomon.[246]

The names given these stones in the biblical text evidently imply a knowledge of a later date than that of the event. It is extremely difficult to establish with certainty what these stones were in actuality.[247] If we may again make reference to the biblical statement that the Israelites brought Egyptian jewelry with them into the Exodus then it stands to reason that the jewelry given by them to Moses for the making of the breastplate and other precious religious paraphernalia[248] was indeed that same Egyptian jewelry. We can, therefore, attempt to reconstruct the gems of the breastplate, first, with the available knowledge of ancient Egyptian stones; second, by taking into consideration the traditional colors of each of the twelve tribes as they are mentioned in connection with the stones as symbols of each tribe.[249] These traditional colors influenced the making of robes for the elders of Israel in *The Ten Commandments,* as discussed in the section on "Hebrew Costume."

For Reuben the stone is sardius and the color red. This checks perfectly with a form of carnelian called sard.[250]

Simeon's gem is the topaz and the color green. The characteristic color of topaz is yellow. It was not known in ancient Egypt and stones so named by classic writers are described by them as having been found on St. John's Island in the Red Sea. The stone found on this island is the peridot, which is of a green color.[251]

The stone for Levi, called carbuncle, is of a red color and, therefore, could not have been an emerald as is suggested on the margin of the Revised Version. The emerald is green and was not known in ancient Egypt. Nor does its color conform with any of the

245. Ex. 28:17-20.

246. a) I Kings 10:11.
b) Jewish Encycl., V, 593.

247. Jewish Encycl., V, 593.

248. Cf. Ex. 35.

249. Jewish Encycl., V, 4, 5.

250. Lucas, p. 448.

251. Ibid., p. 458-459.

three traditional colors of the Levites, which were white, black and red. However, it does agree with the garnet, which, as employed in ancient Egypt, was of a dark red or reddish brown color.[252]

Judah has the emerald and sky-blue color. Again, this stone did not exist in ancient Egypt. To match the blue color ascribed to Judah we have the choice of chalcedony, which often has a bluish tint, or turquoise, which was mined extensively on the Sinai Peninsula.[253]

Sapphire and black are the stone and color of Issachar. Sapphires remained unknown throughout Egypt's ancient history. The tribal color, black, may give us the clue to the stone used in actuality. Haematite, as used for beads and amulets in ancient Egypt, is of a black color with a metallic lustre.[254] It is also suggested that this so-called sapphire may have been lapis lazuli.[255] It is of a dark blue color.[256] Could it have been meteoric iron?

To Zebulun are given the diamond and, for color, white. The diamond was unknown to the jewelers of the ancient Nile Valley. The color white suggests that rock crystal was used.[257]

Dan's stone is the ligure and the color is blue. The Revised Version uses "jacinth" (margin — "amber"), which was a gem of blue color among the ancients.[258] It is a vague term and the margin translation "amber" suggests a yellowish color. According to Lucas, the blue beryl, called aquamarine, was, as far as is known now, not used in ancient Egypt.[259] If it were not for that it would fit the description. Perhaps a rock crystal was used and set in a known Egyptian technique on a base of cement colored blue.

Gad has prescribed for its tribe the agate and gray as color. Agates existed and they do at times have a basic milk-gray color.

The stone of Naphtali, the amethyst, and the color of wine are in agreement with the facts concerning this matter.

Asher has the beryl and the color of pearl. Lucas doubts the employment of beryl in Egypt at the time

252. *Ibid.*, p. 451.

253. *Ibid.*, pp. 448, 460.

254. *Ibid.*, p. 452.

255. *Jewish Encycl.*, V, 594.

256. Lucas, p. 455.

257. *Ibid.*, p. 459.

258. *Shorter Oxford English Dictionary*, ed. C. T. Onions (Oxford, 1933), I, 1055.

259. Lucas, p. 445.

260. *Ibid.*

261. Lucas, p. 458.

262. *Ibid.*, p. 443.

263. *Encycl. Britannica* (14th ed.), XII, 970.

264. *a) Jewish Encycl.*, V, 593-595.
b) *Dict. of the Bible*, pp. 465-8.
c) J. Moffatt, *The Bible: A New Translation* (New York, 1935), pp. 92-93 (Ex. 28:17-20).

of Moses.[260] The suggestion lies at hand that it may have been mother-of-pearl.[261]

The stone for the Joseph tribes is given as the onyx and the color jet black. The onyx is a stone whose color is milk white, alternating with black.[262] The stone fits the needs to some extent.

Benjamin has the jasper ascribed to this tribe, as well as all the previously mentioned colors combined. We have no reason to doubt its employment for the high priest's breastplate, since banded jasper with many colored stripes exists.[263]

We observe that the stones of the breastplate that were known in ancient Egypt also agree with the traditional colors of the tribes of Israel, except the diamond. The others were neither known in that period nor do the tribal colors conform with the physical appearance of these gems, as listed in the Bible.

Other opinions exist as to what these stones may have been.[264] We must repeat that this attempt at a clarification is based on a different probability. It has taken what is known of ancient Egyptian stones and the traditional Hebrew tribal colors into consideration to arrive at a solution.

FOOD AND
ENTERTAINMENT

THE cultural advance of a people can also be measured by its tastes in food and entertainment. The ancient Egyptians have established as impressive a mark in these as they did with their beautiful jewelry or the elegance of their furniture.

Food

As elsewhere in the ancient world the Egyptian considered it perfectly good manners to eat with his hands. Though our Western etiquette demands that we eat certain foods with a fork we must keep in mind that this custom is relatively modern. In France, for example, "as late as the 16th century the court use of forks to eat with was satirized as a novelty."[1]

At a dinner the Egyptian would adorn himself and his guests with flowers. Their heads would be anointed with a cone of perfume.[2] Servants placed food before the diners on platters resting upon "bases and standards."[3] Before and after the meal attendants poured water over the hands of the eaters,[4] a custom still performed in the Near East.

The varieties of food were tremendous, judged by tomb records listing the requirements of the deceased. One of these enumerates ten different meats, five kinds of fowl, sixteen sorts of bread and cake, six varieties of

1. *New International Encyclopaedia* (New York, 1927), IX, 25.

2. W. M. F. Petrie, *Social Life in Ancient Egypt* (London, 1923), p. 106.

3. J. H. Breasted, *History of Egypt* (New York, 1921), p. 88.

4. A. Erman and H. Ranke, *Aegypten* (Tübingen, 1923), p. 221.

wine, four brands of beer, an assortment of fruit and

5. *Ibid.*, p. 219.
a selection of sweets.[5] (Honey was used as the sweet-
6. *Ibid.*,
p. 229.
ening agent in place of the yet unknown sugar.)[6]

When the pharaoh traveled through the land, villages were notified in advance by letter ordering them
to make preparations for the visit of the court. Such
an order requested 15,000 loaves of fine bread of five
different sorts, and of other bread 14,200 pieces; of
assorted cakes 200 pieces; 100 baskets of dried meat;
60 containers of milk and 90 of cream; and baskets of
figs, raisins and other fruit were to be made available.
For the decoration of the royal table 100 flower and

7. *Ibid.*, p. 123.
wreath arrangements were required.[7]

It has become evident to the reader that the Egyptian baker produced a great many kinds of bread. He
baked a great many shapes as well. We find large
oval, triangular, conical and fancy-shaped loaves of

8. W. C. Hayes,
*Scepter of
Egypt*, Part I
(New York,
1953), pp.
97, 156, 264,
305.
bread.[8]

Among the many choices of meat and fowl, goose
seems to have been one of the preferred dishes in ancient Egypt. It was roasted over an open fire suspended from a spit, as were meats and the fish taken
from the Nile or the well-stocked garden ponds. Sometimes meats were also boiled in big pots. When
served, these foods were often decorated with lotus
blooms and the jugs containing beer or wine were

9. Erman and
Ranke, p.
222.
ornamented with flowers.[9] Liquids were sucked from
their containers with the help of reeds, similar to

10. Petrie, p.
102.
straws in use today.[10]

The fare of the average Egyptian was somewhat
simpler. Bread was the staple food. On a military expe-
dition the soldiers were supplied with provisions of
water and twenty loaves of bread per man for a four-

11. J. A. Wilson,
*Burden of
Egypt* (Chi-
cago, 1951),
p. 127.
to five-day period.[11] In one instance the daily ration
of a peasant is described as consisting of four loaves
of bread and two pitchers of beer.[12]

12. Erman and
Ranke, p.
219.
Perhaps the Hebrews' food requirements were as
simple as that. It is very likely that they ate unleavened bread for their daily fare, as do the Bedouins of
the Sinai Peninsula to this day. As a matter of fact, the

bread baked each morning at the monastery of St. Catherine at the foot of Mt. Sinai for free distribution to these Bedouins is unleavened. Such bread is made either of wheat or barley meal or a mixture of the two. Nowadays they also use corn (maize), but that is a later addition to the cereals of the Near East. The dough is made by mixing the flour with water, adding a little salt, and kneading it thoroughly. Depending on the particular custom of each tribe, the dough is made in differing consistencies. If it is a heavy dough it is patted by hand into flat cakes, or, if it is light, it is poured onto the heating surface[13] like our hot cakes. It is this latter method that we use at the Passover meal in the picture *The Ten Commandments*.

13. G. W. Murray, *Sons of Ishmael* (London, 1935), p. 85.

While on the subject of food, something should be said about pork, since neither observing Jew nor Moslem can partake of this meat. Long before their religions came into being, the pig was an "abomination" to the Egyptians. Once a sacrificial animal to their god Horus, it had become taboo to the gods as well as to their followers.[14]

14. J. A. Wilson, in *Ancient Near Eastern Texts* (Princeton, 1950), p. 10.

The Egyptians were fond of drink. It has already been stated in this book that the process of distillation was unknown at that time.[15] Beer and wine, however, were very popular beverages in ancient Egypt. Beer was made from either barley or emmer wheat. Malt and hops were unknown, but flavoring substances may have been added to the brew, such as lupin, safflower, resin or others. The necessary yeast was a wild or cultivated variety.[16]

15. A. Lucas, *Ancient Egyptian Materials and Industries* (London, 1948), p. 33.

The culture of grapes was widespread in Egypt. Wine was made from white and red grapes, from dates and from the sap of the palm trunk. The process of making grape wine was similar to the simple methods practiced by certain European peasants today.[17]

16. *Ibid.*, pp. 16-23.

Although their land produced an abundance of food for the table, Egyptians cherished imported delicacies from Syria, Asia Minor and Mesopotamia. Wines, beer, oil, figs, breads and grapes were among food importations.[18]

17. *Ibid.*, pp. 23-33.

18. Erman and Ranke, pp. 221-222.

Sports and Games

An indication of a people's progress is found when those pursuits that once were the common occupations for survival become professions to some and pastimes to others. This is true of hunting, fowling and fishing in ancient Egypt. At an early time of that land's history professions became established.

Professional fishermen caught huge numbers of fish with dragnets[19] to supply the market, fowlers equipped with broad clapnets[20] delivered fowl for the table, and domesticated cattle brought to the butcher provided meat.[21] In his leisure time, the Egyptian enjoyed going fishing with spear and rod in the Nile or sitting comfortably by his pool angling for fish.[22] He loved to go into the marshy regions of the Delta with his family, gliding through reed thickets on a light papyrus boat and, equipped with a boomerang, try to bring down a duck or some other waterfowl. Sometimes a cat would act as his retriever.[23] Hunting in the desert and adjoining mountains was a popular sport. There, gazelles, antelopes, hyenas and lions, among other animals, were pursued with bow and arrow and the help of a hunting dog, a greyhound known as "saluki." There were those who wanted to catch an animal alive to own as a pet or to add to their zoological gardens. These were roped with a lasso. Rameses II was known to have had a pet lion which followed him like a dog. During campaigns he would lie in front of his master's tent to keep watch at night.[24]

Wrestling was a popular pastime and professionals entertained guests at parties.[25] A pharaoh like Amenhotep II was renowned for his strength in shooting an arrow through a metal target.[26] Ball games were played and little Egyptian girls had dolls to fondle.[27]

A great number of table games were played in ancient Egypt. Among them are those for which specially designed boards and moving pieces were required. Some of these games can be compared with our checkers,[28] while others are of a very specialized character.

19. *Ibid.*, pp. 269, 588.

20. *Ibid.*, pp. 265-266.

21. Hayes, pp. 263-264.

22. Erman and Ranke, p. 269.

23. *Ibid.*, p. 265.

24. *Ibid.*, pp. 271-277.

25. *Ibid.*, pp. 278, 293.

26. Wilson, *Burden*, p. 198.

27. Erman and Ranke, pp. 192, 279.

28. *Ibid.*, pp. 290-291.

Such a one is played by Sethi I and Nefretiri in one of the scenes in the film. This particular game, called "Hounds and Jackals," was adapted from an actual example on exhibit in the Metropolitan Museum in New York.[29]

Music and Dancing

The paintings in tombs, the sculptures, the architecture, the many artifacts, the written hieroglyphs—all of these have helped to bring to life what once was Egypt. But the tunes they sang, the music they played and the rhythm embodied in them have escaped, as a tone struck on a cord disappears when its vibrations cease. No ancient Egyptian music has been recorded in notes—nor Hebrew music—in that long gone age. It is evident, however, that these people sang melodies and played instruments. We know what these instruments were in ancient Egypt. It is even possible to reconstruct their tonal range. But the music created on them has ceased like the last wind-blown ripple on a now still pond.

The instruments played were diverse. There were those to accent rhythm—drums, clappers in the shape of boomerangs, concussion sticks beaten against each other and the sistrum made of metal that was shaken. Among the stringed instruments there were several types of harps, the lyre and the lute. Vertical flutes, double clarinets, trumpets and the oboe made up the wind instruments.[30]

We can assume that the Hebrews were acquainted at least with some of these instruments. On one of the tomb paintings a Semite is shown with a lyre,[31] but generally speaking, factual information is lacking for this early period.

In the picture particular attention is paid to the shofar, traditionally a goat's or ram's horn, which is the only ancient musical instrument that has persisted in Jewish ritual from Bible times to this day. In English translations of the Old Testament the term most widely used for this word is "trumpet."[32] Today the

29. Metropolitan Museum, New York, Carnarvon Room, Exhibit 26.7.1287.

30. C. Sachs, *History of Musical Instruments* (New York, 1940), pp. 86-103.

31. N. M. Davies, *Ancient Egyptian Paintings* (Chicago, 1936), I, Pl. 11.

32. *Jewish Encyclopedia*, XI (New York, 1907), 301.

blowing of the shofar is restricted to religious services in the synagogue. In days of old it served secular purposes as well—for example, that of a signal horn.[33] It is particularly in this last sense, to announce the day of freedom and to call the Israelites to assemble, that it is used in the film.

At the foot of Mt. Horeb we show Moses with his son Gershom in the process of making such a shofar. The basic method of producing such an instrument today is as follows: the tip of the horn is removed and into that end a small opening is drilled till the hollow part of the horn is reached. The horn is smoothed by scraping and then soaked in hot water until it can be bent to the desired shape.[34]

An unusual instrument is sounded in the picture. It is a weapon, a bow. The idea derives from the fact that the wool carder of Palestine performed "his task with the help of a large bow, whose taut cord [was] kept in constant vibration. . . ."[35] "The vibration, oft-repeated, filled his shop with music. . . ."[36] A vibrating bow-cord produces sound—music—and it is for this purpose that we use it on the screen when the Bedouins strike up the band for the dance of Jethro's daughters.

The dance itself, as performed in the picture, is freely adapted from traditional Bedouin dances. The sources read relate that "women dancers let their hair down when performing, and sway their bodies and heads about so that the loose hair swings from side to side in circular motion";[37] the dancer accelerates "her movements according as she herself feels interested in the dance."[38]

At harvest time and special occasions the people of ancient Egypt expressed their joy in dancing.[39] Egyptian aristocracy, however, never appears to have participated in such social activities.[40] Yet dances were a welcome form of entertainment.

Quite early in Egypt's history African dancing pygmies were brought from the land of Punt and given

33. *Ibid.*

34. *Jewish Encycl.*, XI, p. 305.

35. *Ibid.*, p. 511.
36. A. E. Bailey, *Daily Life in Bible Times* (New York, 1943), p. 190.

37. H. R. P. Dickson, *Arab of the Desert* (London, 1949), p. 224.
38. Murray, p. 66.
39. *a*) Erman and Ranke, p. 280.
  b) C. Sachs, *World History of the Dance* (New York, 1937), pp. 29, 229.
40. Sachs, *Dance*, p. 229.

as valued presents to the pharaoh. Later, female dancers from Asia were highly esteemed.[41]

Most interesting are the group dances performed before the pharaoh and his guests, or those presented by aristocrats to make their parties entertaining. These dances performed before such an audience appear to have been of various forms. They can be described generally as simple rhythmical movements, as acrobatic and story-telling dances.[42] Gentle motions, violent steps and kicks, pirouettes and contortions composed the dance. We find lines of dancers performing in unison identical steps and arm and hand motions, as in a chorus. Sometimes two or more dancers combine into a group within the chorus to produce a desired effect. The clapping of hands, the snapping of fingers or the beating of sticks provided the necessary beat. Sometimes an orchestra added music to such rhythms.[43]

Ballet is as modern as ancient Egypt. From tombs as ancient as the Old Kingdom (2800-2250 B.C.) to those of the twentieth dynasty (twelfth to eleventh century B.C.) came the sculptures and paintings that pattern the dance performed in Sethi's throne room upon his jubilee in the picture *The Ten Commandments.*

Each component of the ballet presented in the film is derived from archaeological discoveries; the rising from a seated position, back to back, to a standing one; the strenuous backbend with feet and hands only touching the floor; the rhythmical snapping of the fingers. Particularly noteworthy is the wide upward stride or kick, which required trained skill.[44]

The design for the headdress of the dancers comes from two of these tombs, the tomb of the Vizier Mehou at Saqqara and one located at Deir el Gebrawi. In each instance the hair is shown braided into a long plait to which a ball is attached at the end.[45] It is easy to imagine that when the torso or the head is engaged in a circular motion the whirling hair weighted by the ball will create an extraordinary and colorful picture.

41. *Ibid.,* pp. 16, 230, 231.

42. Erman and Ranke, pp. 280-282. See also Sachs, *Dance,* p. 229.

43. Erman and Ranke, pp. 280-282. Also Sachs, *Dance,* pp. 178, 229.

44. *a)* J. G. Wilkinson, *Ancient Egyptions* (London, 1878), I, 454, 505, 507; II, 54, 68.

b) Art of Ancient Egypt (Vienna, 1936), Pls. 201, 238, 268.

c) Erman and Ranke, Pl. 121.

d) Egypt, Unesco World Art Series (Paris, 1954), Pl. 9.

e) N. de G. Davies, *Rock Tombs of Deir el Gebrawi,* Vol. XI, Part 1 (London, 1902), frontispiece.

45. *Egypt,* Unesco Series, Pl. 121. See also N. de G. Davies, frontispiece; Erman and Ranke, Pl. 121.

The dance seen on the screen still exists in the tombs of Egypt. The instruments that provide the music are there as well. But the melodies that once filled a joyful land with pleasure, laughter and love have vanished into complete stillness, into silence as deep as the rock-hewn tombs of Egypt.

POSTSCRIPT

THE picture *The Ten Commandments* relates the story of Moses and his people; it depicts the lives of great pharaohs and their subjects. Having studied the issues and the people represented in this film, the author now takes the liberty of presenting a few of his own conclusions.

One cannot help but be impressed by the still visible accomplishments of the ancient Egyptians. By a lenient comparison these Nile dwellers lived in a world of many material advantages, not unlike our own. They were a people who had originated and mastered many things from which the world has profited. In their architecture and arts, in their industries and crafts and in their writings, they set examples that prove them to have been a worthy people. They formed a cultured nation for a much longer period of time than has been taken up by the histories of England, France, Germany, Italy or the United States of America. Since the advent of Islam, Egypt has been inhabited essentially by a newer stock of people; nevertheless, the history of that nation has never ceased for over five thousand years.

Somewhat younger by comparison are the Israelites. We meet them on the screen at a stage most critical to their development. Though unbeknown to them at that particular time, they were to influence the history of the world. But in the thirteenth century B.C. they were still a simple, nomadic people, unsophisticated and without time or opportunity to fashion the material records that a settled life would have permitted them to leave for posterity. Yet they brought forth a Moses and, as the centuries went by, the Greater

167

and Lesser Prophets. It was through these men that the fervently insistent, though often shaken, faith in God was soundly established. It was through them that the obedience to His often forgotten Law began to influence mankind.

A few seeds planted in a waterless, arid desert began to bloom, to reseed themselves and flower again and again through the revelations and inspirations carried forth by word of mouth, the written word, the printed book; by the expressions of gifted artists on canvas and in stone; through the inventions of this technological age, the radio, television and the motion picture.

It appears to have been a long road that mankind traveled from the concept of god-kings to theocracies to the freedom under law of a democracy. Yet it is but a day compared to the years it has taken man to start thinking and to form concepts.

The Law that establishes God and the relationships of man to God, and of man to man, is revealed to some in the form of the Ten Commandments. To others it is declared in different words. Yet the idea and ideal of the Law is the same wherever He is worshipped.

BIBLIOGRAPHY

BIBLIOGRAPHY

Albright, William Foxwell. *Archaeology and the Religion of Israel.* Baltimore, 1946.

Apocrypha and Pseudepigrapha of the Old Testament, ed. R. H. Charles. 2 vols. Oxford, 1913.

Arrian. *Anabasis Alexandri,* trans. E. Iliff Robson. 2 vols. Cambridge, Mass., 1946.

Art of Ancient Egypt. Vienna, 1936.

Authorized Daily Prayer Book, trans. and comm. Joseph H. Hertz. New York, 1948.

Baedeker, Karl. *Egypt and the Sudan.* Leipzig, 1914.

Bailey, Albert E. *Daily Life in Bible Times.* New York, 1943.

Barrois, Georges A. "Chronology, Metrology, Etc.," in *Interpreter's Bible,* ed. George A. Buttrick *et al.* Vol. I. New York, 1952.

Bible, translated according to the Ebrew and Greeke . . . London, 1586.

Breasted, James Henry. *History of Egypt.* New York, 1921.

————, in *Cambridge Ancient History,* ed. J. B. Bury *et al.* Vol. II. Cambridge, England, 1931. Chs. 5 and 6.

Buber, Martin. *Moses.* Oxford, 1946.

Budge, E. A. Wallis. *Dwellers on the Nile.* London, 1926.

————. *Kings of Egypt.* 2 vols. London, 1908.

————. *The Nile.* London, 1912.

"Burning Bushes That Grow To-day," *Literary Digest,* April 6, 1929, p. 72.

Campbell, Colin. *Two Theban Queens.* London, 1909.

Capart, Jean, in *Legacy of Egypt,* ed. S. R. K. Glanville. Oxford, 1947. Ch. 4.

Catholic Encyclopedia, ed. Charles G. Herbermann *et al.* 15 vols. New York, 1907-1912.

Cerny, Jaroslav. *Ancient Egyptian Religion.* London, 1952.

Churchill, Winston S. *Amid These Storms.* New York, 1932. "Moses."

Crowfoot, G. M., and Davies, N. de G., "Tunic of Tut'Ankhamun," *Journal of Egyptian Archaeology,* XXVII (December, 1941), 113-130.

Cyclopaedia of Biblical Literature, ed. John Kitto. 2 vols. New York, 1857.

Davies, Nina M. *Ancient Egyptian Paintings.* 3 vols. Chicago, 1936.

Davies, Norman de Garies. *Rock Tombs of Deir El Gebrawi.* Vol. XI, Part 1. London, 1902.

Davis, John D., and Gehman, Henry S. *Westminster Dictionary of the Bible.* Philadelphia, 1944.

Description de l'Égypte . . . pendant l'Expédition de l'Armée Française. 23 vols. Paris, 1809-.

Dickson, H. R. P. *Arab of the Desert.* London, 1949.

Dictionary of the Bible, ed. James Hastings. New York, 1954.

Drioton, Étienne. "Egyptian Religion," in *Introduction to Egyptian Archaeology,* ed. R. Engelbach. Cairo, 1946.

Egypt: Paintings from Tombs and Temples. Unesco World Art Series. Paris, 1954.

MOSES AND EGYPT

Encyclopaedia Britannica. 11th edition. 28 vols. New York, 1911.

————. 14th edition. 24 vols. New York and Chicago, 1936.

————. 24 vols. Chicago, 1951.

Encyclopaedia of Religion and Ethics, ed. James Hastings. 12 vols. New York, 1917-1922.

Encyclopédie Photographique de l'Art. 4 vols. Paris, 1936-1948.

Encyclopédie Photographique de l'Art, Musée du Caire. Paris, 1949.

Engelbach, R. *Problem of the Obelisks.* New York, 1923.

————, ed. *Introduction to Egyptian Archaeology.* Cairo, 1946.

————, in *Legacy of Egypt,* ed. S. R. K. Glanville. Oxford, 1947. Ch. 5.

English-Hebrew Dictionary, ed. J. I. S. Kaufman. Tel Aviv, 1947.

Epigraphic Survey: Medinet Habu. Vol. I, Chicago, 1930. Vol. IV, Chicago, 1940.

Epstein, I. "Foreword" to *Midrash Rabbah,* ed. H. Freedman and Maurice Simon. Vol. I. London, 1951. Pp. ix-xxiii.

Erman, Adolf, and Ranke, Hermann. *Aegypten und Aegyptisches Leben im Altertum.* Tübingen, 1923.

Eusebius of Caesarea. *Preparation for the Gospel,* trans. Edwin H. Gifford. 2 vols. Oxford, 1903.

Fakhry, Ahmed. *Necropolis of El-Bagawat in Kharga Oasis.* Cairo, 1951.

Faulkner, R. O. "Egyptian Military Standards," *Journal of Egyptian Archaeology,* XXVII (December, 1941), 12-18.

Foster, R. J. "Formation and History of the Canon," in *Catholic Commentary on Holy Scripture,* ed. Bernard Orchard *et al.* New York, 1953.

Fox, Penelope. *Tutankhamun's Treasure.* London, 1951.

Frankfort, Henri and H. A. "Myth and Reality," in *Before Philosophy.* Harmondsworth, England, 1951.

Freud, Sigmund. *Moses and Monotheism,* trans. K. Jones. New York, 1939.

Gaster, Theodor H. *Festivals of the Jewish Year.* New York, 1953.

George, Henry. *Moses,* an address delivered in Glasgow, Dec. 28, 1884. New York, n.d.

Gibb, H. A. R., and Kramers, J. H. *Shorter Encyclopaedia of Islam.* Leiden, 1953.

Ginzberg, Louis. *Legends of the Jews.* 7 vols. Philadelphia, 1946-1947.

Griffiths, J. Gwyn. "Egyptian Derivation of the Name Moses," *Journal of Near Eastern Studies,* XII (October, 1953), 225-231.

Haggadah of Passover, trans. Maurice Samuel. New York, 1942.

Hayes, William C. *Scepter of Egypt.* Part 1. New York, 1953.

————. "Daily Life in Ancient Egypt," in *Everyday Life in Ancient Times.* Washington, D.C., 1951.

Heinisch, Paul. *History of the Old Testament.* Collegeville, Minn., 1952.

Herklots, H. G. G. *How Our Bible Came to Us.* New York, 1954.

Herodotus. *History of Herodotus,* trans. George Rawlinson. 4 vols. London, 1862.

Herzfeld, Ernst. "Mythos und Geschichte," in *Archaeologische Mitteilungen aus Iran,* VI (December, 1933), 102-109.

Holy Bible. Authorized King James Version. Cleveland, n.d.

Holy Bible. New Catholic Edition . . . Los Angeles, 1952.

Holy Qur'an, trans. Maulana Muhammad 'Ali. Lahore, 1951.

Hughes, Thomas P. *Dictionary of Islam.* London, 1935.

International Map of the World, 1:1,000,000, sheet NH-36, "Cairo." Survey of Egypt. Giza, 1954.

Interpreter's Bible, ed. George A. Buttrick *et al.* Vol. I, New York, 1952. Vol. II, New York, 1953.

Jeffery, Arthur. "Formation and Transmission of the Old Testment," in *Interpreter's Bible,* ed. George A. Buttrick *et al.* Vol. I. New York, 1952.

Jewish Encyclopedia, ed. Isidore Singer *et al.* 12 vols. New York, 1903-1907.

Jewish People: Past and Present, ed. R. Abramovitch *et al.* 4 vols. New York, 1946-1952.

Jordan, W. G. "The Old Testament and Science," in *Abingdon Bible Commentary,* ed. F. C. Eiselen *et al.* New York, 1929.

Josephus, Flavius. *Josephus,* trans. H. St. J. Thackeray and Ralph Marcus. Vol. IV, *Jewish Antiquities, Books i-iv,* trans. Thackeray. London and New York, 1930.

Koran, trans. George Sale, with introduction by Edward Denison Ross. London, n.d.

Lange, Kurt. *Aegypteñ, Landschaft und Kunst.* Berlin, 1943.

Lauterbach, Jacob Z. *Mekilta de-Rabbi Ishmael.* 3 vols. Philadelphia, 1949.

Lucas, A. *Ancient Egyptian Materials and Industries.* London, 1948.

Marsh, John, and Butzer, Albert G. "Numbers, Exegesis and Exposition," in *Interpreter's Bible,* ed. George A. Buttrick *et al.* Vol. II. New York, 1953.

Meistermann, P. Barnabé. *Guide du Nil au Jourdain* . . . Paris, 1909.

Mekhitarian, Arpag. *Egyptian Painting.* Geneva, 1954.

Midrash Rabbah, ed. H. Freedman and Maurice Simon. 10 vols. Vol. II, *Genesis,* trans. H. Freedman, London, 1951. Vol. III, *Exodus,* trans. S. M. Lehrman, London, 1951. Vol. IV, *Leviticus,* trans. J. Israelstam, London, 1939. Vol V, *Numbers,* trans. Judah J. Slotki, London, 1939.

Miller, Madeleine S. and John L. *Harper's Bible Dictionary.* New York, 1954.

Miller, Olive B. *Picturesque Tale of Progress.* 8 vols. Chicago, 1935.

Mishnah, trans. Herbert Danby. London, 1933.

Moffatt, James. *The Bible: A New Translation.* New York, 1935.

Murray, G. W. *Sons of Ishmael.* London, 1935.

Murray, Margaret A. *Splendour that was Egypt.* New York, 1949.

New International Encyclopaedia, ed. Frank Moore Colby *et al.* 23 vols. New York, 1927.

New Standard Alphabetical Indexed Bible. Chicago, 1936.

New York Times, November 8, 1955, p. 11, col. 2. (Locusts)

Oesterley, W. O. E., and Robinson, Theodore H. *Hebrew Religion.* London, 1949.

Oppenheim, A. Leo. "Babylonian and Assyrian Historical Texts," in *Ancient Near Eastern Texts* . . . , ed. James B. Pritchard. Princeton, 1950.

Ordnance Survey of the Peninsula of Sinai, Sheet 2. Southampton, 1868-69.

Pentateuch and Haftorahs, ed. and comm. Joseph H. Hertz. 2 vols. U. S. A., 1941(?).

Petrie, W. M. Flinders. *Egypt and Israel*. London, 1931.

————. *Researches in Sinai*. London, 1906.

————. *Social Life in Ancient Egypt*. London, 1923.

Philo, Judaeus. *Philo*, trans. F. H. Colson. Vol. VI, Cambridge, Mass., 1950, "Moses." Vol. VII, Cambridge, Mass., 1950, "The Decalogue."

Pope, Hugh, and Bullough, S. "History of the Rheims-Douay Version," in *Catholic Commentary on Holy Scripture*, ed. Bernard Orchard *et al.* New York, 1953.

Power, E. "Languages, Texts and Versions of the Bible," "Archaeology and the Bible," and "Exodus" (Commentary), in *Catholic Commentary on Holy Scripture*, ed. Bernard Orchard *et al.* New York, 1953.

Preble, George H. *Origin and History of the American Flag*. 2 vols. Philadelphia, 1917.

Rappaport, Angelo S. *Myth and Legend of Ancient Israel*. 3 vols. London, 1928.

Rawlinson, George. *History of Ancient Egypt*. 2 vols. Boston, 1882.

————. *Moses, His Life and Times*. New York, 1887.

Riefstahl, Elizabeth. *Patterned Textiles in Pharaonic Egypt*. Brooklyn, 1944.

Robinson, A. E. "Camel in Antiquity," *Sudan Notes and Records*, XIX, 47-69.

Rylaarsdam, J. Coert, and Park, J. Edgar. "Exodus, Exegesis and Exposition," in *Interpreter's Bible*, ed. George A. Buttrick *et al.* Vol. I. New York, 1952.

Sachs, Curt. *History of Musical Instruments*. New York, 1940.

————. *World History of the Dance*. New York, 1937.

Schaefer, Heinrich, and Andrae, Walter. *Kunst des Alten Orients*. Berlin, 1925.

Sculptures of Michelangelo. New York, 1940.

Seele, Keith C. *Coregency of Ramses II with Sethi I and the Date of the Great Hypostyle Hall at Karnak*. Chicago, 1940.

Septuagint Bible, trans. Charles Thomson and ed. C. A. Muses. Indian Hills, Colo., 1954.

Serjeant, R. B. "Sea-Wool," *Ars Islamica*, XV-XVI (1951), 60-61.

Shear, T. L., quoted in W. R. Brown. *Horse of the Desert*. New York, 1947. Pp. 38-40.

Shipley, Joseph T. *Dictionary of Word Origins*. Ames, Iowa, 1955.

Shorter Oxford English Dictionary, ed. Charles T. Onions. 2 vols. Oxford, 1933.

Smith, E. Baldwin. *Egyptian Architecture as Cultural Expression*. New York, 1938.

Steindorff, George, and Seele, Keith C. *When Egypt Ruled the East*. Chicago, 1947.

Strong, James. *Exhaustive Concordance of the Bible*. New York, 1953.

Temples et Trésors de l'Égypte. Art et Style 20. Paris, n.d.

Thompson, R. Campbell, in *Cambridge Ancient History*, ed. J. B. Bury *et al.* Vol. I. Cambridge, England, 1928. Ch. 14.

Universal Jewish Encyclopedia, ed. Isaac Landman. 10 vols. New York, 1948.

Ussher, James. *Annals of the World*. London, 1658.

Westminster Historical Atlas to the Bible, ed. George E. Wright and Floyd V. Filson. Philadelphia, 1945.

Wikgren, Allen. "English Bible," in *Interpreter's Bible*, ed. George A. Buttrick *et al.* Vol. I. New York, 1952.

Wilkinson, J. Gardner. *Manners and Customs of the Ancient Egyptians.* 3 vols. London, 1878.

Wilson, John A. *Burden of Egypt.* Chicago, 1951.

————. "Egyptian Myths, Tales and Mortuary Texts" and "Egyptian Historical Texts," in *Ancient Near Eastern Texts* . . . , ed. James B. Pritchard. Princeton, 1950.

Winlock, Herbert E. *Treasure of El Lahun.* New York, 1934.

————. *Treasure of Three Egyptian Princesses.* New York, 1948.

LIBRARIES AND MUSEUMS CONSULTED

Alhambra Public Library, Alhambra, California
Beverly Hills Public Library, Beverly Hills, California
British Museum, London, England
Brooklyn Botanic Garden, Brooklyn, New York
Brooklyn Museum, Brooklyn, New York
Cecil B. deMille Library, Los Angeles, California
Egyptian Embassy, Washington, D.C.
Egyptian Museum, Cairo, Egypt
Griffith Observatory, Los Angeles, California
Jewish Community Library, Los Angeles, California
Los Angeles County Library, Los Angeles, California
Los Angeles County Museum, Los Angeles, California
Los Angeles Public Library, Los Angeles, California
Louvre Museum, Paris, France
Loyola University of Los Angeles, Los Angeles, California
Metropolitan Museum of Art, New York City, New York
National Gallery of Victoria, Melbourne, Australia
Paramount Pictures Corporation Research Library, Los Angeles, California
Pasadena Public Library, Pasadena, California
San Marino Public Library, San Marino, California
Santa Monica Public Library, Santa Monica, California
South Pasadena Public Library, South Pasadena, California
Stanford University Art Gallery and Museum, Palo Alto, California
Tunis Museum, Tunis, Tunisia
University of California Library, Berkeley, California
University of California at Los Angeles Library, Los Angeles, California
University of Chicago Oriental Institute, Chicago, Illinois
University of Chicago Oriental Institute, "Chicago House," Luxor, Egypt
University of Judaism, Los Angeles, California
University of Southern California Library, Los Angeles, California

INDEX

GENERAL INDEX

A

Aaron, 17, 25, 26, 29, 43-44, 64, 65, 70, 71, 141
  miter of, 45, 142
aba, 141
Abarim, 46
Abiram, 66
Abraham, Abram, 6-7, 11, 17, 32, 63, 67, 87, 95, 97, 148
abrasives, 105
Absalom, 142
Abu Simbel, 61, 116, 119, 120
acacia, 45, 108, 121, 152
acrobats, 111
Adam, 6
Adam and Eve, Books of. See Bible, Old Testament, Pseudepigrapha, Adam and Eve
Adams, John, 37
adhesives, 114, 115
adobe, 104
Adonai, 24, 25
adzes, 113
Ælantic Gulf, 36
Ælfric, 82
Africa, 99, 164
agate, 151, 156, 157
agriculture, 101, 111
Akhnaton, 55, 102, 108, 116, 119, 123, 128
alabaster, 103, 114, 151
Al Beidawi, 16, 43
Albright, William F., 50, 96
Alexander the Great, 37, 62
Alexandria, 15, 52, 75, 78, 80
Al Fatihah, 88
Alfred, King, 82
Allah, 28, 32, 44, 86, 87, 88
Allen, Cardinal, 85
alloys, 113
almond, 121, 149
alphabet, Canaanite, 40
  Hebrew, 40, 79
al-Tanzil, 87
Amalek, 69
Amalekites, 22
Amarna. See El Amarna
Amazon stone, 151
amber, 157
Amenemhet, advice of, 57

Amenhotep II, 98, 162
Amenhotep III, 116
amethyst, 151, 156, 157
Amon, 51, 52, 98
Amon-Ra, 51
Amos, Book of. See Bible, Old Testament, Books, Amos
amulets, 150-151, 154, 155, 157
angels, 33, 36
animals, domesticated, 95-97
anklets, 153, 154
antelopes, 162
Apiru. See Habiru
Apis Bull, 44
Apocrypha. See Bible, Old Testament, Apocrypha
aprons, Egyptian, 132, 135
  Hebrew, 141
'Aqaba, Gulf of, 36, 38
aquamarine, 152, 157
Arabia, 110, 138
Arabs, 67, 104, 110, 126, 141, 142
Aramaean Semites, 64
archers. See archery; army, archers
archery, 139
architecture, 101, 102, 103, 109, 163
Aristeas. See Bible, Old Testament, Pseudepigrapha, Letter of Aristeas
Ark of the Covenant, 45
armlets, 153
arms. See weapons
army, 20, 40, 54, 69, 89-92
  archers, 89, 92
  baggage trains, 92
  campaigns, 7, 20, 55, 56, 58, 71, 92, 162
  cavalry, 89, 98
  chariotry, 5, 35, 89, 90, 91, 98, 111, 117, 130
  conscription, 89
  decorations, 92
  fortifications, 92
  infantry, 89
  insignia, 90
  marines, 89
  mercenaries, 89, 90
  militia, 89
  officers, 20, 54, 55, 59, 69, 71, 90, 92
  organization, 90
  provisions, 92, 160

rewards, 92
Sardinians, 90
spearmen, 89, 90
standards, 90, 91
uniforms, 90, 127, 130, 134, 135
Arrian, 37
arrows, 89, 162
Artapanus, 23
Ascalon, 64
ash, 121
Asher, 91, 142, 157
Ashtaroth, 44, 51
Asia, 55, 61, 92, 96, 97, 125, 126, 129, 165
Asia Minor, 55, 161
Asiatics, 9, 69, 97, 127, 129, 140
assassination, 59. See also Moses, attempted assassination of
asses. See donkeys
Assumption of Moses, Book of. See Bible, Old Testament, Pseudepigrapha, Assumption of Moses
Assyrians, 96, 148
Authorized Version. See Bible, versions, Authorized Version
Avaris. See Tanis
axes, 90, 113
ayat, 87

B

Baal, 51
Babylon, 79
Babylonia, 16, 80, 123
Babylonian Gemara, 16
Babylonian Targum. See Bible, translations, targum
baggage trains. See army, baggage trains
Baka, 21
bakery, 108
balcony, 109
Baldwin, James M., 50
ballet, 165
ball games, 162
balsamum, 149
balustrade, 109
banquets. See feasts
barber, 145
barges. See boats
barley, 29, 161

Baruch, Book of. See Bible, Old Testament, Apocrypha, Baruch; Bible, Old Testament, Pseudepigrapha, Baruch
basalt, 103
bathrooms, 108
battles, 59, 69, 92, 117. See also warfare
beads, 127, 130, 135, 151, 152, 154, 157
beards, 148
    Egyptian, 137, 144-145
    Hebrew, 147, 148
Bedouins, 67, 96, 141, 160, 161, 164
bedrooms, 117
beds, 121, 122, 123
bedsprings, 121, 122
beech, 121
beer, 160, 161
beeswax, 114, 146
beetles, 153, 154-155
belts, 132, 133, 135, 141
Benisch, 86
Benjamin, 91, 142, 158
beryl, 152, 156, 157
Bethel, 45
beverages, 111, 160, 161
Bezaleel, 45
Bible, 5, 6, 7, 9, 11-12, 18, 19, 20, 23, 25, 26, 28, 32, 35, 38, 39, 43, 44, 46, 54, 64, 66, 67, 69, 86, 89, 91, 98, 110, 147, 148, 150, 155, 156, 158
    Apocrypha. See Bible, Old Testament, Apocrypha
    Hebrew text, 6, 17, 24, 36, 40, 68, 70, 75, 78-79, 80, 81, 82, 83, 84, 86
    New Testament, 21, 82, 84, 87
    Old Testament, 6, 7, 13, 15-17, 22, 24, 27, 30, 31, 36-37, 40, 41, 45, 57, 63, 65, 68, 70, 73, 74, 75, 77-78, 87, 92, 95, 112, 140, 142, 143. See also Bible
        Apocrypha, 75-76, 77, 78, 85
            Baruch, 76
            Daniel, 76
            Ecclesiasticus, 75, 76
            Esther, 76
            Judith, 36, 76
            I Maccabees, 36, 76
            II Maccabees, 76

Tobias, 76
Wisdom, 36, 76
Books, Amos, 75
Chronicles, 66
Daniel, 75, 78
Deuteronomy, 31, 45, 74
Ecclesiastes, 78
Esther, 64
Exodus, 8, 16, 22, 39, 65, 66, 68, 149-150
Genesis, 6, 32, 64
Hosea, 75
Judges, 7
Numbers, 30, 66, 68
Psalms, 29, 75, 78, 82
Zechariah, 75, 78
canon, 75, 76
Catholic, 75-76, 77
deuterocanonical. See Bible, Old Testament, Apocrypha
Hebrew, 75, 76, 77, 78
Protestant, 75, 76, 77
Codes. See Bible, Old Testament, Document D; Bible, Old Testament, Document E; Bible, Old Testament, Document J; Bible, Old Testament, Document JE; Bible, Old Testament, Document P
deuterocanonical books. See Bible, Old Testament, Apocrypha
Document D, 74
Document E, 74
Document J, 74
Document JE, 74
Document P, 74
Hagiographa. See Bible, Old Testament, Writings
Hexateuch, 73-74
Law, 75, 77
manuscripts. See Bible, Hebrew text; Bible, translations
Pentateuch, 43, 75, 80, 83
Priestly Code. See Bible, Old Testament, Document P
printed, 83-84
Prophets, 75, 80
Pseudepigrapha, 75, 76, 77
Adam and Eve, 77
Assumption of Moses, 77
II Baruch, 77

III Baruch, 77
I Enoch, 77
II Enoch, 77
IV Ezra, 77
Greek Apocalypse of Baruch, 77
Jubilees, 23, 77
Letter of Aristeas, 77
IV Maccabees, 77
Martyrdom of Isaiah, 77
Psalms of Solomon, 77
Secrets of Enoch, 77
Sibylline Oracles, 77
Syriac Apocalypse of Baruch, 77
Testaments of the Twelve Patriarchs, 77
Writings, 75, 80
translations, Anglo-Norman, 82
Anglo-Saxon, 82
Arabic, 81
Aramaic, 80, 81
Armenian, 81
Bishops' Bible, 84, 85
Breeches Bible. See Bible, translations, Geneva Bible
Coptic, 81
Coverdale, 84, 85
English, 24, 82-84, 85, 86, 163
Erasmus, 83, 84
Ethiopic, 81
Geneva Bible, 84, 85
Georgian, 81
German, 83, 84
Gothic, 81
Great Bible. See Bible, translations, Matthew
Greek, 6, 41, 75, 80, 81, 82, 83, 84
Latin, 76, 80, 81, 82, 83, 84, 85
Luther, 83
Matthew, 84, 85
Midland Psalter, 83
Psalters, 82, 83
Septuagint, 6, 25, 36, 40, 76, 77, 78, 80, 81, 85
Slavonic, 81
Syriac, 81
targum, 79, 80
Thomson, 85
Tyndale, 83, 84, 85
Vespasian Psalter, 82

Vulgate, 76, 77, 79, 80, 81, 82, 83, 84, 85
Wyclif, 83, 84
Vatican Codex, 41
versions, authorized, 84, 85
  Authorized Version, 24, 70, 71, 79, 83, 84, 85, 141, 155-156
  Confraternity Version, 86
  Douay Version, 11, 24, 70, 71, 75, 79, 80, 85
  King James. See Bible, versions, Authorized Version
  revised, 85
  Revised Standard Version, 70, 86
  Revised Version, 85, 156, 157
  Samaritan Pentateuch, 6, 81
Bishops' Bible. See Bible, translations, Bishops' Bible
Bithiah, 18, 20, 21, 65-66, 70, 152
Bitter Lakes, 36, 93
blood, 27, 28, 29, 33, 117, 146
boats, 36, 90, 91, 99, 105, 118, 162
bodkins, 110
bondage, 5, 8-11, 22, 28, 31, 32, 34, 63, 66, 69, 109, 141, 155
bone, 121, 150, 151
Book of the Covenant. See Bible, Old Testament, Books, Deuteronomy
boomerang, 162, 163
boots. See footwear, Hebrew
booty, 33, 92
bowls, 112, 118
bows, 89, 90, 105, 120, 162, 164
boxes. See chests
bracelets, 151, 153
braziers, 123
bread, 159, 160, 161
  unleavened, 28, 29, 30, 160, 161
Breasted, James Henry, 18, 19, 57, 58, 59, 102
breastplate, high priest's, 155-156, 158
Breeches Bible. See Bible, translations, Geneva Bible
brick pits, 21, 103-104, 141
bricks, 8, 25, 26, 101, 103, 104, 106, 108, 109, 110
bronze, 59, 89, 104, 113, 115, 134
Bronze Age, 40, 59
brother-sister relationship, 20, 53
Buber, Martin, 12, 14, 17, 27
Buchis Bull, 44
Budge, E. A. Wallis, 60

building materials, 8, 101, 103-107, 108, 109, 110
buildings, 101, 102, 103, 107-110
bulls, 44, 45, 91, 146
burial, 33-34, 99, 126
Burning Bush, 22, 23-24, 25-26, 68, 144
Buto, 136

C

Caedmon, 82
cakes, 159, 160
calamus, 150
Caleb, 67, 70
calendar, Israelite, 17
camels, 95-97, 110, 140
campaigns, 7, 20, 37, 55, 56, 58, 71, 92, 162. See also army, campaigns
camps, 38, 91, 92, 110
Canaan, 33, 40, 64, 69, 70, 156
Canaanites, 117
canon. See Bible, Old Testament, canon
capes, 133
caps, 142-143, 144, 148
captives. See prisoners
caravans, 95, 97
carbuncle, 156
cardamon, 149
carnelian, 134, 151, 156
carob, 121
carpets, 111
cartouches, 53, 58, 60, 139
carts, 92
cassia, 149, 150
cataracts, Nile, 27
Catholic Church. See Church, Catholic
cats, 146, 162
cattle, 33, 115, 122, 146, 162
cavalry, 90, 98. See also army, cavalry
cedar, 121
chairs, 121, 122, 123
chalcedony, 151, 157
Challoner, Richard, 85
chariots, 5, 35, 37, 89, 90, 91, 97, 98, 99, 111, 117, 139. See also army, chariotry
Charles, R. H., 76, 77
charms, 150-151, 155
Chephren, 117, 120
chests, 45, 122

Chicago Oriental Institute. See Oriental Institute, University of Chicago
chicory, 29
chisels, 104
Christianity, 13
Christians, 30, 31, 55, 77, 78, 80, 81, 86
Chronicles, Book of. See Bible, Old Testament, Books, Chronicles
chrysanthemums, 108
chrysoprase, 151
Church, Catholic, 41, 75, 76, 77, 81, 85
    Coptic, 81
    Lutheran, 41
    Protestant, 75, 76, 77, 85
    Reformed, 41
Churchill, Winston, 36, 43
cinnamon, 149
circumcision, 30
clappers, 163
clarinets, 163
clay. See mud
Cleopatra, 62, 126
cloaks, 46, 129, 130, 132, 133, 135, 140, 141, 142, 144, 156
cloisons, 153
cloth, 125, 126
    Egyptian, 113, 125-127, 128-131, 132-133, 135, 139
    Hebrew, 139-140, 141, 142, 143
    Levite, 142
    Syrian, 125, 129
    tent, 110
clothing, Asiatic, 129, 140
    Egyptian, 111, 122, 126-127, 128-130, 131-136, 137, 138-139, 140, 141, 144, 145, 146, 155
    Hebrew, 139-144, 147, 148, 156
    Semitic, 140, 144
clubs, 90, 138
coats. See tunics, Hebrew
cobra, 26, 115, 135, 136
codes, biblical. See Bible, Old Testament, Document
coffins, 114, 121, 135, 136
Cold War, 59
collars, 153, 154
Colonies, American, 37

colors, Egyptian, 113, 114, 115, 126, 128-131, 133, 137, 145, 156-157
    Hebrew, 141-142, 144, 156-158
colossi, 61, 116, 119, 120
columns, 103, 109
Commandments. See Ten Commandments
commerce. See trade
concepts, religious, 49-53, 59
concussion sticks, 163
Confraternity Version. See Bible, versions, Confraternity Version
conscription. See army, conscription
conspiracy, 19, 20, 21, 54, 58, 60, 66. See also Moses, conspiracy against
Continental Congress, 85
copper, 59, 69, 89, 92, 104, 105, 113, 115, 149, 151
Copper Age, 59
cords, 106
corn, 161
corn flowers, 108
corselets, 134
cosmetics, 148, 149
costumes. See clothing; headdress; jewelry
cotton, 125
Council of Trent. See Trent, Council of
Covenant, Ark of the. See Ark of the Covenant
Covenant, Book of the. See Bible, Old Testament, Books, Deuteronomy
Coverdale, Miles. See Bible, translations, Coverdale
Creation, 6, 52, 73, 109
creator-god, 51
crocodiles, 146
Cromwell, Oliver, 37
crook, 138
Crowfoot, G. M., 130
crowns, 37, 136, 137
crystal. See quartz
curtains, 111
Cush, 70
cushions. See pillows
Cushite, 70
cypress, 121
Cyrillus, Saint, 81

D

daggers, 90
dalmatic, 129

Dan, 91, 142, 157
Dan (city), 45
dances, 111, 164-166
dandelions, 29
Daniel, Book of. *See* Bible, Old Testament, Apocrypha, Daniel; Bible, Old Testament, Books, Daniel
dates, 108, 121, 161
Dathan, 21, 35, 44, 66
daughter of Pharaoh. *See* Bithiah
daughters of Jethro. *See* Jethro, daughters of; Moses, wife of; Sephora
David, 78, 87, 147
Dead Sea, 46
Decalogue, The, 15
Declaration of Independence, 37
decorations, military, 92
Deir el Gebrawi, 165
deities. *See* gods
Delgado, Isaac, 86
Delilah, 147
deMille, Cecil B., 8, 13, 71, 102, 108, 130, 139
DeQuincey, Thomas, 144
deshert, 137
designs, 129, 140-141
    Egyptian, 127, 129, 130, 133, 134-135, 141, 146, 153, 154, 155
    Hebrew, 141, 144
deuterocanonical books. *See* Bible, Old Testament, Apocrypha
Deuteronomy, Book of. *See* Bible, Old Testament, Books, Deuteronomy
diamond, 152, 156, 157, 158
diorite, 113, 120
disease, 28
dittany bush, 24
Divine Presence, 37
document, biblical. *See* Bible, Old Testament, Document
dogs, 162
dolerite, 104
dolls, 162
dolomite, 113
dom palm, 121
donkeys, 92, 95
doors, 103
Douay Version. *See* Bible, versions, Douay Version
drills, 105
Drioton, Étienne, 44

drums, 163
ducks, 117, 130, 162
dung, 103
dyes, 130, 131
dynasties, 8, 53, 89, 96, 133
    VI (2350-2200 B.C.), 96
    XII (1990-1780 B.C.), 57
    XVIII (1570-1320 B.C.), 92, 116, 125
    XIX (1319-1222 B.C.), 55, 95, 96, 97, 103, 129
    XX (1200-1090 B.C.), 58, 61, 165
    XXII (945-745 B.C.), 133, 135
    Empire (1465-1165 B.C.), 49, 58, 61, 90
    Hyksos (1730-1580 B.C.), 56, 97
    Middle Kingdom (2050-1800 B.C.), 101, 123, 129
    New Kingdom (1465-1165 B.C.), 54, 69, 89, 90, 105, 109, 126, 128, 129, 132, 134, 137, 138, 153
    Old Kingdom (2700-2200 B.C.), 49, 96, 107, 109, 121, 128, 129, 144, 165

E

earrings, 153
Easter, 30
Eber, 63
ebony, 121, 122
Ecclesiastes, Book of. *See* Bible, Old Testament, Books, Ecclesiastes
Ecclesiasticus, Book of. *See* Bible, Old Testament, Apocrypha, Ecclesiasticus
Edom, 36
Egypt, culture, 8, 19, 46, 123, 129
    decline, 55, 61, 62
    possessions, 55, 58
Egyptian Museum, 99, 122, 134, 139, 146, 150, 153
Egyptians, appearance, 119-120
    character, 50, 51-52
El, 25
El Amarna, 102, 108, 118
Eleazar, 29, 65
electrum, 113, 133, 151
elef, 35
El Elohe Israel, 25
El Elyon, 25
elephants, 113

El Hai, 25
Elias, 87
Eliezer, 23
Elisheba, 64
Elizabeth II, 54
El-Kab, 136
elm, 121
Eloah, 25
Elohim, 25, 74
El Olam, 25
El Shaddai, 25
emblems. *See* heraldry
embroidery, 127, 130, 135, 140-141
emerald, 152, 156, 157
Empire. *See* dynasties, Empire (1465-1165 B.C.)
Encyclopedia, Jewish, 78
Engelbach, R., 106, 107, 120, 132
England, 83, 84, 85
Enoch, Book of. *See* Bible, Old Testament, Pseudepigrapha, Enoch
entertainment, 111, 159, 162, 163, 164, 165
Episcopal Committee of the Confraternity of Christian Doctrine. *See* Bible, versions, Confraternity Version
Epistles of the Old Testament. *See* Bible, Old Testament, printed
equinox, spring, 29, 30
Erasmus. *See* Bible, translations, Erasmus
Erman, Adolf, 90, 131, 133
Esau, 147
estates, 107, 108
Esther, Book of. *See* Bible, Old Testament, Apocrypha, Esther; Bible, Old Testament, Books, Esther
Ethiopia, 20, 56, 71
Ethiopians, 20, 70, 71
Euphrates River, 63
Eusebius of Caesarea, 15, 20, 21, 23, 71
Everlasting God, 25
exile, 22, 74, 123
Exodus, 5, 6, 7, 8, 19, 22-23, 27, 30, 32, 33, 34, 60, 66, 70, 95, 98, 99, 141, 147, 156
Exodus, Book of. *See* Bible, Old Testament, Books, Exodus
eyepaints, 148-149
Ezekiel, 71

Ezion-geber, 36
Ezra, 16
Ezra, Book of. *See* Bible, Old Testament, Pseudepigrapha, IV Ezra

F

faience, 115, 122, 127, 134, 135, 151
Faiyum, 78, 104
Fakhry, Ahmed, 96
falcons, 135, 136
fans, 90, 139
Father, 46, 55
father-son relationship, 53
fats, 146, 149
feasts, 28, 29-30, 44, 111
feathers, 90, 122, 133, 134, 139
felspar, 151
fibres, 121, 130, 131, 138
figs, 108, 121, 160, 161
first-born, death of, 27, 28, 29, 54, 60, 108, 117
fish, 108, 115, 118, 160, 162
fishing, 162
flail, 138
flint, 105
flood, biblical, 6, 73
    Nile, 27, 51, 117
flowers, 108, 118, 146, 149, 159, 160
flutes, 163
fly-switch, 138
food, Egyptian, 122, 159-160, 161, 162
    Hebrew, 28, 29, 160, 161
footstools, 122
footwear, Egyptian, 138, 139
    Hebrew, 140, 144
"forty," 17
fowl, 33, 159, 160, 162
fowling, 162
Frank, Frederick, 13
Frankfort, Henri, 50
frankincense, 150
Franklin, Benjamin, 37
Freud, Sigmund, 12
Friedlander, 86
fringes, 140
fruit, 108, 118, 149, 160, 161
fugitive, 34
furniture, 121-123, 159

G

Gad, 91, 142, 157
galbanum, 150

galena, 149
games, 162, 163
gardens, 32, 108, 118, 160, 162
Gariss, Jack, 13
garnet, 151, 157
garrisons. See army, fortifications
gates, 13, 33, 102, 107, 108, 116, 118
gazelles, 146, 162
Gebel Musa, 38
Gebel Sijagha, 46
geese, 160
gelatin, 114
Gemara, 16
gems. See stones, precious and semi-precious
generations, 17
Genesis, Book of. See Bible, Old Test-ament, Books, Genesis
Geneva Bible. See Bible, translations, Geneva Bible
George, Henry, 43, 46
Gershom, 22, 23, 27, 164
gesso, 114, 115
Gezer, 64
gifts, 25, 33, 92, 123, 126, 155, 165
Gilgal, 30
girdles. See belts
Giza, 117, 120
glass, 115, 122, 135, 151, 153
glaze, 121, 152
gloves, 139
glue, 114, 115, 122
goat-grass, 29
goats, 140, 146, 163
God, 11-12, 21, 22, 23, 25, 26, 27, 28, 31, 33, 34, 35, 36, 37, 38, 39, 40, 41, 43, 45, 47, 55, 60, 61, 65, 66, 67, 86, 116
    finger of, 38, 39, 40
    names of, 12, 22, 23, 24-25, 28, 30, 32, 34, 35, 36, 37, 38, 39, 44, 45, 46, 55, 64, 68, 74, 86, 88
    voice of, 23, 39-40
God Almighty, 25
god-king, 49-51, 52, 53-54, 55-56, 59, 120
God of Israel, 25
gods, 25, 29, 30, 49, 51
    Egyptian, 27, 44, 45, 49, 50, 51-52, 53, 54, 61, 90, 98, 108, 109, 116, 117, 134, 135, 136, 137, 153, 154, 161
    Hyksos, 51

Semitic, 44, 51
    trinities, 51
gold, 44, 45, 92, 99, 113, 115, 116, 121, 127, 129, 133, 134, 135, 136, 145, 146, 151, 152, 153
Golden Calf, 43-45, 65, 66, 116
Goshen, 9, 26, 93, 103, 109, 110
Gospels. See Bible, New Testament
government, 49, 50, 53, 55, 56, 102
    offices, 54, 92
    officials, 54-55
grain, 29, 51, 99, 108, 161
granaries, 20, 108
granite, 40, 41, 103, 116, 121
grapes, 108, 161
grass, 29, 113, 125, 138
Great Bible. See Bible, translations, Matthew
greaves, 90, 139
Greek Apocalypse of Baruch, Book of. See Bible, Old Testament, Pseude-pigrapha, Greek Apocalypse of Ba-ruch
greyhounds, 162
Griffiths, J. G., 18
gums, 114
gutters, 108
gypsum, 104, 114

H

Habachi, Labib, 9, 56, 102-103
Habiru, 63-64
haematite, 157
Hagar, 67-68
Haggadah shel Pesach, 31
Hagiographa. See Bible, Old Testa-ment, Writings
hair, 152, 155, 164, 165
    camel, 96, 110, 140
    goat, 110, 140
    horse, 146
hairdress, Egyptian, 144, 145-146, 148, 155, 165
    Hebrew, 147-148
    Semitic, 147, 148
halfa grass, 113
Hall of Audience, 108, 117
hammers, 104
Hammurabi, 97
Hananiah, 150
handkerchiefs, 139
harem, 108
Har-em-Hab, 55, 92

harps, 163
Hathor, 44, 61
hawks, 115, 117, 133, 136
ha-yam ha-adom, 36
Hayes, William, 90, 139
headdress, Egyptian, 133, 134, 135, 136, 137, 144, 145, 146, 153, 165
    Hebrew, 142-143, 148
    Semitic, 142
    Syrian, 142
heating. *See* braziers
Hebrews, 5, 9, 15, 17, 20-21, 25, 26, 28, 30, 31, 32, 33, 36, 37, 38, 39, 40, 43, 44, 47, 55, 63, 64, 65, 66, 69, 73, 74, 91, 109, 110, 112, 140, 141, 142, 143, 147, 150, 155, 163, 164
    liberation of, 11, 22, 25, 31, 32, 33, 34, 35, 36, 38, 45, 70, 91, 156, 164. *See also* Jews
hedjet, 137
Heinisch, Paul, 16, 23, 34
hekat, 138
Heliopolis, 44
helmets, 90, 142
hemp, 125
heraldry, Egyptian, 90, 99, 109, 135, 136, 137
    Hebrew, 91
herbs, 29
Hermonthis, 44
Hero, 36
Herodotus, 17, 123, 126
Hertz, Joseph H., 28
Herzfeld, Ernst, 13
He Who has no name, 68
He Who Is, 24
He Who is the Subject of reverence (or fear), 25
Hexateuch. *See* Bible, Old Testament, Hexateuch
Hezekiah, 74
hieroglyphs, 96, 111, 116, 130, 133-134, 138, 153, 163
hinds, 91
hippopotamus, 113, 146
Hitler, Adolf, 59
Hittites, 55, 59, 98
Hobab, 68
holidays, pagan, 30
    religious, 28-31
honey, 149, 160

Hophni, 18
hops, 161
Horeb, Mount. *See* Sinai, Mount
horns (instrument), 31, 32, 33, 163, 164
horses, 89, 97
    chariot, 97, 98
    names of, 98
    riding, 89, 90, 98
Horus, 135, 136, 154, 161
Hosea, Book of. *See* Bible, Old Testament, Books, Hosea
hounds and jackals, game of, 163
houses, Egyptian, 101, 102, 103, 107-109
    Hebrew, 110
hunting, 129, 162
Hur ben Caleb, 29, 67
huts, 66, 103
hyenas, 162
Hyksos, 51, 56, 61, 97, 127
hypostyle hall, 60
hyssop, 28, 29

I

I Am, 24
I am He Who IS, 24
I AM THAT I AM, 11, 24, 68
I AM WHO AM, 11, 24
idolatry, 39, 44, 66, 74
idols, Egyptian, 28, 108
    Hebrew, 43, 44, 65, 66, 116
incarnation, 44, 136
incense, 149-150
infantry, 90. *See also* army, infantry
inlay, 122, 139, 152, 153, 154
insects, 27-28, 53, 92, 153, 154, 155
insignia, 90, 127, 139
    royal, 133, 134, 135-138, 155. *See also* army, insignia
intrigue. *See* conspiracy; Moses, conspiracy against
invasions, 20, 51, 96
iris, 149
iron, 59, 134, 151, 157
Iron Age, 59
Iron Curtain, 59
Isaac, 11, 32, 87
Isaiah, Book of. *See* Bible, Old Testament, Pseudepigrapha, Martyrdom of Isaiah
Ishmael, 67-68, 87
Isis, 136

Islam, 13, 19, 33, 67, 86, 87
Israel, 23, 34, 54, 64, 65, 69, 74, 91, 96, 110, 140, 155, 156, 158
Israel (Jacob), 64, 87
Israelites. See Hebrews; Jews
Issachar, 91, 142, 157
It philosophy, 50
ivory, 113, 121, 122, 139

J

jacinth, 157
Jacob, 11, 64, 87
jade, 152
jadeite, 152
Jallalo'ddin, 45
Jamnia, 78
jasmine, 108
jasper, 151, 156, 158
Jefferson, Thomas, 37
Jehovah, 24
Jeremiah, 87
Jeroboam, 7, 45
Jerome, Saint, 80-81
Jerusalem, 7, 16, 30, 31, 74, 79
Jerusalem Gemara, 16
Jerusalem Targum. See Bible, translations, targum
Jesus, 15, 30, 87
Jethro, 22, 23, 67-68, 111
    daughters of, 11, 22, 68, 70, 164
    names of, 68, 87
    son of, 68
jewelry, 150
    Egyptian, 99, 111, 112, 118, 136, 150-156, 157, 159
    Hebrew, 155, 156
Jewish Antiquities, 15
Jewish Publication Society, 86
Jews, 16, 29, 31, 43, 55, 63, 64, 77, 80, 81, 86, 143, 148, 161. See also Hebrews
Jochebed. See Yochabel
Jonah, 87
Jordan River, 30, 45, 46, 63, 141
Joseph, 5, 32, 33, 87, 91, 142, 158
Josephus, Flavius, 15, 18, 19, 20, 21, 24, 25, 33, 37, 39, 40, 67, 70, 71
Joshua, 33, 46, 69, 78, 98
Josiah, 30, 74
jubilees, 56, 106, 165
Jubilees, Book of. See Bible, Old Testament, Pseudepigrapha, Jubilees

Judah, 91, 142, 157
Judah, Kingdom of, 7, 64, 74
Judaism, 13, 31, 143
Judges, Book of. See Bible, Old Testament, Books, Judges
Judith, Book of. See Bible, Old Testament, Apocrypha, Judith
Julius, Pope, 79
juniper, 121

K

Kabah, 67, 68
Kadesh, 59
Kahun, 102, 107, 108
Karnak, 18-19, 57, 60, 106, 117, 119
Kenite theory, 68, 69
Keturah, 67
Khamsin, 28
khepresh, 137
khepri, 154
Khnum, 27, 116
kilts, 127, 129, 131, 132, 133, 134
kingdom, 33, 74
King James Version. See Bible, versions, Authorized Version
kings, 7, 49, 64, 71, 74, 82, 98, 117, 123. See also pharaohs
kitchens, 108, 111
kohl, 149
Korah, 66
Koran, 16, 19, 21, 22, 23, 25, 26, 27, 28, 32, 34, 36, 41, 43, 45, 65, 67, 68, 69, 70, 86-87
    divisions of, 41-43, 69-70, 87-88
    names of, 87
Kremlin, 54

L

labor, 8, 9, 34, 66, 69, 109
laborers, 9, 56, 107, 108, 113, 127
ladanum, 138
lambs, 28, 29, 30, 31, 33
lamps, 112, 123
lapis lazuli, 151, 157
Lasky, Jesse, Jr., 13
Last Supper, 31
lasso, 162
lathes, 121
laundries, 131
law, 12, 16, 73, 82
    canonical. See Bible, Old Testament, Law

Egyptian, 54, 56
giving of the. *See* Ten Commandments, tables of stone
God's. *See* Ten Commandments
Hebrew, 28, 29, 74, 112, 142, 143, 147, 150
Moslem, 86
laying on of hands, 46
lead, 149
leather, 73, 89, 90, 98, 99, 121, 122, 127, 129, 134, 135, 137, 140, 141, 142, 152
leopards, 115, 127
leprosy, 43
lettering. *See* alphabet; writing
Letter of Aristeas, Book of. *See* Bible, Old Testament, Pseudepigrapha, Letter of Aristeas
lettuce, 29
level, 106
levers, 106
Levi, 91, 142, 156
Levi, David, 86
Levites, 157
Liberty Bell, 47
Libya, 56
ligure, 156, 157
limestone, 103, 104, 114, 115, 152
linen, 121, 122, 125, 126, 129, 130, 131, 133, 140, 152
lintels, 28
lions, 91, 92, 115, 117, 122, 146, 162
Living God, 25
lock of youth, 145
logic, 50, 61
logos doctrine, 52
loincloths, Egyptian, 127, 132
Hebrew, 140, 141
longevity, 6-7, 17
looms, 105, 125, 127
loot, 92, 125
Lord, 24, 25, 28, 29, 31, 32, 34, 35, 38, 39, 44, 45, 86, 88
lotus, 108, 109, 146, 160
Louvre, 117, 133
Lucas, Alfred, 96, 105, 113, 121, 126, 146, 157
lupins, 161
lutes, 163
Luther, Martin, 83, 84
Lutheran Church. *See* Church, Lutheran
Luxor, 27, 61, 106, 116, 120, 134
lyres, 163

M

ma'at, 53, 54
Maccabees, Book of. *See* Bible, Old Testament, Apocrypha, Maccabees; Bible, Old Testament, Pseudepigrapha, IV Maccabees
Mackenzie, Aeneas, 13
madder, 131
magic, 26, 150, 151
malachite, 148, 149, 151
mallets, 104
malt, 161
mandrake, 91
manna, 45
mantles. *See* cloaks
maqui bush, 24
Marcus, Ralph, 40
marines. *See* army, marines
marriage, 53
marsh sea, 36
Martin, Gregory, 85
Martyrdom of Isaiah, Book of. *See* Bible, Old Testament, Pseudepigrapha, Martyrdom of Isaiah
masks, 115, 137
masons, 104, 106, 113
Masorah, 79
Matthew, Thomas. *See* Bible, translations, Matthew
matting, 131
measurements, 40, 109, 149, 150
meat, 28, 29, 159, 160, 161, 162
Mecca, 67, 68, 87
Medinah, 87
Medinet Habu, 102, 134
Mediterranean Sea, 26, 58
Mehou, 165
Memnon, 116
Memphis, 44, 52, 107
Memphite theology, 52
mercenaries. *See* army, mercenaries
Mered, 65, 66, 70
Merneptah, 60, **61**, 64, 140
Mesopotamia, 161
metals, 44, 45, 59, 69, 89, 92, 99, 104, 105, 112, 113, 115, 121, 127, 129, 130, 133, 134, 135, 136, 137, 145, 146, 148, 149, 151, 152, 153, 157, 162, 163
casting, 115

Methuselah, 6
Metropolitan Museum of Art, 98, 150, 154, 163
Michelangelo, 79
Middle Ages, 82
Middle Kingdom. See dynasties, Middle Kingdom (2050-1800 B.C.)
Midian (people of Arabia), 68, 96
Midian (son of Abraham), 67
Midian (land), 11, 16, 22, 23, 27
Midland Psalter. See Bible, translations, Midland Psalter
Midrash, 15-16, 39-40, 66, 143
Midrash Haggadah, 16
Midrash Halakah, 16
Midrash Rabbah, 16, 19, 20, 21, 22, 23, 65, 70, 91
midwives, 70
Migdol, 92-93
militia. See army, militia
milk, 160
minerals, 113, 149, 151, 157
mines, 44, 69, 92, 157
Miriam, 67, 70, 71
mirrors, 148
Mishnah, 16, 28
Mississippi, 34
mixed multitude, 33-35
Mnevis Bull, 44
Moffatt, James, 23, 74
Mohammed, 32, 44, 86
molds, 103, 115
molten sea, 45
monotheism, 55, 61, 73, 86
Montu, 134
mordants, 131
mortar, 8, 104
Mosaic law, 31, 43, 75
Moses, 8, 9, 11, 13, 14, 15, 18, 19, 23, 26, 33, 39, 40, 41, 43, 46, 47, 58, 69, 75, 79, 80, 95, 103, 109, 111, 112, 129, 134, 140, 141, 142, 147, 156, 158
   age of, 7, 16-17
   appearance of, 17, 46, 79, 80
   attempted assassination of, 21
   birth of, 6, 7, 11
   brother of, 17, 25, 26, 29, 43, 45, 64, 65, 70, 71, 141, 142
   builder, 20, 33, 56
   character of, 12, 20, 21, 22, 46
   conspiracy against, 20, 21, 66
   death of, 46

   death sentence of, 22
   early years of, 8, 11, 12, 18, 20
   education of, 19, 46
   exile of, 22
   father-in-law of, 22, 23, 67, 68
   horns of, 79-80
   imprisonment of, 21
   in Midian, 11, 16, 22, 23, 27
   Jethro's brother-in-law, 68
   killing of Egyptian, 11, 19, 21, 66
   lawgiver, 11, 13, 15, 37, 47, 143
   leader of Egyptian army, 20, 56, 71, 134, 145
   leader of Hebrews, 21, 26, 29, 31, 32, 33, 35, 37, 38, 43, 44, 45, 55, 56, 60, 66, 69
   leprous hand of, 43
   mother of (Egyptian), 18, 19, 20, 21, 65-66, 70, 152
   mother of (Hebrew), 11, 71
   name of, 18, 65, 87
   Nefretiri, relationship with, 20
   nomad, 22
   paintings of, 41, 79
   parentage of, 20
   prince of Egypt, 12, 19, 20, 55, 56, 92, 129, 134, 145
   prophet, 25, 78, 143
   sculptures of, 79
   shepherd, 22, 23
   shoes of, 45
   signs, 25, 26, 27, 35, 43, 68
   sister of, 67, 70, 71
   slave, 21
   sons of, 22, 23, 27, 164
   staff of, 25, 26, 43, 45
   successor to throne, 18, 19, 20
   tomb of, 46
   traditions about, 13, 14, 16, 18, 20-22, 25, 27, 29, 70, 71
   wife of, 22, 23, 27, 70-71
"Moses," article by W. Churchill, 36
Moslems, 55, 67, 86, 87, 161
mosque at Mecca, 67
Most High God, 25
mother-of-pearl, 152, 158
motion pictures, 5, 13, 95
   art department, 102
   code regulation, 44
   color, 130
   costume, 130, 137, 139
   photography, 130
   set design, 102, 108, 109, 116, 117

Mount Sinai, *See* Sinai, Mount
moustaches, 144, 148
mud, 101, 103-104, 106, 108, 109
music, 111, 163, 164, 165
  instruments, 163-164, 166
myrrh, 149

N

nails, 115
names, effacement of, 57, 58
Naphtali, 91, 142, 157
Napoleon I, 117
Narration of the Story of the Passover.
  See Haggadah shel Pesach
Nash Papyrus, 78
navy, 36, 90
Nazarites, 147
Near East, 49, 59, 73, 112, 139, 143,
  145, 159, 161
Nebo, Mount, 45-46
necklaces, 151, 153, 154
Nefretiri, 20, 27, 60-61, 99, 117, 119,
  126, 133, 139, 145, 163
Negroes, 33, 99
Nekhbet, 135, 136, 153
nemes, 136
New Kingdom. *See* dynasties, New
  Kingdom (1465-1165 B.C.)
New Year, 17
New York Times, 28
Nicholas of Hereford, 83
Nile Delta, 9, 26, 34, 51, 56, 60, 69,
  97, 102, 103, 162
Nile River, 8, 26, 27, 28, 49, 51, 61,
  62, 99, 102, 103, 104, 106, 108,
  109, 112, 116, 117, 125, 131, 140,
  157, 160, 162
Nisan, 17
Noah, 6, 87
nomads, 22, 64, 67, 95, 110, 112, 141
Norman conquest, 82
Nozaki, Albert, 102
Nubia, 89
Numbers, Book of. *See* Bible, Old Tes-
  tament, Books, Numbers

O

oak, 121
oars, 99
oats, 29
obelisks, 56, 57, 60, 106, 107, 116
oboes, 163
ochre, 149

officers, army. *See* army, officers
oils, 123, 147, 148, 149, 150, 161
ointments, 146, 148, 149-150
Old Kingdom. *See* dynasties, Old
  Kingdom (2700-2200 B.C.)
Old Testament. *See* Bible, Old Testament
oleander, 108
olives, 91, 150
olivine, 151
On the Life of Moses, 15
onycha, 150
onyx, 151, 156, 158
opal, 152
"Opening, The," 88
oppression. *See* bondage
Oriental Institute, University of Chicago, 40, 105, 134
Osiris, 117, 136
ostriches, 139, 151
oxen, 45, 91
Oxford University, 85
"Ozymandias," 116

P

painting, 25, 52, 61, 102, 104, 106,
  111, 112, 113, 114-115, 117-121,
  127, 128, 129, 131, 133, 135, 137,
  138, 139, 140, 142, 144, 145, 146,
  163, 165
paints, 113
palaces, 25, 54, 101, 102, 107-109,
  111, 116, 118, 123
Palestine, 7, 34, 56, 61, 64, 77, 80, 164
Palestine-Syria, 34, 56
Palestinian Gemara, 16
Palestinians, 140
palms, 108, 109, 113, 121, 138, 146,
  161
Pamphylian Sea, 37
papyrus, 46, 73, 78, 99, 109, 113, 117,
  138, 162
Passover, 17, 28-31, 60, 65, 66, 69,
  161
patriarchs, 7, 67, 73, 95
pearl, 152
pectorals, 136, 153-154, 155
Penitential Psalms. *See* Bible, Old Testament, printed
Pentateuch. *See* Bible, Old Testament,
  Pentateuch

pepperwort, 29
Pereira, Hal, 102
perfumes, 138, 148, 149-150, 159
peridot, 151, 156
per-o, 54
Per-Ramses, 9, 56, 60, 102, 103
persea, 121
Pesach. *See* Passover
Peshitta, 81
Petrie, W. M. Flinders, 27, 35, 44, 96, 97
pharaohs, 5, 7, 8, 11, 16, 17, 18, 21, 25, 26, 27, 28, 32, 35, 36, 37, 40, 65, 70, 90, 92, 108, 111, 123, 127, 129, 133, 136, 137, 138, 145, 155, 160, 165. *See also* Akhnaton; Amenemhet; Amenhotep; Har-em-Hab; Merneptah; Rameses; Sethi; Tutankhamon
bodyguards of, 90
character of, 32, 54, 55, 56, 58, 59, 60
divinity of, 49, 50, 51, 52, 53-56, 59
duties of, 54, 55-56
forms of address, 54
Philistines, 63
Philo Judaeus, 15, 18, 19, 21, 22, 23, 33, 35, 39, 40, 46, 52
Phinehas, 18
picks, 104
pigments, 113, 114
pigmies, 164
pigs, 161
Pihahiroth, 93
pillar of cloud, pillar of fire, 35, 37, 40
pillows, 111, 121, 122
pine, 121
Pinna marina, 126
Pisgah, Mount. *See* Nebo, Mount
Pithom, 8, 36
plagues, 8, 26-28, 29, 43, 95, 117. *See also* first-born, death of
planes, 121
plaster, 104, 113, 114
Plato, 52
pleating, 130, 131
Pliny the Elder, 131
plumb rules, 106
plywood, 121-122
poetry, 57, 71, 73, 116, 121
pomegranates, 108
pools, 108, 118, 160, 162

poppies, 108
population, Egypt, 34
  Palestine, 34
  Syria, 34
  Transjordan, 34
pottery, 112, 113, 114, 115
prayers, Hebrew, 143
  Moslem, 88
precious stones. *See* stones, precious and semiprecious
Preparation for the Gospel, 15
priests, Egyptian, 54, 127, 135, 145
  Hebrew, 65, 68, 74, 140, 142, 147, 155, 158
printing, 82, 83-84
prisoners, 9, 34, 69, 125, 148
Promised Land, 11, 30, 31, 32, 33, 46, 141
prophets, 32, 67, 70, 78, 86, 87
Prophets. *See* Bible, Old Testament, Prophets
Protestant Church. *See* Church, Protestant
Psalms, Book of. *See* Bible, Old Testament, Books, Psalms
Psalms of Solomon, Book of. *See* Bible, Old Testament, Pseudepigrapha, Psalms of Solomon
Psalters. *See* Bible, Old Testament, Books, Psalms; Bible, translations, Psalters
Pseudepigrapha. *See* Bible, Old Testament, Pseudepigrapha
Ptah, 18, 52
Ptahmose, 18
pulleys, 99, 105, 106
punishments, 57, 66
Punt, 164
Purvey, John, 83
Putiel, 18
pylons, 57, 102, 106, 107, 117
pyramids, 52, 62, 101, 107, 109-110, 117, 120

Q

Qantir, 9, 56, 103
quarries, 104-105
quartz, 105, 114, 151
quartzite, 103
queens, 53, 133, 135. *See also* Cleopatra; Nefretiri

R

Ra, 51, 136
Raamses (city), 8, 9, 33, 56, 102-103, 107, 116, 117
Raguel, 68
raisin, 160
Rameses I, 8, 54, 55, 60, 137
Rameses II, 8, 9, 19, 21, 25, 26, 27, 35, 36, 37, 40, 53, 54, 57, 58-59, 60-61, 64, 66, 91, 98, 102, 106, 107, 115, 116, 117, 119, 120, 121, 125, 126, 129, 134, 135, 136, 137, 145, 162
  character of, 54, 59, 60
  children of, 60, 61, 108, 117, 145
  wife of, 60-61, 117, 119, 126, 133, 145
Rameses III, 59, 134, 137
Ramesseum, 102, 116
ramp, 105, 106
Ranke, Hermann, 90, 131, 133
Ras Safsafeh, 38
razors, 147, 148
Re, 136
Red Sea, 26, 35-37, 38, 40, 60, 66, 91, 92, 134, 156
reeds, 103, 108, 125, 129, 160, 162
Reformation, 77, 82
Rehoboam, 7
religion. *See* Christianity; concepts, religious; god-king; Islam; Judaism
Rephidim, 69
resins, 114-115, 149, 151, 152, 161
Reuben, 91, 142, 156
Reuel, 68
Revelation, The, 87
Revised Standard Verson. *See* Bible, versions, Revised Standard Version
Revised Version. *See* Bible, versions, Revised Version
Revolution, October (1917), 59
rewards, 92
Riefstahl, Elizabeth, 125, 126, 127, 129, 131, 132, 133, 135
rings, 153, 154
rites, Egyptian, 117
  Hebrew, 28-31, 74, 163-164
  pagan, 29, 30
robes. *See* cloaks
Robinson, A. E., 96
rock crystal. *See* quartz
rockers, 106
rod. *See* Moses, staff of

Rogers, John, 84
rollers, 105, 116
Roman Empire, 15, 62
ropes, 96, 99, 105, 106, 110, 142
rouge, 149
ruby, 152
rudders, 99
ruku, 87
rush, sweet, 149

S

Sabbath, 20, 43
sacrifices, animal, 29, 30, 31, 45, 161
saddlery, 111
safflowers, 161
sails, 99
Saint Catherine, monastery of, 38, 41, 161
Saint John's Island, 156
Sale, George, 69-70
salt, 123
saluki, 162
Samaritan Pentateuch. *See* Bible, versions, Samaritan Pentateuch
sammur, 126
Samson, 142, 147
Samuel, 78
sanctuaries, portable, 45
sandals, 138, 144
Sand-Dwellers, 97, 140, 141
sandstone, 103, 121
sandstorms, 28
Sanhedrin, 19
sapphire, 152, 156, 157
Saqqara, 165
sard, 151, 156
Sardinians, 90
sardius, 156
sardonyx, 151
Sargon II, 98
saws, 105
scaffolds, 106
scarabs, 153, 154, 155
scepters, 136, 138
Schild, Ewald, 24
scimitars, 90
scribes, 35, 73, 74, 95, 135
Scriptures. *See* Bible
Scriptures of Islam. *See* Koran
scrolls, 46
  Dead Sea, 78
sculptors, 79, 113, 114

sculpture, 18-19, 44, 52, 57, 58, 59, 61, 79, 82, 105, 111, 112, 113, 114, 115, 116-117, 118-120, 127, 128, 129, 131, 133, 135, 139, 144, 163, 165
Seal of the United States, 37
seals, 37, 154
"sea-wool," 126
Secrets of Enoch, Book of. See Bible, Old Testament, Pseudepigrapha, Secrets of Enoch
Seder, 29, 31
Seele, Keith C., 60, 89, 95, 97, 135
sekhemti, 137
Semites, 9, 33, 34, 45, 63, 64, 97, 129, 140, 141, 142, 144, 147, 148, 163
Sephardic Jews, 31
Sephora, 22, 23, 27, 70-71
Septuagint, See Bible, translations, Septuagint
sequins, 127, 133
serpentine, 113
serpents, 25, 26, 91, 115, 135, 136, 137, 146
servants, 107, 108, 159
Seth, 51
Sethi I, 8, 9, 19, 20, 21, 51, 53, 54, 55, 56-57, 58, 60, 92, 98, 102, 106, 116, 117, 120, 129, 134, 135, 137, 154, 163
  character of, 54, 55, 56, 57, 58
shaving, Egyptian, 144, 145, 146, 148
  Hebrew, 147
Shechem, 91
sheep, 22, 28, 29, 30, 31, 33, 34, 110, 126
sheiks, 22, 68
shekels, 149, 150
Shelley, Percy Bysshe, 116, 121
Shem, 63
shepherds, 22, 23, 138
Sherden. See Sardinians
Sheshonk, 7
shields, 89
Shipley, Joseph T., 151
shirts. See tunics
Shishak, 7
shittim, 45
shoes. See footwear; Moses, shoes of
shofar, 31, 33, 163-164
shrines, Egyptian, 27, 99, 108, 117
  Hebrew, 67, 68, 112
  Moslem, 67, 68

Shu'aib, 87
Sibylline Oracles, Book of. See Bible, Old Testament, Pseudepigrapha, Sibylline Oracles
sidder, 121
sifrim ganozim, 76
sifrim hisonim, 76
signs, See Moses, signs
silk, 126
silver, 113, 115, 133, 134, 151, 152
Silvia of Aquitaine, 38
Simeon, 91, 142, 156
Sinai, Mount, 23, 33, 36, 37-38, 40, 41, 63, 65, 69, 80, 91, 92, 110, 161
Sinai Peninsula, 37-38, 44, 69, 141, 157, 160
Sinuhe, 123
sister-brother relationship, 20, 53
sistrum, 163
size. See glue
skins, animal, 126, 127, 139
skirts, 140
slaves, 20, 21, 32, 34, 69, 92, 109, 155
sleds, 105, 106
sleepers, 105
Smith, Miles, 85
snake charmers, 26
snakeroot, 29
Sokar, 108, 117
soldiers. See army, uniforms
Solomon, 7, 36, 45, 78, 87, 156
son-father relationship, 53
sorcery. See magic
spearmen. See army, spearmen
spears, 89, 90, 162
spelt, 29
sphinx, 33, 43, 117, 119
spices, 150-151
sports, 98, 162-163
squares, 106
stables, 98, 108
stacte, 150
staff, 25, 26, 45, 139
standards, Egyptian, 90-91
  Hebrew, 91
statues, 79, 98, 105, 107, 112, 113, 115, 116, 117, 119, 120, 121, 133, 135, 138, 144
steatite, 113
Steindorff, George, 60, 135
stele, 64, 140

Stephen, 19
stones, precious and semiprecious, 44, 69, 92, 121, 122, 134, 135, 145, 151-152, 153, 154, 155-158
stools 122
storerooms, 108
storms, 27, 28
straw, 25, 26, 103, 151
streets, 107-108
Suez, 36
Suez Canal, 26
sugar, 160
Sumerian King List, 6
sun-god, 51, 53, 136, 154
surah, 43, 69-70, 87
Sut-Plant, 53
swaggerstick, 90
swamps, 99, 162
sweets, 160
swords, 37, 90
sycamore, 108, 121
symbols, 35, 53, 109, 117, 135, 136, 137, 150, 153-154, 156
Syria, 34, 55, 56, 61, 161
Syriac Apocalypse of Baruch, Book of. See Bible, Old Testament, Pseudepigrapha, Syriac Apocalypse of Baruch
Syrians, 125, 140

T

tables, 122
tabut, 45
talismans, 151
Talmud, 16
tamarisk, 121
Tanis, 56, 102
tapestries, 127, 129
targum. See Bible, translations, targum
Taverner, Richard, 84
tempera, 114
Temple (Jerusalem), 30, 31, 45, 74, 79
Ten Commandments, 11, 12, 33, 38, 39, 43, 78, 83
    division of, 40-43
    tables of stone, 38, 39, 40, 41, 43, 44, 45, 80
    traditions about, 41

Ten Commandments, The (motion picture), 5, 8, 9, 12, 13, 15, 19, 20, 21, 22, 23, 24, 25, 26, 27, 29, 31, 33, 34, 35, 37, 39, 40, 41, 44, 45, 46, 47, 53, 54, 55, 56-57, 58, 60, 61, 65, 66, 67, 68, 69, 70, 71, 89, 90, 91, 95, 98, 99, 102-103, 104, 106, 107, 108, 109, 110, 111, 116-117, 122, 126, 128, 129, 130, 132, 133, 135, 137-138, 139, 141, 142, 143, 144, 145, 147, 148, 151, 152, 153, 154, 155, 156, 161, 163-164, 165, 166
tent-dwellers, 110
tents, 22, 23, 35, 92, 110-111, 162
Ten Words. See Ten Commandments, division of
Testaments of the Twelve Patriarchs, Book of. See Bible, Old Testament, Pseudepigrapha, Testaments of the Twelve Patriarchs
textiles. See cloth; cotton; hair; linen; silk; wool
Tharbis, 71
Thebes, 61, 98, 101, 116, 133, 134
theocracy, 61
Thompson, R. Campbell, 95, 96, 97
Thomson, Charles, 85
thorn bush, 23
Thou philosophy, 50
thrones, 5, 58, 60, 121, 134, 165
    succession to, 18, 19, 20, 53, 55, 56, 57, 58
thunder, 27, 28
Thut-mose, 18
time reckoning, 6-8, 17, 32
Timsah, Lake, 36
Tishri, 17
titles, military, 92
    royal, 53, 54, 57, 58, 59
Tobias, Book of. See Bible, Old Testament, Apocrypha, Tobias
"Toilette of the Hebrew Lady," 144
tombs, 25, 46, 61, 79, 101, 102, 103, 109, 111, 115, 126, 127, 128, 129, 131, 133, 134, 135, 142, 144, 152, 153, 159, 163, 165, 166
tools, 104-106, 107, 113, 115, 121
topaz, 156
Torah, 80, 87, 143
towers, 92, 107, 117
trade, 97, 126

traditions, 13-15, 59, 67, 73
  about the Commandments. *See* Ten
    Commandments, traditions about
  about the Hebrews, 11, 15, 16, 32,
    34, 36, 63, 65, 66, 67, 70, 71, 73,
    75
  about Moses. *See* Moses, traditions
    about
  Moslem, 87
transportation. *See* boats; camels;
  chariots; donkeys; horses; wagons
trays, 123
treasure cities, 8, 9, 20, 33, 56, 60,
  102, 103, 106, 107, 116, 117
trees, 45, 91, 108, 109, 113, 121, 146
Trent, Council of, 76
tribes, 73, 138, 161
  Hebrew, 9, 33-34, 64, 68, 140, 141,
    156, 157-158
  Semitic, 34
tribute, 20, 25, 125, 129
Troy, 126
trumpets, 163
tunics, Egyptian, 90, 127, 129, 131,
  132, 133, 134
  Hebrew, 141, 143
turquoise, 44, 69, 92, 151, 157
Tutankhamon, 115, 122, 127, 129,
  131, 132, 133, 134, 136, 137, 153
Tyler, Walter, 102
Tyndale, William. *See* Bible, translations, Tyndale

U

unicorn, 91
uniforms. *See* army, uniforms
Union of Soviet Socialist Republics,
  54, 81
universe, 6, 50
University of Chicago Oriental Institute. *See* Oriental Institute, University of Chicago
uraeus, 135, 136, 137
Urim and Thummim, 91
Ussher, James, 6

V

Valley of the Kings, 101
Valley of the Queens, 61, 133, 134
varnish, 114
vases, 112
Vatican Codex. *See* Bible, Vatican
  Codex

vegetables, 29, 108
veils, 143
veneer, 122
Venus de Milo, 120
Vespasian Psalter. *See* Bible, translations, Vespasian Psalter
villas, 101, 107, 108, 109, 123
viziers, 55, 165
volcanoes, 36, 38
Vulgate Bible. *See* Bible, translations,
  Vulgate
vulture, 135, 136, 137, 153

W

Wadi Tumilat, 9, 26, 36, 93
wagons. *See* carts
walls (building), 101, 104, 107, 108,
  111, 118
walls (city), 107
warfare, 20, 37, 55, 56, 58, 59, 69, 89,
  91, 92, 96, 98. *See also* army, campaigns; battles; compaigns
Washington, George, 120
weapons, 89, 90, 115, 138, 162, 164
weaving, Arabian, 110
  Egyptian, 105, 125, 126, 127, 129,
    130, 133
  Hebrew, 140
  Syrian, 129
wedges, 104
wells, 11, 22, 92
wheat, 29, 51, 161
White House (United States), 54
White Wall, 107
whitewash, 114
wicks, 123
wigs, 146, 148
Wilcoxon, Henry, 13
wilderness, 11, 33, 91, 110, 112
willows, 121
Wilson, John, 34, 49, 50, 59
wind, 28, 35, 37, 111
wine, 149, 160, 161
Winlock, H. E., 151, 155
Wisdom, Book of. *See* Bible, Old Testament, Apocrypha, Wisdom
wood, 44, 45, 103, 104, 105, 113, 115,
  116, 121-122, 151
wool, 110, 125-126, 130, 139, 141,
  146, 164

wrestling, 162
writing, 38, 39, 40, 46, 73, 74
   Egyptian, 95, 111, 116, 130, 133-134, 138, 153, 163. *See also* alphabet; hieroglyphs
Writings. *See* Bible, Old Testament, Writings
Wyclif, John. *See* Bible, translations, Wyclif

X

Y

Yahweh. *See* YHWH

yam suph, 36-37
yeast, 161
Yemenite Jews, 31
yew, 121
YHWH, 11, 24-25, 55, 64, 68, 74
Yochabel, 71

Z

Zamzam, 67
Zebulun, 91, 142, 157
Zechariah, Book of. *See* Bible, Old Testament, Books, Zechariah
Zipporah, 70
Zobaa, 28

REFERENCES TO THE BIBLE

OLD TESTAMENT

Genesis

3:7	p. 84
5:5	6
5:27	6
9:29	6
10:21	63
10:25	63
12:16	95
13:5	110
13:14-15	32
14:13	63
14:23	144
15:13	17, 28, 32, 69
15:16	17
16:11	67
24:26	91
24:65	143
25:1-2	67
25:7	7
25:12-18	67
25:25	147
25:27	110
30:14	91
32:28	64
37:3	140
45:10	9, 26, 109
49:9	91
49:13	91
49:17	91
49:19	91
49:20	91
49:21	91
49:27	91
49:28, *et passim*	64
50:25	33

Exodus

1:1	63
1:8	5
1:8-11	32
1:11	8, 102
1:11, *et passim*	54
1:14	8, 9
1:22	11
2:2	11, 16
2:3	11
2:10	11, 12, 18, 19
2:11	16, 21, 69
2:12	11, 19, 21
2:15	11, 22
2:15-25	22
2:16	68
2:16-	11
2:18	68
2:21	22, 70
2:22	23
3	22
3:1	37, 68
3:3	22
3:5	140, 144

3:6	11	14:21-22	35
3:7-	11	14:24	35
3:8	69	14:27-31	35
3:12	37	15:20	70
3:14	11, 24, 68	17:8	22
3:21-22	33	17:9	69
4:1-23	22	18:2	23
4:17	25	18:2-5	23
4:20	22, 27	18:2-6	27
5:1-	25	19:18	38
5:6, et passim	66	19:20	37
5:21	26	20	39
6:9	26	20-	11
6:20	71	20:1-22	38
6:23	64	20:2	41
6:25	18	20:2-17	39
7:7	16, 17, 64	20:13-15	40
7:10	25	20—23	82
7:10-	25	23:15	30
7:11	26	23:31	36
7:13, et passim	27	24:4-8	39
7:20	27	24:16	38
7—10	26	25:10	45
8:22	26	25:16	45
9:3	95	28, etc.	140
9:22-26	27	28:4	142
10:21	28	28:17-20	156
11:2-3	33	28:37	142
11:5	27, 60	28:40	142
12:14-20	28	30:23-24	150
12:25	32	30:25	149
12:29	28, 108	30:32	150
12:29-30	27	30:34	150
12:35	155	30:35	149, 150
12:35-36	33	30:38	150
12:37	35	31:18	38, 39
12:37-38	34	32	66
12:38	33	32:1-	43
12:40	32	32:1-6	65
12:40-41	69	32:19	39, 44
12:41	110	32:20	66
12:48	65	32:26	44
12:48-49	29	34:1	39
13:3	34	34:18	30
13:5	30	34:29	80
13:19	34	34:35	80
13:21-22	40	35	156
14:2	93	37	45
14:6-	5	Leviticus	
14:10-12	35	19:27	147
14:11-12	66	21:5	147
14:15-31	37	23:5-6	29
14:19-20	35, 40		

25:10	47
Numbers	11
1:52	110
2:2	91
6:5	147
6:18	147
9:1-4	30
10:29	68
12:1	70
13:6	70
13:17	70
16	66
20:26	65
24:24	63
Deuteronomy	11
6:4	34, 78, 86
10:1-5	45
10:2	39
16:5-6	30
16:7	30
22:12	140
27:20	140
32:49	46
32:49-52	46
33:8	91
34:1-6	46
34:6	46
34:7	7, 46
34:9	46
Joshua	
5:2-11	30
Judges	
1:16	69
4:11	68
4:18	140
6:2	96
13—16	142
16:19	147
I Samuel	
1:3	18
16:12	147
17:5	142
II Samuel	
14:25, 26	142
18:9	142
I Kings	
7:23	45
7:25	45
8:6-8	45
9:26	36
10:11	156
11:40	7
12:28-29	45
14:21	7
14:25	7
20:32	142
22:10	13
II Kings	
1:8	140
22:8-10	31
23:21-23	30
I Chronicles	
2:19	67
4:18	65, 70
12:33	91
II Chronicles	
35:1-18	30
Nehemiah	
3:8	150
9:38—10:29	75
Psalms	
45:8	150
90:10	7
90—100	29
91	29
91:6	29
104	52
106:16-20	67
Proverbs	
7:17	150
Canticles	
1:12-14	150
3:6	150
4:10	150
5:11	147
Song of Solomon. *See* Canticles	
Ezekiel	
44:20	147
45:21	31
Micah	
7:5-6	57

NEW TESTAMENT

Acts	
7:22	12, 19, 20, 46
Hebrews	
11:24-25	21

REFERENCES TO THE HOLY QUR'AN

1:1-7	p. 88	10:75	32
2:50	36	10:90-92	36
2:127	67	17:101	43
2:243	34	18:60	69
2:248	45	19:54	67
3:3	87	20:77-80	36
3:17	86	20:87-94	65
5:12	32	26:10	32
5:23	69	27:7	22
6:155	43	28:4	32
7:85-93	68	28:5-6	33
7:107	25	28:9	19
7:127	27	28:15	21
7:129	32	28:22-28	68
7:130-135	26	28:23-28	22
7:131	28	28:27	23
7:142-147	41	28:29	22
7:145	43	28:34-35	65
7:148	65	40:78	87
7:148-151	44	90:3	67